Emily Dickinson's Imagery

BY REBECCA PATTERSON

Edited, with an introduction by Margaret H. Freeman

The University of Massachusetts Press   Amherst, 1979

Copyright © 1979 by
The University of Massachusetts Press
All rights reserved
Printed in the United States of America
LC 79-4024   ISBN 0-87023-272-X

Library of Congress Cataloging in Publication Data
Patterson, Rebecca.
Emily Dickinson's imagery.
Bibliography: p.
Includes index.
1. Dickinson, Emily, 1830–1886—Style.   2. Figures
of speech.   I. Freeman, Margaret H.   II. Title.
PS1541.Z5P28   811'.4   79-4024
ISBN 0-87023-272-X

CONTENTS

INTRODUCTION

The controversy that surrounded Rebecca Patterson's first full-length study will not be lessened by this one. Readers will no doubt still be provoked by her thesis of Emily Dickinson's lesbian attachment to her sister-in-law Sue and her friend Kate Scott (Turner) Anthon; they may not agree that "there is no more erotic poetry in the English language." Serious critics of her poetry, however, will have to deal with Patterson's scholarship on both counts. Certainly, the evidence she presents from an intense scrutiny of the poetry reinforces other psychological studies, and her analysis of recurrent words and images, often sound and illuminating, is a major contribution to a comprehensive study of Emily Dickinson's imagery.

Rebecca Patterson's work over the past thirty years encompassed many aspects of Emily Dickinson criticism and in some respects anticipated particular developments. The intense interest in "the myth of Amherst" when edited examples of Emily Dickinson's poetry first appeared inspired the publication of many articles and books dealing with particulars of her life and speculations about a possible "lover." [1] This emphasis on biography was perhaps abetted by the fact that her poetry was difficult to assimilate to popular nineteenth- and twentieth-century norms. It was not until the publication of Thomas H. Johnson's scholarly edition of all the poetry discovered by 1955, which followed, as best it could in printed form, the actual manuscript marks and which provided all the variants, that attention could turn seriously to the poetry itself. [2]

Although recent theoretical concerns, emerging primarily from studies in the psychology of consciousness, structuralism, and linguistics, are developing new approaches toward the interrelationships of artist, text, and reader, most Emily Dickinson criticism since 1955 has concentrated on biography or textual analysis. Such criticism has reached a level of scholarship in both these areas, thereby contributing a fuller and richer understanding of the poet and her work. It is now no longer possible to hold a simplistic view of a life frustrated by an illicit love affair with a married man or to dismiss the poetry as "minor."

In the area of biography, two major approaches emerge. The first emphasizes data external to the poetry in its search for information. Studies such as George Whicher's *This Was a Poet,* Jay Leyda's *The Years and Hours of Emily Dickinson,* and Johnson's *Emily Dickinson: An Interpretive Biography* established the tradition of this first approach, which culminates in the recent publication of Richard Sewall's two-volume biography, *The Life of Emily Dickinson.*[3]

Since so little factual information is available about the details of Emily Dickinson's personal life and experiences, a biographer like Sewall turns to what is known about those around her, trusting that an understanding of what her family and friends were like will provide clues to Emily Dickinson's own character. Thus, Sewall devotes the major portion of both volumes to a study of her immediate family and friends and their relationship to the poet. The account he gives is as concise and clear a picture as I can imagine of the life around the poet. In the end, however, the omission of any confrontation with different analyses concerning the poet herself, whether it is Clark Griffith's thesis of a father complex, Patterson's on homosexuality, or John Cody's on mother deprivation, is disappointing.[4] In particular, Sewall's conservative attitude in retreating to the earlier position of Whicher and Johnson that an actual male lover existed, and even opting for Samuel Bowles as his choice, limits our further understanding, ignoring as it does the very real possibilities presented by our increased knowledge of repression in psychological processes and its occurrence in nineteenth-century society. Be that as it may, Sewall's exhaustive study of information that has come to light since the earlier biographies is a welcome and significant addition to Emily Dickinson scholarship.

The second biographical approach relies primarily on internal information by using the poetry and the letters for its data. This more speculative approach is evidenced in the work of such writers as Albert Gelpi, Clark Griffith, William Sherwood, Genevieve Taggard, and Rebecca Patterson.[5]

When Patterson's thesis of Emily Dickinson's lesbian attachments first appeared in 1951, reviews ranged from outright hostility to enthusiastic acceptance.[6] Though much of the criticism justifiably questioned the speculative nature of Patterson's thesis, with respect to both lack of a theory relating poetry to biography and the assumption of an unproven chronology, her hypothesis that Emily's "lover" was female rested on just as much evidence (or lack of it) as other, "more acceptable" theories that have variously identified Charles Wadsworth, George Gould, Edward Hunt, or Samuel Bowles as the (male) object of the poet's affection and has thus lent a healthy skepticism to all subsequent attempts at identification. As more psychologically oriented studies appeared, some justification for Patterson's approach was provided, although the focus shifted from an emphasis on possible actual occurrences (which probably never can be proven) to an exploration of the inner processes of the poet's psyche. The most recent exponent of this approach is John Cody, whose book-length study appeared in 1971.[7]

In his very balanced evaluation of the myths that had grown up around the poet, Cody gives a succinct account of the reasons why critics have spoken out so strongly on the question of Emily Dickinson's eccentricity. The fear that her poetry, in its defiance of accepted norms, would initiate hostile responses caused her first editors to downplay stories of her strangeness, and this approach was followed by subsequent critics. The time has come, Cody thinks, to put the record straight, especially in the light of our twentieth-century knowledge that lucidity and genius are not denied to those who experience mental breakdowns. In effect, he entertains an old idea that "madness is to genius close allied" and offers some evidence from the world of psychiatry that takes us a long way toward seeing Emily Dickinson as the rich and complex person she must have been. Cody is, naturally enough, strongest in the area of his own field of psychiatry. By employing the method of psychography—the discovery of psychological processes through the writings of the "patient"—Cody concludes that the poet experienced early deprivation of a mother's affection, a deprivation that caused psychic imbalance, preventing her from achieving a healthy heterosexuality and causing instead a "cultivation of older women throughout her life" which served as a defense against incestuous, erotic thoughts about her brother and her father.[8]

The most significant aspect of Cody's study, however, is the question of whether Emily Dickinson suffered a nervous breakdown. Depending primarily upon analyses of certain poems, Cody claims that the poet has given us a documented description of the actual inner processes experienced in a mental collapse. If he is correct, Emily Dickinson does indeed have a secure place among those women writers who, as David Porter has commented, write "obsessively" about loss and deprivation.[9] More particularly, she joins the list of exclusively female writers in the modern period who have dealt specifically with the experience of insanity, writers such as Sylvia Plath, Margaret Atwood, and Doris Lessing.[10] What distinguishes Emily Dickinson from all these, furthermore, is significant: where they show us the *external* attributes associated with mental collapse, Emily Dickinson describes in detail the *internal* emotions experienced in the process. In this respect, she ranks only with Shakespeare in English literary tradition.

Whether or not Emily Dickinson had actually to undergo a real breakdown to express the feelings attendant to it is debatable: Cody is least convincing when he tells us that poets can imagine only events, not feelings. One need only recall Aristotle's theory of catharsis, Keats's negative capability, or Coleridge's theory of the imagination to explode the naive presumption of a direct correlation between experience and emotion. Great writers inspire us precisely because of their ability to put in words feelings we only dimly perceive and cannot well express. Dickinson's poetry inspires us because it makes the feeling concrete at the same time as it delocalizes it, thereby removing it from its source. The "pain" may be physical, it may indeed be mental or emotional, but all Emily Dickinson tells us is that it is "great." Likewise, we are not told what kind of "success" is counted "sweetest," only that those who do not have it think it so.

In the final analysis, then, Cody's work needs a theory of poetry. Perhaps his weakest point comes at the conclusion of his study when he argues that without Emily Dickinson's emotional deprivation and psychic imbalance we would not have such great poetry. No explanation of process is offered here (though it is close to the madness-genius idea discussed earlier). One might just as well argue that her ellipses and hiatuses are sloppy because of her lack of emotional control, that the poetry would be greater if the opposite were true (as some critics have argued, and some still do).

Despite these limitations, Cody shows exceedingly well the poet's psychological sensitivity in the poems he quotes. His thesis that Emily Dickinson's lover was more fantasy than fact is persuasive. To prefer one's own company *is* considered abnormal from society's perspective: such an attitude undermines its very existence. Certain documented events in Emily Dickinson's life, such as her love for her nephew Gilbert, are given a coherent explanation in Cody's study, and the chronology of such events with respect to her psychological development is clarified. Cody achieves perhaps the greatest advance in our understanding of the poet by showing how other critics' theories, such as homosexuality, father complex, and necrophilia, are interrelated in his description of the poet's personality.

Unless new information on the events of Emily Dickinson's life comes to light, or a better theory of how the "persona" of poetry is related to the person of the poet is formulated, it is clear that little more can be said concerning the poet's life. Scholarly research over the years has dispelled, once and for all, the popular myth of the reclusive nun, replacing it with a picture of a gifted, if eccentric, woman, witty but not pretty, fond of her family, her friends, her books, her plants, and her dog, a woman who in her adolescent years had all the nineteenth-century desires and expectancies of a healthy girl but who, for whatever reason, never married, who matured emotionally and intellectually through some crisis in her late twenties, and who had, above all else, a passion for poetry.

Indeed, if it were not for her poetry, we would not be concerned with what Emily Dickinson was like, much less know she ever existed. Since the publication of Johnson's editions of the poetry and the letters, much careful work has been done on the fundamental problems they present:

the establishment of a text and a chronology, the poems' groupings in fascicles and packets, the clarification of manuscript markings and line ends.

Although Edith Perry Stamm presented an intriguing theory that the manuscript marks were performance indicators, like those found in nineteenth-century school rhetorics, most critics remain unconvinced.[11] The most comprehensive treatment of her punctuation so far is that of Brita Lindberg-Seyersted.[12] After discussing all the theories previously held, from irrelevance to music, she concludes that it "was not a consistent system; it was a conscious, but impressionistic method of stressing, of arranging the rhythmical units of her verse; sometimes the adding of meaning to the linguistic units; and it was the creation of the moment, seldom deliberated."[13] As edited versions of the poems show, the markings are, even when printed as a dash, essential to the reader's apprehension of the poem, as is indeed her just as random capitalization.[14]

If her capitalization and punctuation are random, the existence of variants for words, phrases, and entire lines seems even more so. Editors of her poetry are forced to make choices that the poet herself apparently was not prepared to do. Differing versions of poems in fair copies sent to friends or included in the fascicles and packets she bound together give few clues that one might be preferred over another. Even within the bound volumes, variants are often written in. Often, the originals seem just as valid as the suggested substitutions. Richard Howard has concluded that Dickinson's refusal to choose was an indication of her poetic philosophy of "play" and that she is most like that other Victorian poet, Gerard Manley Hopkins, in her delight in "the polymorphous-perverse."[15] Such deliberate indiscrimination in refusing to believe in only one way of expressing her world makes doubly difficult the attempt to determine development, progression, or chronology.

The dating of the poems will always be conjectural. Johnson, who with Theodora Ward's help painstakingly undertook the task, says so himself.[16] And yet so much has been made to hang upon the chronology of the poems that a certain amount of skepticism may be forgiven. Johnson, for example, comments on the year 1862: "In no other year did she ever write so much poetry."[17] Even if R. W. Franklin's revisions are taken as a guide, a study of the fascicles and packets attributed to that year makes dubious the strength of Johnson's claim.[18] Of the 387 poems that appear in the nineteen fascicles and packets, 61 have more than one copy. For only thirteen of these can it be reliably determined that they were in existence by a certain date (and only nine of these by 1862). The thirteen poems occur in eight of the fascicles only, leaving a total of eleven fascicles and packets (224 poems) dated by handwriting evidence alone.[19]

What conclusions may be drawn? There is very little independent evidence for the dating of the poems; even if Ward's handwriting analysis is correct, one can conclude only that the poems ascribed to the year 1862 had been written by then, not that they were written in or even close to that year. Despite Johnson's disclaimer,[20] we know too little of the poet's practice to assume that she placed newly written poems into fascicles, and there is some evidence that this was not always her practice. Some poems appearing in different handwriting (and therefore assigned to different years) occur in the same fascicle; the fact that 366 poems are assigned to 1862 handwriting argues more for a year of collation than for one of creation.[21] Though very few poems can be dated reliably before 1858, it may nevertheless be the case that the poet's creative drive began much earlier than we have so far assumed.

Johnson's datings are the result of educated guesswork, and no critic may forget that. It makes the task of tracing Emily Dickinson's poetic development especially difficult. Much more work needs to be done in this area, following the initial endeavors of Johnson, Ward, and Franklin, before such dating-dependency claims as have been made about the poet or her poetry can be substantiated. Despite such problems, recent scholarly research has made great progress in our understanding of the kind of poet Emily Dickinson was and the underlying forces and themes that determined her craft. As recognition of her standing as a major poet steadily grows, so does a deeper understanding of her place in English and American literary tradition.

The important advances that have been made in reconstructing Emily Dickinson's own groupings of poems increase the possibilities of moving away from a fragmented approach to the corpus toward a more comprehensive and coherent analysis. The reconstruction, as far as is possible, of the fascicles and packets has led Ruth Miller, for example, to develop a theory of thematic structure for the poems' groupings. She suggests that the poet found her inspiration to order her poems in the works of William Wordsworth and especially Francis Quarles, a seventeenth-century emblematic poet, who accompanied his poem groups with etchings. As with her use of other sources, however, Emily Dickinson imposes her own particular perspective: after comparing fascicle 32 with Quarles's Emblem 10, Miller concludes that the poet "borrows from Quarles in order to alter, to put straight, to rectify not the language but the thoughts of the poet she has under scrutiny. We find not parallels but refutation." [22]

Early evaluations of her poetry as Emersonian, modern, or metaphysical have been replaced by intensive examination of the extent to which the poet shows aspects of such attitudes or movements. For example, Judith Banzer's conclusion that Emily Dickinson was well acquainted with the metaphysical poets and that parallels exist between their poetry and hers is placed under scrutiny first by Ruth Miller, who argues that in fact such poetry appeared too little and too late to have had much influence,[23] and second by Robert Weisbuch, whose careful analysis of her craft reveals that the similarity, though there, is only superficial.[24]

Weisbuch's study is a masterly description of the emergence of Emily Dickinson's individuality as a poet from the wellsprings of her cultural heritage in Puritan Calvinism, Emersonian transcendentalism, and nineteenth-century romantic and postromantic thought. In like manner, he shows that the poet's persona, far from being "Emily Dickinson of Amherst," or even the simple personas of the child, the lover, the sufferer, and so on, is a complex interraction between the oracular, defined as the rebellious transcendental seer, and the confessional, or suffering, skeptical bard through the third persona of mediation or connective thought.[25]

The exploration of such structural themes has given Emily Dickinson scholarship new sophistication and new directions. No longer dismissing, as her earliest critics did, the apparently distorted syntax, the fractured rhymes, or uneven rhythms of her poetry, critics of Emily Dickinson's prosody have set into motion a closer and more critical scrutiny of her language techniques, with remarkable results. David Porter's study of the early poetry, charting as it does the major routes of development in "metrics and rhyme, imagery and diction, speaker and language usage,"[26] has been further elaborated by Brita Lindberg-Seyersted in *The Voice of the Poet* and more recently by Sirkka Heiskänen-Mäkelä in an intensive examination of Emily Dickinson's poetic dialectic.

In the course of this study, Heiskänen-Mäkelä does for the later poetry what Porter did for the earlier and reveals how much the poet has refined her technique of phonetic patterning and elliptic metaphor. Finding much of the later poetry difficult, many critics have underrated it; Heiskänen-Mäkelä's contribution distinguishes more clearly and precisely those elements that succeed: "Dickinson's late manner was the most concise of quatrain form; it was the antithetic, syllogistic use of parallelism; frequently it was the suggestive, euphonic circle of a spell. What seems lost to this manner is the dynamic presence of immediate inspiration; what is gained by it, is distance: dedication to the distinct contour."[27]

Modern linguistic scholarship has only very recently, and still quite sparsely, turned its attention to literary forms.[28] Perhaps as a result, little has yet been written on the poetry of Emily Dickinson from the perspective of language theory. What has been accomplished so far, however, reinforces the observations of the prosodists in showing to what extent the poet exploited all aspects of her language in formulating her major themes and creating her personal voice. Thus, Donald C. Freeman, using the methodology of generative metrics, shows that the awkwardnesses critics saw in the poet's rhythmic patterns result from the influence of the native tradition in her poetry;[29] Irene Nims confirms the critics' tonal readings of several poems by exploring their underlying syntactic structures;[30]

Elizabeth Perlmutter shows how Emily Dickinson's use of the existential sentence differs from other lyric poets of the nineteenth century in creating "a wholly new lyric form, in which the poetic ego is rigorously excluded from the cognitive structure of the poem;" [31] and Archibald Hill uses language strategies to confirm his intuition that one poem is more successful than another.[32]

Perhaps the greatest advance in Emily Dickinson criticism has been made in the movement away from discussions of her poetry in terms of such "surface" themes as religion, love, nature, and death to an exploration of their underlying thematic patterns, such as indirection and indeterminacy, deprivation and destitution, expectancy and afterness. The progress made in the symbolist criticism of the Geneva school and the work of structuralism is reflected in such studies as David Porter's discussion of the poet's "preoccupation with afterknowledge, with living in the aftermath" [33] and Roland Hagenbüchle's close analysis of Emily Dickinson's synecdochic/metonymic metaphors, in which he explores the extent to which the poet's ambivalence and indeterminacy are deliberate.[34] Such studies advance our understanding of Emily Dickinson as a poet who was at home with those who refuse to accept a shallow explanation of human existence, who thought deeply and much about the questions of philosophers, and who had come to her own conclusions about the nature of the world and the human psyche. The fact that the poet has long enjoyed an international reputation, despite the ambivalences and difficulties that critics have seen in her work, indicates the extent to which her poetry speaks to the basic and universal questions of human existence and experience.[35]

The results of Rebecca Patterson's thirty years of dedication to Emily Dickinson scholarship, in the context of this very selective review and as set out in this collection of her writings, are impressive. In her later work, Patterson developed more extensively the patterns of imagery in both the poems and the letters that she had originally identified in *The Riddle of Emily Dickinson* and that were crucial to her thesis. By bringing these together with further elaborations and placing them within the framework of unconscious symbolism, Patterson provides a more coherent picture than she has previously given of her thesis that all the poet's images and word associations are linked to the central theme of erotic love transforming into erotic death. It is the most thorough attempt so far to provide a comprehensive analysis of Emily Dickinson's use of particular and recurrent images, and it traces, more than any other study so far attempted, the relationship of such imagery to the poet's reading, with the result that Emily Dickinson is perceived more clearly as a Victorian poet, indebted to Emerson, the English romantics, and the Brownings and closer to Blake and Hopkins than to Wordsworth or Whitman.

What emerges so remarkably from Patterson's extensive knowledge of the books Emily Dickinson read is how much the poet, whose knowledge of the world depended primarily upon her reading, reached levels of insight and understanding that often surpassed the authors of her sources, and how much she was able to fashion out of these contexts her own personal voice. Patterson's study goes far beyond the question of "borrowing" in its explanation of how the poet turned her readings into raw material for her art. By restricting her analysis to word associations, Patterson makes it clear that her objective is not to discuss poetic influences on Emily Dickinson but rather to reveal poetic relationships with the intent of deepening the contextual meanings surrounding the poet's word choices. As a result, perhaps the major achievement of this book, though incidental to Rebecca Patterson's conscious thesis, is the extent to which it firmly places and defines Emily Dickinson as a poet within nineteenth-century tradition.

In her first chapter, Patterson places the masculine element of Emily Dickinson's character within its proper nineteenth-century perspective, when women and especially artists took on male roles, women like Charlotte Cushman, George Sand, and George Eliot. Emily Dickinson's reluctance to publish is given further perspective in Patterson's discussion of the local climate that was so hostile to women writers.

In the second chapter, the implications of Emily Dickinson's assumed masculine identity are explored in a discussion of the unconscious processes at work in the imagery of her poetry. It is here that Patterson's indebtedness to Cody and the other psychiatrists and psychologists mentioned in her preface becomes clear. It is the most biographically oriented of the chapters and formally presents her major argument that the poet's recurrent imagery is a symbolic expression of her unconscious erotic feelings.

Patterson's analysis of the various patterns in word and image goes some way toward providing the theory of poetry that Cody's study lacks. The succeeding chapters trace the particular image patterns, from the use of jewel, scientific, and color words to geographical place-names and landscapes, developing their interrelationships and building the pattern of erotic symbolism. The book concludes with a discussion of the complex interlocking of images into the cardinal-points symbolism.

Patterson's style is a discursive one, which develops its themes through suggestions and examples, prodding her readers to work out for themselves the conclusions and implications of her analysis. It is a comprehensive style, in which other themes continually and sometimes incidentally intrude, but these are fascinating in their own right: the dating of the poetry,[36] Emily Dickinson's reading and her position in nineteenth-century poetry and thought; the fact that T. W. Higginson, her life-long correspondent and future editor, actually saw very little of the poetry after 1862 while the poet was alive; the thesis that Emily Dickinson died as a symbolist poet in 1865.[37] If one regrets the lack of explicitness in determining how the imagery is transformed into a coherent symbolism, one nevertheless admires the meticulousness and depth of scholarship revealed. And Patterson has the gift of a graceful and witty style, rare in the plethora of current scholarship.

Although Patterson's style does not lend itself to an analytic methodology, there is some evidence that she was moving in the direction of defining the type of symbols the poet used as representations not of archetypes of the external world but of the poetic consciousness itself, thus opening the way for symbolist and structuralist interpretations. The relationships she has drawn in this study provide a rich source for more formal studies of Emily Dickinson's symbols.

Rebecca Patterson died before her manuscript was ready for publication. I trust that the expectations of her family and the University of Massachusetts Press in entrusting me with the task of preparing this book for publication have been fulfilled. The ordering of the chapters is quite different from the original manuscript: Patterson's technique of developing toward her final interpretation resulted in placing the chapter on "The Geography of the Unconscious" last. Moving it forward, I think, will give readers a better sense of the underlying theme throughout the discussions of the various image patterns in succeeding chapters. As it presently stands, the book progresses from the biographical forces that moved Emily Dickinson to the poetic sources of her inspiration, an emphasis on the poet's achievement in distancing her personal suffering and experience and transforming it into great poetry that Rebecca Patterson, I am sure, would have wanted.

I am indebted to David Porter for his continuous support and criticism; to Aaron Fischer for his diligent library hunts; to Nancy Silber for typing what was in parts a difficult manuscript; to Jonathan H. Collett, Donald C. Freeman, and Albert Rabil, Jr., for their comments and suggestions on the first draft of my introduction; to Beth and Roger Freeman for their help with the index; and to my husband, whose support and encouragement throughout was crucial.

Margaret H. Freeman
State University of New York, College at Old Westbury

AUTHOR'S PREFACE

A preface is an opportunity to pay debts, and my own are many and heavy. My initial, heaviest debt is to the late Millicent Todd Bingham, Emily Dickinson's scholarly editor, whose enthusiastic letter stirred a bored and lonely housewife (with an unused Ph.D.) to renew interest in research. In an effort to deserve such kindness, I plunged anew into my study of Emily Dickinson's letters and poems—and of everything written about her—and very shortly I found myself trapped in an agonizing dilemma. The poet's suffering in the early 1860s could not be written off as an embarrassing but transient schoolgirl episode. On the contrary, it was deep and tragic as life—it *was* her life. I had either to forget all about her or to transform a personality (my own) as conventional, priggish, and puritanical as that of any of her biographers. Unfortunately, I could not forget her. I was compelled to swim for my life in bitter waters of humility.

In our earliest correspondence, Mrs. Bingham suggested that I become acquainted with Richard Sewall. Since Professor Sewall and I were both working at Yale, an interview was quickly arranged, and with it began the second most important influence on my life and work. I read him a manuscript outlining my theories, and his response was instant and warm: "You are right," and after a moment, "And that is a real tragedy." We saw each other occasionally but more often conferred by telephone. On one such occasion, we discussed a trip I needed to make to a possible source of Dickinson letters and to fresh information. "It's money, isn't it?" said Mr. Sewall. I admitted that my husband's G.I. school allowance and our slender savings did not allow for scholarly travel. After a brief silence, "You could probably do it on fifty dollars." I thought that on fifty dollars I could manage two such trips. "Oh, hell," said Mr. Sewall grandly. "What's fifty dollars? You'll have my check in the morning."

My two first trips to Cooperstown were very profitable, although in one respect I was late by a hair breadth. Only two months earlier, my hostess had burned the last of the curious little letters in the odd handwriting signed by an unknown "Emilie." Here I should like to attest to my affectionate memory of two other great influences on my work, Margaret Johnson and Katherine Anthon Wood, the grandnieces of a close friend of the poet. Unhappily, the tenor of my research could only bring distress to them, and the affectionate gratitude so strong in my own heart remains, I am afraid, one-sided. There was tragedy to spare in the life of Emily Dickinson, so much that it has reached out to envelop many other lives.

I have never repaid Mr. Sewall his fifty dollars because it pleases me to remain in his debt, and perhaps I think he has had his money's worth. After his initial enthusiasm, he came under the influence of his conservative colleagues, and toward the middle of our acquaintance he complained that I could not write about Emily Dickinson's color words without hidden biographical reference. Quite correct. I agree with R. P. Blackmur that she used the materials of her life as her subject matter and that it is impossible to analyze her aesthetics in ignorance of the true facts of her experience. Of late years, Mr. Sewall has come uneasily closer to my interpretation, and he even feared I would think his biography superficial. I do consider it reserved, understandably so, but a most valuable contribution to Dickinson study.

Mrs. Bingham also initiated my acquaintance with Theodora Ward, granddaughter of the poet's beloved Elizabeth Holland and scholarly editor of the Harvard *Letters of Emily Dickinson*. Though I do not share Mrs. Ward's Jungian proclivities, I do consider her *Capsule of the Mind* one of the most insightful, commonsensical studies of the poet. As a woman, she could. at least write about another woman without male vanities, male fears, and male oedipal hang-ups.

Turning to a man who did produce a very useful, indeed an indispensable, work, I recall with gratitude that Jay Leyda left the manuscript of his *Years and Hours of Emily Dickinson* at my London lodgings, thus giving me an early acquaintance with a book whose pages are now worn with my turnings. I have also made a careful study of the Amherst microfilm of Dickinson manuscripts which he edited, and I regret that the editor of the Harvard *Poems* did not make better use of Leyda's dating. For example, Mr. Leyda pointed to what is almost certainly a packet of poems copied in the late seventies in identical handwriting and on identical stationery that the Harvard *Poems* broke up and dispersed over a period of *six years!* The integrity of this packet is of serious biographical importance.

It would be a mistake, however, to suppose that I am now or have ever been interested in the biography of Emily Dickinson except as a necessary preliminary to understanding her work. As she herself said, "My life has been too simple and stern to embarass any" (letter 330). Indeed, it affords about as much material as the experience of some life-termer in a penitentiary. Her real biography is her poetry and, to a far less extent, her letters. In her correspondence, she too often romanced the truth—"posed," her brother said—and it must be read with great caution.

My real interest has always been in her remarkable handling of language—the elaborate, complex interweaving of images, metaphors, and symbols. That is the concern of my present book, and it brings me to my most important and recent set of obligations. The persons I shall name have all read, advised, corrected, and approved my manuscript, although of course they are not to be held responsible for any errors or omissions on my part. In the second chapter and at intervals throughout the book, I go deeply into the poet's unconscious symbolism. I should not have ventured into a field so foreign to me without the advice and encouragement of distinguished professionals. I am profoundly indebted to Dr. Hilda Rollman-Branch, psychiatrist, Los Angeles; to Dr. Mark Kanzer, psychiatrist, and Dr. Harry Slochower, psychologist, both of New York, and especially to Dr. John Cody, psychiatrist, Hays, Kansas, whose own psychological study of Emily Dickinson was published by Harvard University Press. For his unswerving support, I am deeply grateful to Arlin Turner, professor at Duke University and editor of *American Literature*. Richard Sewall of Yale University, author of the newest and best biography of Emily Dickinson, has read the published articles here collected with mingled approval and uneasiness but with an honest admission that I cannot be ignored. David Porter, University of Massachusetts, Amherst, and author of a fine study of Dickinson's early poems, has read my manuscript with a generous absence of criticism. My last reader, Barton St. Armand of Brown University, now at work on his own Dickinson book, has been a warm source of encouragement.

I am indebted to Robert Lambert for sending me a Xeroxed copy of Samuel Bowles's review of J. G. Holland's *Miss Gilbert's Career;* to the New York Historical Society at Cooperstown for prompt information on the Cooperstown fire, which corrected the dating of a Dickinson letter; to the Springfield (Mass.) Public Library for the records of this fire in the *Springfield Daily Republican;* and to my good friend Myra Himelhoch for many years of criticizing and curbing my excesses and for her exact and scholarly redating of the carelessly dated letters and poems to the Bowles family in the Harvard *Letters of Emily Dickinson*. Finally, I am most grateful to the librarian and staff of the Houghton Library, Harvard University, for permitting me to examine their invaluable collection of Dickinson materials.

Permissions

The thesis of Emily Dickinson's attachment to Kate Scott (Turner) Anthon first appeared in *The Riddle of Emily Dickinson* (Boston: Houghton Mifflin, 1951). Earlier versions of chapters 1, 3, 5, 6 (the Latin American section), and 7 originally appeared in the following publications: "Emily Dickinson's 'Double' Tim: Masculine Identification," *American Imago,* 28: Winter 1971, pp. 330–62. "Emily Dickinson's Jewel Imagery," *American Literature,* January 1971, pp. 495–520. Copyright 1971 by Duke University Press. "Emily Dickinson's Palette I," *Midwest Quarterly,* Summer 1964, pp. 271–91. "Emily Dickinson's Palette II," *Midwest Quarterly,* Autumn 1964, pp. 97–117. "Emily Dickinson's Geography: Latin America," *Papers on Language and Literature* (Southern Illinois University), Fall 1967, pp. 441–57. "Emily Dickinson's Cardinal Points Symbolism I," *Midwest Quarterly,* Summer 1973, pp. 293–317. "Emily Dickinson's Cardinal Points Symbolism II," *Midwest Quarterly,* Autumn 1973, pp. 31–48.

The quotation from W. B. Yeats is from "The Circus Animals' Desertion" from *Collected Poems of William Butler Yeats* (New York: Macmillan, 1966), Copyright 1940 by Georgie Yeats, renewed 1968 by Bertha Georgie Yeats, Michael Butler Yeats, and Anne Yeats. Quotations from the poems of Emily Dickinson are reprinted by permission of the publishers and the Trustees of Amherst College from *The Poems of Emily Dickinson,* edited by Thomas H. Johnson, Cambridge, Mass.: the Belknap Press of Harvard University Press, copyright © 1951, 1955 by the President and Fellows of Harvard College, and from *Poems of Emily Dickinson,* edited by Martha Dickinson Bianchi and Alfred Leete Hampson, copyright 1914, 1942 by Martha Dickinson Bianchi; copyright 1929 by Martha Dickinson Bianchi, copyright © renewed 1957 by Mary L. Hampson; and copyright 1935 by Martha Dickinson Bianchi, copyright © renewed 1963 by Mary L. Hampson. Quotations from the letters reproduced by permission of the publishers from *The Letters of Emily Dickinson,* edited by Thomas H. Johnson, Cambridge, Mass.: the Belknap Press of Harvard University Press, copyright © 1958 by the President and Fellows of Harvard College.

Notes on the Text

Numbers in parentheses are those of the poems in the three-volume variorum edition of *The Poems of Emily Dickinson,* ed. Thomas H. Johnson (Cambridge: Harvard University Press, Belknap Press, 1955). Numbers preceded by the letter L and by the letters PF are those of the letters and prose fragments, respectively, in the three-volume *Letters of Emily Dickinson,* ed. Thomas H. Johnson and Theodora Ward (Cambridge: Harvard University Press, Belknap Press, 1958). Emily Dickinson's spelling in quotations from the poems and letters has been preserved throughout.

ONE ❧ THE BOY EMILY

"I was born a tomboy," Charlotte Cushman remembered. Uneasily, her biographer explained that the word *tomboy* was applied to any little girl especially lively and independent and was but the forerunner of a host of unpleasant epithets used to keep down the aspiring woman of the midnineteenth century. The great actress, who had earned her freedom from the pettier conventions, went on imperturbably to recall that as a child she had cracked open the heads of all her dolls "to see what they were thinking about," had possessed neither skill nor inclination for making dolls' clothes, but loved tools and handled them skillfully and had a passion for climbing trees. She had also earned her tomboy epithet.[1]

Among her most celebrated roles were such breeches parts as Romeo, Hamlet, and Cardinal Wolsey. The sculptor Paul Akers was especially struck by the "passionate tenderness" of her Romeo, and several critics praised her interpretation. Biographer Emma Stebbins tried to argue that these indecorous roles were more or less forced upon the actress, but the latter had a good deal of independence in choosing her vehicles and played her breeches parts with convincing gusto. An old school friend, meeting Charlotte after many years, recalled how the actress went over the old times "when, as she said, we were boys together, albeit I had no such penchant for a masculine masquerade as she, with the glory of her Romeo behind her, might reasonably entertain."[2] This preference went back to a period much earlier than her Romeo. Remembering a schoolgirl performance of the operetta *Bluebeard,* the friend could still picture Charlotte as the young soldier-lover in white trousers, close jacket, and red sash and could hear the beautiful clear voice singing joyously, "Fatima, Fatima, Selim's here."

It was a strange, androgynous age in which the sexes, separated by wide differences in education, duties, place of occupation, and status, seemed to be striving furiously, often at cross-purposes, even unconsciously, to bridge a painful chasm. Costume was an important symbol of the difference. Bettina Brentano writes in great excitement to Frau Rath von Goethe to guess what the tailor is making for her: "A pair of trousers? Yes!— Hurrah! (Other times are coming now) and a waistcoat and coat too... and then I throw myself into a chaise, and courier-like travel day and night through the entire armies, between friend and foe; all the fortresses unbar at my approach, and thus on to Berlin." Back in Frankfurt and the glorious adventure five months in the past, she looks often and wistfully at her *Bubenkleider,* yellow waistcoat, gray trousers, and brown coat, remembers climbing a spruce tree and looking over the countryside; remembers going into the stable to help the postboy saddle the horses, fetch saddle and stirrups from the wall, and run in front with the whip; remembers walking to the smithy arm in arm with an old Prussian soldier who wondered that such a young lad should be traveling so far. "And these little freedoms," she concludes with a sigh, "made me childishly happy, as I have seldom ever been." [3]

The November 1861 *Atlantic* carried a long article by Julia Ward Howe reviewing and commenting on George Sand's autobiography (to which Emily Dickinson alluded in letter 234). During her youth, as Mrs. Howe observes, George Sand had sometimes scandalized the neighborhood by wearing a boy's dress of blouse, cap, and trousers. In Paris she adopted male attire on a plea of poverty but with this revealing admission: "I cannot express the pleasure my boots gave me. I would gladly have slept with them on. With these little iron-shod heels, I stood firm on the pavement. I flew from one end of Paris to the other. I could have made the circuit of the world thus attired." Although Mrs. Howe did not wish to be "understood as relaxing in any degree the rigor of repudiation which such an act deserved," she could not help adding wistfully, "Yet it is imaginable, even to an undepraved mind, that a woman might sometimes like to be on the other side of the fence." Moreover, she was not going to fling mud "at a sister's crowned head," especially a forehead that "Elizabeth Browning's hands were not too pure to soothe...chiding while they soothed." [4] The allusion is to a pair of sonnets Mrs. Browning wrote to that "large-brained woman and large-hearted man," pitying the attempt to deny her "woman's nature with a manly scorn, / And break away the gauds and armlets worn / By weaker women in captivity," but urging her to wait patiently "Till God unsex thee on the heavenly shore"—a consolation somewhat on the order of the heavenly bleaching that awaited the good little pickaninny.[5]

Bettina Brentano and George Sand were among the idols of Margaret Fuller, author of the feminist *Woman in the Nineteenth Century,* and like them she seemed curiously teased by the idea of wearing trousers. "George Sand smokes, wears male attire, wishes to be addressed as 'Mon

Frere,'" she observes, then notes with approval that Goethe's "Mignon and Theresa wear male attire when they like, and it is graceful for them to do so."[6] With some ambivalence, her friend Emerson recalls, "She had a feeling that she ought to have been a man, and said of herself, 'A man's ambition with a woman's heart, is an evil lot.'" And he quotes these lines from Margaret Fuller's poem "To the Moon":

> But if I steadfast gaze upon thy face,
> A human secret, like my own, I trace;
> For, through the woman's smile looks the male eye.[7]

Nowadays it may be difficult to understand what all the bother was about; yet there is no mistaking the symbolism of this drive toward male freedom by a number of unusually gifted and aggressive women. It could be limited to the adoption of a masculine pseudonym, the George Eliot of Mary Ann Evans, the Currer, Ellis, and Acton Bell of the Brontë sisters, or the stark simplicity of "Dickinson" with which the American poet signed a number of her letters. Elizabeth Browning is another case in point, perhaps surprisingly to readers of her *Sonnets,* for the romantic circumstances of her private life (which she insisted on living quite publicly) have somewhat obscured a remarkable aggressiveness and ambition. All through her childhood, she told her friend Miss Mitford, and even before reading Mary Wollstonecraft at the ripe age of twelve, she had been indignant against nature for making her a woman and had "resolved to dress up in men's clothes as soon as ever I was free of the nursery, and go into the world 'to seek my fortune.'" How she would do it she did not know, but she rather inclined toward being page to "poor" Lord Byron. As to the "pudding-making and stocking-darning theory" of woman's activities, she admitted to being as incompetent as she was contemptuous; writing was her business.[8]

Her admiration of Byron, whose language, themes, and attitudes recur in her work, was another tie to George Sand. The latter's Lelia borrows her name from Don Juan's protégée and is so clearly a female Manfred as to make one critic complain that the author was giving her readers "du lord Byron au kilo."[9] Bettina Brentano was Byron's contemporary but wrote all her books after his death and reflected his influence. In short, as Byron and his publisher well knew, most of his readers were women.

If Byron was singularly attractive to the disadvantaged women of the early nineteenth century, it may have been because they were singularly attractive to him. He usually sought out clever, bookish, rather aggressive women. Of Madame de Staël he thought so highly at one time that he gave her the supreme accolade: "she ought to have been a man." He had also his circle of intimate male friends, for whom his feelings were consistently tenderer than for any woman he knew. In his twentieth year he proposed, half seriously, that he and a young chorister at Cambridge retire

to some secluded vale and set an example of constancy to put the celebrated Llangollen ladies to the blush, and there were other such romantic
friendships in his life.[10] Perhaps this androgynous element in his nature
accounts for his strong interest in the hermaphroditic sculptures at the
Uffizi—marble figures with maternal breasts and male sex organs.

Tennyson's *The Princess,* which had a marked influence on Emily Dickinson, is a striking example of the androgynous spirit of the age. The
Prince, fair and blue-eyed, with a girl's yellow ringlets, and subject to
peculiar fits, disguises himself and two companions as women and invades
the forbidden grounds of the college his childhood fiancée, Princess Ida,
has set up to educate women to be the equals of men. By the end of the
story, he has persuaded this six-foot Amazon with her watchdog leopards
to abandon women's rights for woman's duties as his mother-*cum*-bride,
and her surrender rids him of his troublesome epilepsy. It is a curious story
but hardly more curious than the respectful sympathy expressed by some
readers for the supposed widow who wrote *In Memoriam* to honor her
fallen soldier-husband. In these and other strange ways the age sought to
heal the painful split in its psyche.

2

Amid the trash accumulated in the mental attics of her
neighbors, one legend about Emily Dickinson has the look of truth. A
woman who in early years sewed for the Dickinsons heard the young
Emily say she was afraid of death, the dead were so soon forgotten—"But
when I die, they'll have to remember me." [11] Whether the words were
ever spoken or not, she undertook to live by them. An intelligent, talented,
extremely ambitious girl, she wanted to make her mark (in the beginning
she scarcely knew how) for the same reason that an ambitious man wants
to make his—to affirm in the face of death that she at least *was*. But here
she came in conflict with her age, which was inhospitable to gifted men
and flinty toward the woman who did not know her place. Woman's place
was narrowly defined and did not include a literary career.

An increasing number of women, it is true, were entering the literary
marketplace and sometimes doing well—"a damned mob of scribbling
women," Nathaniel Hawthorne wrote bitingly—probably because an increasing number of women were receiving some education, and then as
now they were the principal audience for fiction.[12] But women could not
write for this audience of their own without dragging a heavy weight of
apology. In the late 1840s Lydia Maria Child began to think it was no
longer absolutely disreputable for a woman to write, but she would have
found scant comfort in a Mrs. S. C. Hall, whose article in the September
1850 *Harper's* made such defense as seemed possible for erring Jane Porter,

author of *Thaddeus of Warsaw* and *Scottish Chiefs*.[13] "Happy is the country where the laws of God and nature are held in reverence," Mrs. Hall
wrote darkly. Her tone implied that Miss Porter had prospered at the
expense of the "strength and glory of England," which "are in the keeping
of the wives and mothers of its men," so that "when we are questioned
touching our 'celebrated women,' we may in general terms refer to those
who have watched over, moulded and inspired our 'celebrated' men."
There might be a *few* women who achieved fame without neglecting their
"domestic and social duties," yet in her individual capacity "the *woman*
would have been happier had she continued enshrined in the privacy of
domestic love and domestic duty." [14] Mrs. Child may not have seen this
ponderous put-down, but Emily Dickinson read it.

In his introduction to Elizabeth Browning's poems H. T. Tuckerman
was somewhat more indulgent, as became an introducer, to the feminine
writers of verse. He considered genuine verse "an excellent safety-valve."
True, he had "heard the publication of a lady's effusions regretted by one
of her sex, on the ground that she had 'printed her soul,' " and the objection was "not without significance to a refined nature." Happily, her audience would be so slender, and of this small number there would be so
very few able to discover the personal experience hidden in the mere
observation, that he apprehended no grave harm. At the same time, it
seemed well to "acknowledge that authorship, as a career, is undesirable
for a woman." Susan Dickinson owned this 1852 edition, and Emily read
the introduction, for she outraged Helen Hunt Jackson by asking her how
she could bear to "print her soul." [15]

In the late fifties Josiah G. Holland, husband of Emily's good friend,
pleased a wide audience with his abuse of the feminists as "masculine
young women ... abnormal women ... who bemoan the fate which drapes
them in petticoats, who quarrel with St. Paul and their lot." [16] He now
undertook to crush them once for all with a novel that would deflate their
pretensions and restore them in grateful humility to the domestic hearth.
The heroine of *Miss Gilbert's Career* decides to write books, to reveal her
life in poetry and capture the adoration of the world, to become a great
painter, a prison visitor, a missionary, a public speaker, and feminist: "She
would have a career of some kind." And while she daydreams for a golden
hour, the charms of domestic life fade, and the idea of marriage, of the
wife's duties, of the necessary subordination to the husband, becomes
"repulsive." To her father, Fanny bursts out:

I wish to God I were a man! I think it a curse to be a woman....
A woman has no freedom, and no choice of life. She can take no
position, and have no power, without becoming a scoffing and a by-
word.... I say that I will not accept this lot, and that I do not believe
my Maker ever intended I should accept it.

Her father merely orders her to stop insulting him and disgracing herself. When she confides to a woman friend that she has written a novel, the latter is not helpful but appalled. Miss Hammett would shudder at the thought of her name becoming "public property." She could not bear to be talked about "in private parlors and public places" or to coin "my heart's best emotion and my sweetest imaginations into words which the world can use as a glass by which it may read my life." She assures Fanny that a woman's true world is the small one of the heart and that someday she will give everything in the world and indeed in the universe to win the love of one good man. Fanny persists in her folly, and by the early age of twenty-seven has achieved success and the wisdom to see that it is all ashes and vanity. Sublimely, she now throws away wealth and fame and marries an impecunious, self-educated clergyman, having learned that to give humble support to a good man is a woman's true career.[17]

Without doubt Emily Dickinson and her sister-in-law read their friend's book, as a duty if not a pleasure, and they must have laughed at its monstrous silliness—yet uneasily and perhaps angrily, for the work mimics youthful daydreams with stinging ingenuity. Representative even in its silliness of a whole climate of contemptuous hostility, *Miss Gilbert's Career* helps explain the mysterious excitement of some letters written by the poet in her ambitious youth. To Jane Humphrey she confides that she has "dared to do strange things—bold things," has "heeded beautiful tempters," and though she does not think herself "wrong," she could make her friend "tremble" for her "and be very much afraid, and wonder how things would end." She would like to sit at Jane's feet and "confess" a secret experience that has beguiled her with its sweetness and given her life an aim, and she coyly invites Jane to guess what she means (L35). The language would suggest a clandestine love affair. Only from the evidence of further letters and the squeamishness of a Miss Hammett is it possible to understand that the twenty-year-old girl was daring to write poetry and dream of fame.

Late in the same year, a letter to Abiah Root throws a stronger light on Emily's ambitions and fears. Her friend is "growing wiser" than she and nipping fancies that Emily lets blossom, even though they may come to nothing or bear a bitter fruit: "The shore is safer, Abiah, but I love to buffet the sea—I can count the bitter wrecks here in these pleasant waters, and hear the murmuring winds, but oh, I love the danger!" (L39). By this time she has probably read Emerson's "Heroism," for her imagination appears to be fired by his strong encouragement of a woman's ambition, especially in such lines as these: "O friend, never strike sail to a fear! Come into port greatly, or sail with God the seas!"[18] His figure is adapted in turn from a daring passage in Bettina Brentano's *Günderode,* and the whole paragraph is a tribute to ambitious womanhood as exemplified in Bettina and must have rung bells in the mind of young Emily Dickinson.[19]

In an earlier letter to Abiah, written not long after the mystifying letter to Jane, the would-be poet speaks of "dreaming a golden dream, with eyes all the while wide open." She has been burdened with kitchen duties, owing to the illness of her mother, but "God forbid" that the kitchen ever be hers, and "God keep [her] from what they call *households*," except of course the heavenly household above; and she makes her disaffection still clearer by scornfully alluding to Abiah's presumed interest in "*boots,* and *whiskers*" (L36). For a girl of her times, this is not so daring as it is hopelessly unrealistic. In very different language, Samuel Bowles congratulates a friend on the birth of a son: "I am glad it is a boy. Boys are institutions. They have a future, a positive future. Girls are swallowed up, —they are an appendage,—a necessary appendage, it may be,—probably they are,—but still they are appendages." [20] In an age when girls were swallowed up—destroyed as human beings—the only alternative, regardless of internal convulsions and suffering, was for the very intelligent, very gifted girl to turn into a boy.

Martha Dickinson Bianchi called her Aunt Emily an "instinctive feminist," indignant from her youth "at being counted as *non compos* in a man's world of reality." The evidence cited by Mrs. Bianchi is some uncomplimentary remarks directed at the type of professor who would someday write the poet's biographies, for Emily Dickinson had met a good many Amherst professors and had taken their measure. "Most such are Manikins," she wrote to a friend, "and a warm blow from a brave Anatomy, hurls them into Wherefores—" (L901). Mrs. Bianchi remembers her Aunt Emily summoning her to an upstairs window "to peep at a new Professor.... 'Look dear, he is pretty as a cloth Pink!' her mouth curling in derision," and on a like occasion looking down at a stranger sent to call on her and dismissing him unreceived with the comment, "His face is as handsome and as meaningless as the full moon." [21] Those biographers who picture the secluded poet as a Lady of Shalott fatally smitten by a glimpse of the passing Lancelot have overlooked the derisive gestures from the tower window. They have also overlooked the fact that Emily is never the Lily Maid, she is Lancelot. "Her devotion to those she loved," Mrs. Bianchi remarked slyly, "was that of a knight for his lady." [22]

3

In general, the biographers and editors of Emily Dickinson have been content to ignore the poet's masculine claims, although these claims bulk large. Again and again, the poet describes herself as a boy— a boy possessed, moreover, by an unappeasable desire to return to the mother, symbolized by such objects as houses, rooms, food, nectar, and the like; but neither this symbolism nor the boy identity has attracted much notice. A partial but interesting exception is Theodora Ward's *Capsule of the Mind,* with its gingerly excursion into the poet's masculine alter ego. The approach is Jungian, and Ward specifically mentions Jung as her authority for stating that such mental power as a woman possesses belongs to her masculine side, whereas the feminine element in a man is "soul." She finds this idea borne out in the more "philosophical" poems (many of them in the form of "definitions" and employing the "phraseology of the text books") written in the years 1863–65, after the poet had suffered a tragic love affair and had extracted from the now-vanished lover "the masculine element that set her mind free." This masculine power of textbook and definition appears also to be the more lyrical power of the years 1860–62. Speaking of the poet's double, the boy Tim, in an 1860 poem beginning "We dont cry—Tim and I" (196), Ward observes that Emily's "shy masculine counterpart ... 'reads a little Hymn'—an act that is prophetic of his true function" as the part of her mind that creates.

Like other biographers, Ward betrays a troubled concern with the childish tone of many poems. Of one beginning "God permits industrious Angels— / Afternoons—to play—" (231), she says the image of the boy playing with the angel could not have originated in the mind of a thirty-year-old woman "but was certainly carried over from the impressions of childhood."[23] She has failed to observe what is going on in the poem. This schoolboy has been summoned from a game of "Marbles" to play the game of love with an enchanting angel and stranger, two names Emily Dickinson repeatedly gave the lost beloved, with an obvious reference to the Bible: "Be not forgetful to entertain strangers; for thereby some have entertained angels unawares."

Mrs. Ward is equally positive that young Tim was an imaginary companion invented by a child of five or six. She notes the curious childlike language, the poet's surprising regression, "at a time when her creative flood was reaching its height, ... to the mood of a lonely child, burdened with a secret fear," and the odd fact that, instead of projecting herself into an imaginary companion of the same sex, the little Emily invented for her alter ego a boy named Tim. Possibly Ward knew that George Sand, a writer whom Emily admired, created in her own little girlhood "a sort of angel-companion," a boy named Corambe, whom she enveloped in mythology and worshiped at a little shrine in the wood. The coincidence is a striking one, but the poet could not have been influenced by this account of George Sand earlier than late October 1861, when she received the November *Atlantic.*[24] The handwriting of her poem seems to belong quite definitely to late 1860, and the actual composition may have been earlier, for about February 1859 the Tim identity made its appearance.

During the early months of 1859, Sue Dickinson entertained her old school friend, Kate Scott Turner, and Emily spent many of her evenings with them. Apparently one such visit was prolonged until nearly midnight, and the poet was fetched home by her overbearing father. In a note sent to her sister-in-law the following morning she wryly describes herself as an "unfortunate insect" and her father as a "Reptile." Pasted above the joking message is a woodcut clipped·from the *New England Primer* showing a youth (Emily) pursued by an upright, wolflike creature with a forked tail, the "Reptile" of her misleading caption (L214). Although she cut away the letterpress, she doubtless reminded Sue and Kate, or they remembered, that the woodcut illustrated the letter *T* and these verses: "Young Timothy / Learnt sin to fly." There is no evidence that the little Emily ever "played with" an imaginary little Tim, but it is quite clear that the twenty-eight-year-old woman playfully identified herself with the Puritan youth Timothy fleeing from "sin."

Another interesting hint of Tim has escaped Mrs. Ward's notice. At some unknown time, but surely not long after February 1859, the poet excised the name "Timothy" from the title page of 1 Timothy in her personal copy of the Bible and probably used it as a signature to a letter sent to one of her more irreverent friends—very likely her sister-in-law or the latter's friend Kate, who would recognize the allusion.[25] Still another hint of playing at masculinity occurs in a letter of 2 March 1859 to Elizabeth Holland. Commenting on the news that Dr. Holland is returning from a lecture tour, the poet observes that Mrs. Holland can now doff her "weeds for a Bride's Attire," adding: "Am told that fasting gives to food marvelous Aroma, but by birth a Bachelor, disavow Cuisine." Bachelor Emily goes on to describe, half playfully, a painful degree of tension and excitement brought on by the departure of some cherished person (L204). Although Mrs. Holland doubtless took the compliment for herself, another letter written almost at the same time, probably the same evening, suggests that the poet owed the idea of the "weeds" as well as her ill-concealed excitement to Sue's beautiful school friend, Kate Turner, whose invariable black made a strong impression on the sensitive poet. The young widow had just ended a two-months visit with Sue and had gone on to friends in Boston, and Emily was writing a first letter to her only a few hours later.

In early 1859 the poet found still another reason for wishing status as a boy. The February *Atlantic* published T. W. Higginson's most celebrated feminist article, an attack on entrenched prejudice under the sardonic title, "Ought Women to Learn the Alphabet?" In his reply he cited example after example of brilliant women who made their mark because they had been given the opportunities of boys, among them Florence Nightingale and sculptor Harriet Hosmer, scholarly Queen Christina of Sweden and her scholarly friend Madame Dacier. Of Elena Cornaro, professor of six languages at the University of Padua, he observes, "But Elena Cornaro was educated like a boy, by her father"; and Clotilda Tambroni, "the first Greek scholar of Southern Europe in her day ... was educated like a boy, by Emanuele Aponte." "And so down to our own day, who knows how

many mute, inglorious Minervas may have perished unenlightened, while
Margaret Fuller and Elizabeth Browning were being educated 'like boys'?" [26]
When Emily Dickinson wrote to Higginson three years later, "I went to
school—but in your manner of the phrase—had no education" (L261), she
was not humbling herself to his sex but admitting a fear that she did not
measure up to these brilliant women educated "like boys."

Higginson's essay continued to reverberate among these young women.
About mid-February 1862, Sue Dickinson commissioned Bowles to get her
a photograph of this champion of women's rights, and when Higginson's
"Letter to a Young Contributor" appeared in the April 1862 *Atlantic,*
Emily greeted the article like a message from a trusted friend and invited
his criticism of her writing. Although she was speedily disillusioned about
his critical ability and sent him very few poems after 1862, she continued
to write to him as a kindly man and a staunch friend to women.

Sue Dickinson was at least a covert feminist and, like Emily, responded
to the strong feminist element in *Aurora Leigh.* Mrs. Browning might
speak deprecatingly of the "Woman's Question" as of some current American fad, but she made a substantial contribution to feminine self-respect
by creating a heroine who earned her living and held her own in a world
of men, as did Mrs. Browning herself. In her copy of the poem, Sue
Dickinson (less probably, Emily) marked with approval the heroine's
haughty words to her cousin Romney:

> You think a woman ripens as a peach—
> In the cheeks, chiefly.

And she marked passages asserting that a woman must have intellectually
satisfying work:

> Otherwise she drops
> At once below the dignity of man,
> Accepting serfdom;

and again:

> Three years I lived and worked. Get leave to work
> In this world,—'tis the best you get at all;
> For God, in cursing gives us better gifts
> Than man in benediction.[27]

Nor would it escape her attention, or Emily's, that the fairytale ending was
accompanied by some peculiar and perhaps gratifying circumstances. For
Aurora accepts her cousin as a husband only after she has convicted him
of pitiable folly, harangued him by the good hour, forced him to his knees,
and symbolically castrated him—in precisely the same manner as Charlotte
Brontë tames her Rochester, that is, by blinding him. When Emily acquired her own copy of *Aurora Leigh,* she marked it much less exuber-

antly than Sue had done, but among her marked passages are ten lines beginning "The works of women are symbolical," in which Mrs. Browning heaps scorn upon servile feminine activities.

In Tennyson's reactionary treatment of the feminist movement, *The Princess,* Sue discovered the line, "You hold the woman is the better man," and improved it by bracketing the last six words, "the woman is the better man." Another bracketed passage has a puzzling relationship to a letter written by Emily to Bowles in late 1862 (L277). After she refused to see him, he sent her a "little Bat" with the obvious intention of reminding her of some earlier discussion or argument. The passage marked in the poem is Princess Ida's proposal to put love on the shelf like so many bats:

Love is it? Would this same mock-love, and this
Mock-Hymen were laid up like winter bats,
Till all men grew to rate us at our worth,
Not vassals to be beat, nor pretty babes
To be dandled, no, but living wills, and sphered
Whole in ourselves and owed to none. Enough!

But Sue's most startling avowal of feminism was the belated use of her maiden name, S. H. Gilbert, on the flyleaf of an 1859 edition of a book by Bettina Brentano von Arnim. It may have been a deliberate repudiation of her husband; if an unconscious slip, then it is still more revealing. And it was in this atmosphere of defiance and self-assertion that the boy Emily struggled into poetry.

The poet's boyishness was a recognized part of the family jokelore, as shown by her own comments about being told to behave better "when I was a Boy" (L571) or about little Ned inheriting "his Uncle Emily's ardor for the lie" (L315) or by the signature "Brother Emily" in a letter to her Norcross cousins (L367); and these cousins knew that Emily herself found it "criminal...to be a boy in a godly village" and unhopefully hoped to be "forgiven" (L234). Nor was this boyishness completely unknown to outsiders. On reading the poem, "A narrow Fellow in the Grass" (986), Samuel Bowles delightedly asked where "that girl" got her knowledge of farming and Sue Dickinson laughingly replied, "Oh, you forget that was Emily '*when a boy*'!" [28] Sue's joking answer was intended to remind Bowles of earlier incidents, for he too was aware of Emily's masculine identity.

In late June 1877, in an unusually reminiscent mood (her old friend Kate had once more been visiting in the house next door), the poet signed a letter to Bowles, "Your 'Rascal,'" adding, "I washed the Adjective" (L515). She was alluding to a passage in *The Old Curiosity Shop* in which Dickens explains that Mr. Brass was in the habit of treating his sister Sally like another man, a feeling "so perfectly reciprocal, that not only did Mr. Brass often call Miss Brass a rascal or even put an adjective before the rascal, but Miss Brass looked upon it as quite a matter of course." And Dick Swiveller, Mr. Brass's clerk, is so accustomed to the manliness of Sally Brass that he "would sometimes reward her with a hearty slap on the back, and protest that she was a devilish good fellow, a jolly dog, and so forth." Later in the story, the masculine Miss Brass is reported to be disguised as a sailor or as a soldier in the foot guards.[29]

An 1861 letter in which Emily Dickinson calls Bowles the "Swiveller" and signs herself the "Marchioness" suggests that labeling each other as characters in *The Old Curiosity Shop* was a game with them (L241). The temptation to call Emily a mannish "Sally Brass" or "Rascal" (Dickens says "provoking rascal" and hints at a stronger adjective) would be most likely to arise upon any suggestion of feminist sympathies, and about 5 August 1860 the poet was clearly on the aggressive and open to the charge of being Sally Brassish. In Amherst to report the August commencement, Bowles was taking a little time off to refresh himself at the house of his friend Austin Dickinson, when a discussion arose that waxed almost as hot as the weather. Months later he would write with some pride to his close friend Maria Whitney that she and two or three unnamed women had given him a new understanding of the disabilities of their sex. It can be no more than a guess that the unnamed women were Emily and her sister-in-law and probably Kate Turner, but it is a certainty that the conversation that August day turned on the position of women and that Bowles was annoyed. In her letter of apology Emily hopes that Bowles will forgive and respect his "little Bob o' Lincoln" (L223). Characteristically, she is a boyish bird.

A self-educated man, Bowles was grateful to Sue Dickinson for developing his taste in literature. She was his "Queen of Pelham," "Queen of the Tropics," the "most graceful woman in Western Massachusetts"; and he was kind in his way to the less attractive Emily, on whom he bestowed the less attractive title of "Queen Recluse." As for the beautiful "Mrs. Kate," he licked his lips when writing to Austin about her and pursued her as if he had some hope of catching up.[30] "Amherst furnishes the beauty—the world comes to adore," he said of them in his commencement report.[31] These then were the women—queens, all of them—who converted him to the cause of women's rights that August day and persuaded him to treat *Miss Gilbert's Career* less tenderly than he might otherwise have done. His review begins with generous quotation and neutral comment (Dr. Holland, albeit a canting prig in Bowles's opinion, was useful to the *Springfield Republican*), but in the final paragraph the reviewer hears "the cold, clear voice of some gray-eyed 'woman of the nineteenth century' triumphantly asking the author of *Miss Gilbert's Career*" whether there can be any just, rational distinction between "man's work" and "woman's work."[32] Had Sue introduced Bowles to Margaret Fuller's

Woman in the Nineteenth Century? Whatever the source of his interest, he would quote from Fuller's work again.[33]

4

Although "Tim" as a conscious double belongs to about 1859, Emily's unconscious boy self would be a far earlier development, no doubt as early as the discovery of the favoritism shown to her slightly older brother, when she may have been no more than three or four years old. From infancy she must have identified and competed with Austin only a little less passionately than Elizabeth Barrett with her brother Edward, and if Austin had drowned like young Barrett, Emily might have been plunged into as desperate and guilty an invalidism. In a poem beginning "A loss of something ever felt I," she declares that her earliest memory is of being a "Mourner" among the other children, "Bereft" of a nameless something, "bemoaning a Dominion" from which she is "the only Prince cast out" (959). With the slight flicker of an old resentment, she tells Higginson: "When much in the Woods as a little Girl, I was told that the Snake would bite me, that I might pick a poisonous Flower, or Goblins kidnap me" (L271); and a poem of late 1871 begins, "So I pull my Stockings off / Wading in the Water / For the Disobedience' Sake" (1201). She knew well that little boys were not told to stay out of the woods or forbidden to go barefoot. After her mother died, in late 1882, she wrote with poignant regret of the childhood "rapture of losing my shoe in the Mud and going Home barefoot, wading for Cardinal flowers and the mothers reproof," adding that this reproof had been "more for my sake than her weary own for she frowned with a smile" (PF117). At long last she appeared ready to forgive her mother that mysterious injury for which she had always blamed her.

More was involved than a deeply unconscious rivalry with her brother. The customs of an age bore down with oppressive weight on lively, playful little girls. Perhaps these girls did not fade and die in such calamitous numbers as midcentury witnesses reported, but the death rate was alarmingly high. Exercise was discouraged, and the cumbersome clothes were in themselves an unhygienic prison. The remarkable kinesthetic imagery of Emily Dickinson's poetry may be simply the violent eruption of energies too long repressed. It is not just that her verbs incessantly run, leap, climb, swim, row, wrestle, grapple, and grasp, or creep, crawl, clutch, stagger, push, strive, struggle, and strain, or dance, caper, swagger, clasp, quiver, strike, and stab; or that her nouns and adjectives are only a little less energetic and that storm, earthquake, maelstrom, and volcanic eruption run riot. The whole body of her poetry throughout 1859-65 (but hardly at all afterward) seems to be working with a violent energy. She is a gun-woman firing herself in manic passion; her house-body rocks in a kind of orgasm; she suffers, exults, prefers a look of agony because "it's true" (754, 638, 241). The "Essential Oils" of poetic greatness do not come easily; like a perfume, they are "wrung" or "expressed by . . . Screws" (675). Exposure to any great amount of the poetry written during these crucial years can become a wearing experience.

"Cramped, curbed, repressed in every natural desire or impulse," Mrs. Bianchi said of her aunt, but she added correctly that this was a general condition applying no less to her stolid and indifferent companions.[34] A recurring note in poems and letters is the poet's unavailing search for a playmate. Her friend Abby Wood, she writes, shortly after her twentieth birthday, "is more of a woman than I am, for I love so to be a child" (L39). Or Abiah Root has always been dignified, but Emily liked to "cut a timid caper now and then" (L91). Defensively she began to call herself "old-fashioned." Play is the key word to her figurative childhood. "Blessed are they that play," she writes, "for theirs is the kingdom of heaven" (L690). It is her preferred attitude toward life (she and her soul go out to play, 1120), or would be her preferred attitude if pain did not make her soul put its playthings up (244). When Higginson asked about her poetry, she answered that it was her only playmate (L513), and of a friend now estranged from her she wrote sadly that they had been "playfellow" hearts (1098).

When Susan Gilbert came to live in Amherst, the young girl at last had a friend clever and witty enough to return the balls as they were driven into her court. The experience while it lasted was delirious. Writing to Jane Humphrey in early 1850, Emily was ready to find the path of duty "very ugly indeed," to reach out for the things that "Satan covers . . . with flowers," to laugh at the sewing society and its good works and to be cheerfully undisturbed by the thought that she had been "set down as one of those brands almost consumed" (L30). It was the juvenile persiflage of a happy heart. Three years later, the delirium ended with Sue's engagement to Austin Dickinson, and the "younger brother" wrote a desperately unhappy letter begging remembrance for "the Youth, the Lone Youth, Susie, you know the rest!" (L102). The letter suggests that the boy Emily was known to Sue in their early twenties, although no other evidence exists in the relatively small number of letters that Sue preserved. To Austin, the poet wrote in early 1854, "Well—we were all boys once, as Mrs. Partington says" (L152).

There are no boy poems in handwriting earlier than 1860, and two of the three examples of that year may be dismissed as casual: "School Boys" hunt pine cones in the bough overhead (161); "Death . . . Never was a Boy," that is, a boy like herself (153). The Tim poem of late 1860 is the first clear assertion of her new masculine identity. A poem written late in the next year, "Over the fence—," describing the temptation of some strawberries, seems indebted both to Julia Ward Howe's wistful glance over the fence of boyhood and to love's seducing strawberries which Bettina regretfully left uneaten.[35] Emily could climb the fence—and berries are "nice"; but if she spoiled her apron, God would scold. On second thought, she guesses he would try to climb too, "if He were a Boy"—like Emily (251). Another 1861 poem, "Did we disobey Him?," confesses her inability to forget. If the lover were such a dunce, Emily would continue to "Love the dull lad—best—." Can the other person not love the dull lad Emily? (267). In a poem probably written in late 1861, "The nearest Dream recedes—unrealized" (319), "School Boy" Emily is "Homesick for steadfast Honey" but admits that no bee "brews that rare variety."

Of these 1860 and 1861 poems, except for the Tim poem, it may be said that the poet does not unequivocally identify herself as a boy. The comparison with God is not completed; the "dull lad" is shifty and evasive; the schoolboy is as elusive as his bee. Beginning with 1862, however, she quite clearly and deliberately adopts the boy identity for specific poems. In "There's been a Death, in the Opposite House" (389), she remembers —"when a Boy"—watching a house of death, seeing a mattress flung out, wondering "if it died—on that," finding in the minister's stiff walk a suggestion that this man now owns the mourners—"And little Boys— besides—." Perhaps the boy identity struck her as peculiarly suited to graveyard themes. In a letter of 25 April 1862 to T. W. Higginson, she speaks of a terror she has suffered "since September" and adds, "and so I sing, as the Boy does by the Burying Ground—because I am afraid—" (L261). An 1864 poem, "Who occupies this House?" (892), describes the graveyard as a "curious Town" with houses old and new. The poet would not care to build among such silent inhabitants; she would prefer a place where birds assemble and "Boys" like herself are "possible." Another 1864 poem, "How the Waters closed above Him" (923), might suggest an attempt to poetize some local tragedy. It describes feelingly the solitary anguish of the drowning youth, the pathos of his "unclaimed Hat and Jacket," the ironic beauty of the pond spreading her water lilies "Bold above the Boy." This boy is Emily herself perishing beneath her symbolic lilies.

Several boy poems written about 1862 deal with the pain of lost love. The first of these describes the attractive power of the distant, feminine moon over a masculine—and curiously juvenile—sea: with her "Amber Hands" she "leads Him—docile as a Boy—." In the final stanza, this inconstant moon is transmogrified into a beloved "Signor" and the poet identifies with the "Boy" sea (429). In a second 1862 poem she appears to represent herself as a masculine "Black Berry," which wears a "Thorn in his side" (like Christ, with whom she identifies) but stoically conceals the pain and goes on offering his berries to the passerby. There is no mistaking the tender self-pity of the final line, "Brave Black Berry" (554). In like manner she murmurs "Brave Bobolink" over a boyish bird (a self-symbol, as in her August 1860 letter to Bowles) whose longed-for nesting tree has been cut down (755). In another 1862 poem she is once more locked within the lonely prison of herself, dreaming of the pools in which she splashed when "Memory was a Boy" (652). An early 1863 poem, which makes a detailed contrast between loveless North and erotic South, says that "playing Glaciers—when a Boy" taught her to long for the fire of love (689). She sent a copy of this poem to Samuel Bowles, reminding him once more of Emily "when a boy" (L283).

After 1865, the love theme being effectually dead, and with it most of her symbolism, she used the boy identity to voice her opinions on religious or moral subjects. According to a Christmas poem that illustrates her rather curious palship with Jesus, the road to Bethlehem has been considerably improved "Since He and I were Boys" (1487). An 1879 poem to which she gave one of her rare titles, "Diagnosis of the Bible, by a Boy" (1545) expresses a strong and increasing hostility toward the religious instruction she had received in childhood. "Boys that believe," she says, "are very lonesome" or even "bastinadoed," and the "Boys" that do not "are lost." The "Boy that lived for 'Ought to'" might go to heaven at death, and then again he might not; after all, God had treated Moses unfairly (1201). Besides the boy poems already described, there are poem 968 with its "Excellenter Youth" and poem 717 about the "Beggar Lad" who cries, "Sweet Lady—Charity," to a bowing, smiling, feminine world taking its cruel "Cambric Way." Finally, there are some fifteen or sixteen poems in which she confers on herself various masculine titles of nobility. Since she may call herself indifferently girl, bride, or earl within the same poem, the titles earl, duke, prince, or king must have a reduced sexual significance, as have also boy, lad, and youth, but they do manifest a preference for the important male role. The belted earl is a more striking figure than his appendage, the countess.

In a rather curious poem, "He" puts the "Belt" around her life, and she hears the "Buckle snap." Since she—or perhaps "He"—folds up her "Lifetime" as a "Duke" would fold the title deed to a kingdom, the poem appears to have a religious flavor, but it is the religion of erotic love so constant throughout her poetry. The oddity consists in depicting herself as a medieval nobleman undergoing investiture or "belting" at the hands of his sovereign (273). In another poem the now-indifferent beloved will regret not speaking to "that dull Girl" when the latter becomes an "Earl"; but what with "Crests," with "Eagles" on her "Buckles" and on her "Belt," with "Ermine' as her familiar wear, the new-made "Earl" will be indifferent too (704). In "The Malay—took the Pearl— / Not—I—the Earl," the Malay has got away with the "Jewel" that "Earl" Emily desperately wanted (452). Of a wild rose, she says she would rather "wear her grace" than be "Duke of Exeter" or have an "Earl's distinguished face," although in one of her marriage poems it is precisely like an "Earl" that she wants to hold her "Brow" (138, 473). Rejoicing in some unspecified happiness, she calls herself "Prince of Mines," but in a poem about childhood suffering she is a "Prince cast out" of his dominion (466, 959). An "Earldom out of sight" is the bird in the bush she eschews for the bird, or the "Dollars," in hand; and she wonders how an "Earl" may feel when with her "Crumb" she thinks herself a "Sovereign" (1093, 791). After the virtual disappearance of the love theme in 1865, the few royal-name poems concern themselves with death and are of a more general nature.

Masculine titles are only part of the evidence pointing to a boyish side. It has been noticed that she links the forbidden sport of wading to her little-boy self, plays a boyish game of marbles, wrestles with an "Angel" —no doubt the one who interrupts the marble game—and wrings a blessing from this "Stranger." She is the "Loaded Gun" that roams in "Sovreign Woods" with her curiously passive "Master" and hunts the "Doe," although at night she stands ascetically on guard instead of resting her head on the womanly bosom of the "Eider-Duck's / Deep Pillow" (754). The incessant activity—struggling, striving, wrestling, rowing, climbing—is equally boyish. According to a poem sent to her sister-in-law, she showed another woman "Hights she never saw" and asked her, "Would'st Climb ...With *me*?" but the other woman's "face withdrew" (446). Another climbing poem begins: "Love—thou art high— / I cannot climb thee"; but if there were two of them and they were "Taking turns—at the Chimborazo," they might stand up "Ducal" at last (453). A poem interpreted as erotic by all but the prudish begins "Wild Nights—Wild Nights! / Were I with thee" and then describes how blissful those nights would be. The "Heart in port" would have no further use for compass or chart, though oddly it would continue to go to and fro on the water—"Rowing in Eden" (249). An interesting and related image occurs in the second stanza of the poem about climbing Chimborazo. Love is not only a high mountain, it is also a great deep she cannot cross alone; but if there were two of them, "Rower, and Yacht," they might one summer reach the sun (453). Since this extremely active woman took a passive position seldom and with great reluctance, she is presumably the "Rower" and the other person is the "Yacht" in which she rows.

Except in a few of the last poems, the imagery so far examined has been conspicuously and persistently juvenile. She is a boy, a lad, a childish prince; even her earls tend to be childlike or girlish. In her letters as well as in her poems, a tendency to revert to childhood under particular pressures can be detected again and again—for example, when Susan Gilbert became engaged to Austin Dickinson and hence "lost" to Emily, or when Kate Turner apparently sought to reduce a perfervid attachment to a calmer goodwill. On the former occasion, Emily wrote painfully to her brother: "How to grow up I dont know" (L115). It would appear that certain needs and desires became acceptable, that is, tolerable, to the poet if they were given a childish context. In short, she could think of herself quite comfortably as a boy, freed not only of the onerous restrictions laid upon little girls but relieved also of the frightening demands of womanhood. On the other hand, she dared not wish to be a man and indeed repudiated the idea with a curious ferocity in the opening stanza of a poem somewhat neglected by the explicators:

Rearrange a "Wife's" affection!
When they dislocate my Brain!
Amputate my freckled Bosom!
Make me bearded like a man! [1737]

To become a man involves, first, a destructive alteration of the brain, followed by gruesome major surgery that evokes surprising parallels with the castration fears common to men, and, finally, the humiliation of suffering a disfiguring growth upon one's smooth and cherished skin. A male reader would have to be remarkably naive to suppose these lines express a simple admiration of his sex. Indeed they are so hysterical, so much in excess, as to suggest a particular occasion, a monition to some friend who might be showing an interest in the bearded and less amply bosomed. The manuscript has been destroyed, presumably by Mrs. Bianchi, but not before it was copied by Mable Loomis Todd and listed among the contents of packet 8. Most of the contents of this packet appear to have been written in the late fall of 1861, when the now-estranged Kate Turner was once more visiting her friend Sue next door, and one reproachful poem of this group (221) was sent across the lawn to her. If only (the poems imply) they could have gone on being boys together! In default of such happiness on earth, Emily was driven to fix her eyes upon that life beyond death when, as Elizabeth Browning suggested in one of her scolding sonnets to George Sand, earthly sexual distinctions would be ended and they could be boys together for all eternity.

5

A girl with a strong masculine drive may identify, quite unconsciously, with the hero rather than the heroine of a book, and it is clear that Emily Dickinson made such identifications frequently and even consciously. She was "entangled Antony" to Sue's Cleopatra, on one occasion to Mrs. Todd's, and perhaps to the Cleopatra of other friends. This masculine role playing involved her more covertly with another Shakespearean character. An 1863 poem affirms that had "the 'Romeo' left no

Record / Of his Juliet" the story would still have been enacted in the theater of the human heart (741). Here she is as much identified with the impassioned youth as ever Charlotte Cushman was. The celebrated actress played this most notorious of her male roles during the Boston season of 1851–52 (but probably after Emily returned to Amherst from her visit to Boston in 1851) and again in the spring of 1861, as Samuel Bowles reported to his Dickinson friends, but of course the poet did not need the newspaper accounts to see herself in the part. In an 1862 poem, "I could die—to know—," she imagines the estranged lover walking the streets of some large city, perhaps Boston or New York, and wishes desperately that she had "the Charter of the least Fly" (570). The allusion is to Romeo's complaint that "more courtship lives / In carrion flies than Romeo. They may seize / On the white wonder of dear Juliet's hand / And steal immortal blessing from her lips"; and this allusion relates her poem to still another written probably a little earlier, "I envy Seas, whereon He rides" (498).

The contents of packet 6, in which poem 498 occurs, have been assigned to early 1862, but this date applies only to the finished copies; the original composition may go back to late 1861. It is worth noting that a much loved friend, now estranged, had just completed a visit to Amherst and, as in times past, had apparently gone on to friends in Boston and then proceeded by packet to New York. The sea voyage described in the poem is not a long one, for the beloved makes the voyage in a single verse and then is off the boat and into a carriage. As in Romeo's lines and in the poem "I could die—to know—," this poem laments the privilege of *seeing* enjoyed by every object, animate or inanimate, except the luckless poet-Romeo. The following lines are especially significant:

I envy Nests of Sparrows—
That dot His distant Eaves—
The wealthy Fly, upon His Pane—
The happy—happy Leaves—

There is an echo of Keats's "Ah, happy, happy boughs that cannot shed / Your leaves" and, with a change of birds, a probable reminiscence of the love song of Tennyson's Prince, "O Swallow, swallow... Fly to her, and fall upon her gilded eaves"; but the "wealthy Fly" appears to be Romeo's.

The most startling of her identifications springs from her attitude toward religion, and here the going is not easy, partly because her first editor suppressed, distorted, and lied about her work (and later anthologists and literary historians have been too lazy to take an independent look), partly because an earnest group of younger (male) scholars have attempted with innocent complacency to see her as a Bride of Christ.[36] If they had read what Emily herself was reading, they might have caught the point, though not so sharply as Elizabeth Browning's Aurora Leigh, whose cousin Romney taunts her with women's role as doting mothers, wives, madonnas, and saints, but—

> We get no Christ from you,—and verily
> We shall not get a poet in my mind.

Sue Dickinson gave her sister-in-law an *Imitation of Christ,* and the latter wrote one poem in the bridal vein, "Given in Marriage unto Thee" (817), but she did not prolong an unnatural posture. Apparently she attached no more historical reality to Jesus than to Noah (whom "no one credits"), or the "Grandame's story" of Eve and the Garden of Eden, or the "Romance" of Moses, or even the whole "antique Volume" of the Bible, written as it was by "faded Men" (403, 503, 597, 1545). Since her brother Austin could describe his mistress as his "Jesus," it is apparent that these Dickinsons used religious language with uncommon freedom. Jesus was a symbol, approved or disapproved according to circumstances.

As a child, Emily wondered who "the Father and the Son" were and what they had to do with her. When told in a "portentous" manner, with an inference "appalling" to childhood, she reflected that at least the two could be no worse than they were painted. In an earlier version, it is still clearer that the child, hitherto protected by the infant sense of immortality, is now introduced to the idea of its own death as the consequence of original sin (1258). Another poem demands whether heaven is an "Exchequer," since men are so often reminded of what they "owe," adding brusquely that she is no "Party" to the negotiation (1270). As a member of the Trinity, Jesus fares little better than God. He shares in the responsibility for that negotiation—original sin–mortality–atonement—to which she refused to be a party. Remembering the punishment she and her sister Lavinia received for a childish bit of sacrilege, she observes with ferocious humor that the little girls thought Jesus hateful to get them into trouble when they "had done nothing but crucify him and that before [they] were born" (PF51). In her childhood, she writes to Mrs. Holland, when the clergyman asked those who loved Jesus to remain for communion her flight kept time to his words (L412). But on another occasion, or the same one remembered differently, she could hardly refrain from thanking the clergyman for his courteous invitation, although she now believes the name of Santa Claus would have evoked much livelier transports (L926).

One of her poems pays a curious, backhanded compliment to Jesus as the more appealing member of the Trinity. He is a kind of divine confidence man, a John Alden who might win for himself the love he has come to woo for Miles Standish–God, if the latter did not affirm with "hyperbolic archness" that they two were one (357). More somberly, she writes that she distrusted Jesus' account of his father, and turned away from his promise of heaven, but when he confided that he "was ac-

quainted with grief," then she listened (L932). Although she did not explicitly name the crucified Christ with Moses and Isaac as another instance of God's bullying cruelty, the idea often seemed close to expression.
As a symbol of suffering humanity, Jesus was dear to her, and as a suffering woman, she felt no sacrilege in identifying herself with him. Some two
dozen poems use the language of the Passion to describe her own suffering
or that of her lover or, in one instance, the "transporting anguish" of Charlotte Brontë's death (148).

A few of these poems have already been mentioned, among them the
one about the blackberry with a thorn in his side and another describing
the road to "Bethlehem" (Golgotha) traveled by the "Boys" Jesus and
Emily (554, 1487). Sometimes she assumes the name of one of the disciples
in relation to a beloved conceived as Jesus. A packet 6 poem of early 1862,
or perhaps late 1861, accuses the lover of racking her with suspense, wring-
ing her with anguish, stabbing her even while she begged forgiveness, and
it ends by exclaiming, "Jesus—it's your little 'John'! / Dont you know—
me?" or "Why—Slay—Me?" (497). Here she drew upon the curious and
widespread nineteenth-century conception of a humanly intimate, well-
nigh erotic relationship between the beloved disciple and the Master in
whose bosom he lay. Years later she chose another disciple's name for
comic rather than tragic effect. Courted by the widowed Judge Otis
P. Lord, she had the delicate problem of putting off her elderly wooer yet
retaining the flattery of his interest. In one of her evasive letters she calls
herself his "little Simon Peter"—with the punning implication that she
denies her Lord! (L645).

More commonly the poet compares herself with Jesus. An early poem
sent to Mary Bowles speaks with apparent humility of making the first
overtures of friendship, but since the poem equates Emily with Christ,
the effect is scarcely humble (85). Recalling Elizabeth Browning's sonnet
"The Look," she compares herself with Christ who "merely 'looked' at
Peter" by the temple fire; and a poem of the same late 1860 packet an-
ticipates that in the "schoolroom" of the sky Christ's account of Peter's
denial will help her forget a similar anguish (203, 193). Late the following
year, she expects Christ's crucifix to enable him to guess at one of the
"smaller size" (255). Kneeling on Sue's doorstep, she raps as patiently and
unweariedly as Jesus (317). If the lovers are to be punished, says another
poem, then her guilt is the greater because of her great love—"base as
Jesus—most" (394). Asked whether her love is as strong as Jesus', she
dares to answer, with a possible double entendre, "Prove it me / That He
—loved Men—/ As I—love thee—" (456). Here the pauses enforced by
the dashes appear to reserve their full weight.

She is a female Jesus—"Queen of Calvary," "Empress of Calvary" (348,
1072). If the beloved doubts other proofs of her love, then she has nothing
left to show except "Calvary" (549). When she passes "Calvary" she gets

a "piercing Comfort" from observing the fashions of the cross and how they are worn, fascinated by the thought that some are like her own (561). Christ was indeed crucified for all men, and yet she knows of a "newer—nearer Crucifixion" (553). Perhaps the "Reefs in Old Gethsemane" will "Endear the Shore beyond"; she might have loved earth too well "without the Calvary" (313). In this world she and her beloved must bind each other's crucifix and take their earthly farewell, but in another world they will rise to a "Marriage, / Justified—through Calvaries of Love." (322). They will look back from heaven in play at "Old Times—in Calvary" (577). A quatrain declaring that news of her friend Mrs. Helen Hunt Jackson would make her "Gethsemane" "Gay" implies that Gethsemane has long been her settled home. Written in late 1878, this quatrain marks the last appearance of her important Passion symbol, and indeed the only one after 1862; the most intense phase of her agony was short-lived (1432).

Apparently her worst suffering began about April 1861 and continued into the early months of 1862, for the poems and letters of this period are well-nigh frantic. Among the earliest is a poem alluding to Easter, 31 March 1861, and lamenting the going down of her "*Faint* Star of Bethlehem," which may be her hope or the defaulting lover or both (236). A poem of the same period, "I think just how my shape will rise—" (237), uses religious language so boldly as to suggest that she may be addressing God himself. A closer look shows that she is praying to be "*forgiven*" by a godlike lover, to "rise" into a human heaven, and to be considered the "Sparrow" of this god's care. The poem follows immediately on the idolatrous "Easter" poem which asks that "some God—*inform* Him" (the lover), and is no more extravagant than poem 640, which declares that her lover's "Face / Would put out Jesus'," that this human deity so "saturated Sight" that she had no eyes for the "sordid excellence" of paradise. In an undated poem, most likely written in early 1861 (at the same time as 236 and 237, and equally extravagant), she imagines that her lover is suffering as much as she, that both are enduring a crucifixion only a little less agonizing than Jesus' in that it is shared (1736).

It was very near this time, either in late spring or in early summer 1861, that she wrote the first of her anguished letters to an unknown "Master." "I heard of a thing called 'Redemption,'" she writes. "You remember I asked you for it—you gave me something else. I forgot the Redemption in the Redeemed" (L233). A variant of a "Redemption" poem which appears to bear on these lines exists in a transcript made by Sue. All surviving manuscripts begin "To see her is a picture," but only Sue's copy reads that to be "undone" by knowing this other woman "Is dearer than Redemption," even though failure to receive this "Redemption" has made a mockery of the melody that Emily's life could have been (1568).[37]

The letters contain two other identifications with Christ associated with the only paintings the poet ever mentions. No doubt her reading made her aware of the nineteenth-century infatuation with Raphael's Sistine Madonna, yet it was appropriate that *this* woman should speak of *this* painting in just the tone she used. To Higginson, who was abroad, she wrote that to have seen "the Dresden Madonna, must be almost Peace—" (L553). Now it is no surprise to discover that every man desires in his heart to be the only child (male, naturally) of a virgin mother, but it seems at first a little odd to find the same desire in a woman's heart.

Another clue to the interpretation of her work must be advanced before considering her last identification with Christ, and that is that she hated with as much passion as she loved, and perhaps a little more so. The real pity is that she so often had to dissemble her hates, even to herself, instead of venting them and making rootroom for the growth of new feelings. In the early spring of 1853 she was full of suppressed rage, hurt, depression. She was losing her adored friend to her brother and rival, and she could not emigrate or fight a duel or even express an honest anger; she was obliged to be pleased. On 24 March 1853 a rather subdued letter to Austin informed him that she did "drop in at the Revere" a good many times the day before; that is, she mentally eavesdropped on his proposal to her friend Susan Gilbert (L109). In a restrained letter congratulating him on his engagement, she thanked him for putting her mind at rest and added, "I really had my doubts about your reaching Canaan" (L110). Her wording suggests that she was recalling hymn writer Isaac Watts's "gloomy doubts" about crossing over into the land "Flowing with milk and honey" (a peculiarly apt metaphor for a young man dreaming of his bride).

Subsequent letters grow increasingly more desolate and wintry, full of regret for the lost privileges of childhood: "I wish we were children now. I wish we were *always* children, how to grow up I dont know" (L115). Shortly afterward she was feeling "so tired" and "lonely" and "very old every day" (L123), indications of a neurotic fatigue brought on by frustration and suppressed rage. A few months later she heard "a splendid sermon from that Prof Park" which, to her excited mind, electrified the entire congregation (L142). Edwards Amasa Park was famous for his "Judas" sermon; that she heard this sermon appears certain from a letter to her Norcross cousins twenty years later: "The loveliest sermon I ever heard was the disappointment of Jesus in Judas. It was told like a mortal story of intimate young men. I suppose no surprise we can ever have will be so sick as that" (L385). That she reacted to Sue's engagement as a betrayal is the plain meaning of the evidence. There were to be other Judases, however.

"With the sincere spite of a Woman," the young Emily Dickinson wrote on a scrap of paper in ink and handwriting which her editors assign to about 1850 (PF124). And Jay Leyda has discovered the program of an oratorical exhibition of 26 November 1850 on which Emily wrote, among other comments: "This night is long to be remembered. New things have happened. 'The crooked is made straight.' I am confided in by one—and despised by an *other!* and another still!" Late in the next month she was writing to Abiah Root about difficulties with another friend, Abby Wood: she and Abby see little of each other, take different views of life, might disagree, and then Abby is now so grown-up and holy—"goes among the poor...shuts the eye of the dying." But after this little fling Emily begs for Abiah's interpretation of Abby (L39). Some fifteen months later her joy in the revival of this friendship is the best indication of how deeply she had been hurt. "I often see Abby—," she writes, "oftener than at sometimes when friendship drooped a little. Did you ever know that a flower, once withered and freshened again, became an immortal flower,—that is, that it rises again?" (L91).

Unfortunately, the flower proved mortal after all. Abby was indeed growing up and planning to marry Daniel Bliss and accompany him to Syria for years of active missionary work. When Mrs. Bliss returned to Amherst in the summer of 1873, Emily at first refused to see her or to talk with her except unseen from an adjacent room. Mrs. Bliss sensibly declined these conditions, and they met at length in a fashion more becoming to old acquaintances. There is a poem of about that time which the editor suggests may be Emily's comment on her old friend's visit. It shows her unvarying sensitivity to the signs of age, for the poem is particularly concerned with Abby's graying hair, "I saw that the Flake was on it" (1267). But if this poem is about the old friend, so also is the strange and terrible poem inscribed on the verso, "Art thou the thing I wanted?" (1282). Using her familiar equation of food with love, the poet curtly orders the friend to be gone, to tease some lesser palate, some hunger she has not goaded so long. Through years of starvation, the mystery of "Food" has grown until Emily has perforce "abjured" it, since when she has subsisted without love—"like God"!

6

On 15 April 1862 Emily took the fateful step of sending a brief note with four poems to T. W. Higginson for his criticism. She knew, or believed she knew, that the creative eruption that had shaken her these past months was of great value, but she had urgent need of a word outside herself. Apparently Higginson thought her poems little better than doggerel, but he did answer, offer criticism, ask questions about her reading, and invite more poems. In later years she would twice tell him that without knowing it he had saved her life.

Answering him on 25 April from the sickbed to which the convulsions of the past few days had driven her, she wrote that she had "a terror—since September" and had created poems in order to save herself. Compulsively, she rehearsed the significant emotional events of her life, the loss of Sue, the death of her good friend Ben Newton—"Then I found one more—but he was not contented I be his scholar—so he left the Land" (L261). Very near this time, and for her private relief, she may also have written the second of her anguished "Master" letters, in which she wonders painfully whether her "Backwoodsman ways" offended the exquisite beloved and begs to be taught "patrician things" (L248). Perhaps on the same day she wrote also to Mary Bowles and, under the guise of understanding Mary's grief over her husband's absence, poured out her own chaotic suffering: "Not to see what we love, is very terrible.... The Eyes and Hair we chose—are all there are—to us—." She noted that it was a warm, pleasant day in late April and Vinnie and Sue were making hotbeds, though much plagued by robins. Earlier she had watched Sue pull her lively little boy "in a Cab," accompanied by the dog Carlo and cats from both households. "The Frogs sing sweet—today— They have such pretty—lazy—times—how nice, to be a Frog!" (L262). On the same day she answered a letter, the first in many months, from the beloved friend whom she always associated with frogs.

They had seen each other as recently as the past October and November, during Kate Turner's visit to Sue, and had been pleasant and polite to each other; but the sad burden of the poetry was that Kate no longer responded. Why then had Kate reopened the dialogue, some twelve and a half months after the letter that had spelled the end of their friendship? Perhaps because things are never finished off so neatly as one planned them to be, perhaps because she was still shaking with superstitious awe after a night of blazing terror. From the evening of 10 April until well into the following day, a huge fire engulfed Cooperstown, New York, and came very close to Kate's family home. This fire was reported in the *Springfield Republican* of 12 April, where Emily read about it some days before Kate wrote.

The latter dated her transcript of Emily's reply "April 1860," but the "1860" is a slip of her pen. In late April 1862 "Sue's little boy" was a child of ten months, sitting up in his cart, thrashing the bushes with his stick, and taking an active interest in Carlo, the cats, the scurrying poultry, and a colt in the Dickinson barn to which he was pulled "demi-daily." Finally, there is no mistaking the April 1862 date of the great fire of Cooperstown or the ties between this letter and those to Higginson, Mary Bowles, and "Master." Apparently this letter also contained poem 332, "There are two Ripenings," which also survives in a transcript made by Kate. It is a rather touching effort to persuade the lost friend that some things—or people— ripen chiefly in the cheek like a peach, whereas a "homelier maturing," that of a nut in its "Bur," is disclosed by "teeth of Frosts" in "far October Air"—presumably the air of Kate's visit to Amherst the preceding October.[38] In a sense, it harks back to poem 296, "One Year ago—jots what?"

(which Kate may or may not have seen), insisting that the poet is no longer the baby she was accused of being; but of course the primary reference is to the remarkable ripening of her talent under the past winter of adversity.

If this voice out of a long silence so disrupted the poet's scanty composure as to put her to bed and cause her to moan aloud to Mary Bowles, indulge in a rhapsody of grief in Master letter 248, and make uninvited disclosures to a stranger like Higginson, it is noteworthy that she wrote to Kate herself with extraordinary restraint, as if she were trying to coax a shy bird and dare not raise her voice. Nevertheless, a careful examination of letter 317 shows that she did not relieve her feelings by slipping in a good deal of innuendo, some of which her friend surely was not expected to understand.

She begins by thanking Kate for her letter, admitting that "it *was* relief"; she had been silent so long that Emily had "got a bad whim." She begs Kate not to "leave Emily again, it gnarls her character!" She asks, "*Will* folks get rested, Katie?—You spoke of 'Heaven' you know. 'I' will take *so many beds*"; and she ends, "So tired, Katie." The tension and fatigue manifested here and throughout this letter link it to Master letters 233 and 248, where just such neurotic fatigue and suffering are described, and are reminiscent of the much earlier reaction to Sue's engagement. They are the price she paid for the civilized surface of her letter. At this time she wrote her powerful renunciatory poem, "I cannot live with You" (640), in which the words to Katie, "You spoke of 'Heaven' you know," reappear as "For You—served Heaven—You know" and in which the last word is "Despair."

It was humanly inevitable that the suffering woman would at times suspect the interference of others, especially her sister-in-law. The several references to "treason" in the poems may reflect darkly, not so much on Kate's default as on possible machinations of Sue Dickinson, who in truth could not have been altogether pleased when her own strongest admirers formed an intimacy which for two years largely excluded her. Now, in this April 1862 letter, a sly allusion to "you & me & Vinnie & the 'other house'...the *Israelites* & those *Hittite* folks" reads like a covert attempt to detach Kate from her reestablished loyalty to Sue. Unquestionably it is an attack on Sue, for Emily well knew the roll call of the Canaanite tribes who blocked the path of the Chosen People into the land flowing with milk and honey. Years later, in a letter to Mrs. Holland, she made another comically garbled allusion to "the Jebusites and the Hittites" and explicitly identified them with unpleasant relatives (L473). Yet by all the evidence Sue did try to help her sister-in-law through an agonizing period, even to the point of enlisting Samuel Bowles's cooperation in getting two of Emily's poems into his *Springfield Republican*.

Bowles came to Amherst only two or three times a year, and then rarely for more than a few hours at a time, but he was on friendly terms with all three women, being particularly close to Sue Dickinson, and the professed admirer of her handsome friend. In the work of Sue's daughter, there is a striking vignette of Kate and Bowles playing wild games of battledore and shuttlecock "to the *crescendo* of Emily's counting" or with "Emily convulsing their onlookers by her superfluous antics added to their game." [39] Whatever Sue's actual words may have been, the intent of this anecdote was to show Emily's anxious determination not to be left out. The time came, of course, when she could no longer hold her own. In June 1861, some few weeks after the rupture between the two women, Bowles gallantly visited Kate in Cooperstown and boasted afterward of his kind reception. The situation is at least reminiscent of late fall 1854, when Austin had gone west to visit Sue and Emily could only cry, "He will see you, Darling! What I cannot do. Oh *could* I!" (L176). There could be no question of Bowles marrying the "flirtatious widow," and since the latter regarded marriage as a woman's necessary career but was otherwise sexually cool, it is most unlikely that the Malay took this pearl. In allowing his attentions, however, she had the power to wring her friend's heart. For a brief period in the winter of 1861–62, Emily clung to Bowles like some tortured youth to his more successful rival, although there may have been covert defiance in sending him "Title Divine" with its pathetic claim to a kind of marriage between herself and the lost friend. After his return from Europe in the late fall of 1862 she refused to see him, and apparently she did not see him again until her father's death in 1874. She ceased to write to him, and he stopped alluding to her in his letters. When he and Sue arranged to publish her "Snake" poem in February 1866, she wrote to Higginson with forthright anger, "it was robbed of me—" (L316), and she did not except Bowles from the charge.

In her letter of late April 1862 to Kate, there is another apparent hint of a jealous hostility toward Bowles. She says she has read about Katie's fire "in the 'Midnight Cry'—Vinnie's favorite journal—." The *Midnight Cry* was a defunct paper of the Millerite sect. Emily had read about the fire in the *Springfield Republican,* a newspaper so identified with its editor-publisher that for many people Bowles simply *was* the *Republican,* and this identification underlies Emily's jeer at his newspaper as a Millerite rag relished by simpler minds like her sister Vinnie's.

When Kate returned to Amherst in October 1861, to remain until sometime in November, she came because she owed Sue the courtesy of a visit after the birth of Sue's baby Ned. Apparently she reached Amherst from Cooperstown and was joined later in her visit by Gertrude Vanderbilt, with whom she returned to her sister's home in Flatbush, New York, not far from Mrs. Vanderbilt's. The scanty evidence suggests that Emily was not in Sue's house as constantly as on earlier visits, and the walks she had previously enjoyed with the tireless Kate would have been given over even if the weather had been pleasant. It was not pleasant. Emily remembered the severe storm and heavy rain on the evening she and Vinnie arranged to have Kate properly to tea. "Come & have tea with us again Katie!" she wrote the following April. "How it rained that night!" Very possibly, the poem "Wild Nights—Wild Nights! Were I with thee" (249) that went into packet 8 in October or November 1861 was written on this stormy night after the tea party ended and the guest was gone.

Recalling that tea party in her April letter, Emily took special note of a painting—the only famous work of art, other than the Sistine Madonna, she mentions anywhere; and in a letter as tightly composed as any of her poems, where no word was accidental, she wrote:

> We must take many a tea together in a Northeast storm o' Saturday nights, before Da Vinci's Supper!
> So tired, Katie, so good night Speak, will it more to
>
> Emily—[L317]

At a new Last Supper, a new Christ had broken bread with the beloved Judas. And this letter survived because Kate remembered the real picture and missed the damning allusion.

7

Among Shakespeare's plays the tragedy of *Othello* occupies an important and curious place in the mind of Emily Dickinson. To judge from quotations in her letters, it is the theme of jealousy that absorbs her. With the "throe of Othello," she imagines "others possessing" her absent friend Mrs. Jonathan L. Jenkins (L506). Regretting the absence of still another woman friend, she writes: "Othello is uneasy, but then Othellos always are, they hold such mighty stakes" (L948). Congratulating Mrs. Holland on the birth of a grandchild, she assumes her friend will now have less time for her and adds: "We will try to bear it as divinely as Othello did, who had he had Love's sweetest slice, would not have charmed the World" (L882). In letters 538 and 622, she quotes from Brabantio's bitterly reluctant surrender of Desdemona: "I here do give thee that with all my heart / Which, but thou hast already, with all my heart / I would keep from thee." Twice she attempts to quote the Duke's counsel to Brabantio: "The robb'd that smiles steals something from the thief" (L478, L937), and there are other less significant references to Othello scattered through her letters. The lines she remembers from the play—and she rarely quotes with a text under her eyes—appear to be those that made the deepest imprint at the most crucial period of her life.

In 1857 Emily's father bought a new set of Shakespeare, and some years later she apparently made it her own, even going so far as to mark certain favored passages in *Othello,* the only play so treated in the Dickinson Shakespeare. The tone, substance, and consistency of these bracketed passages, all of which are given below, are a guarantee that the markings are hers:

> *Brabantio.* I here do give thee that with all my heart
> Which, but thou hast already, with all my heart
> I would keep from thee. For your sake, jewel, ... [1. 3. 193–95]
> *Iago.* Poor and content is rich, and rich enough;
> But riches fineless is as poor as winter,
> To him that ever fears he shall be poor:
> Good heaven, the souls of all my tribe defend
> From jealousy! [3. 3. 171–75]
> *Othello.* If she be false, O, then heaven mocks itself!
> I'll not believe't. [3. 3. 278–79]
> He that is robb'd, not wanting what is stolen,
> Let him not know't, and he's not robb'd at all. [3. 3. 342–43]
> It is the cause, it is the cause, my soul,—
> Let me not name it to you, you chaste stars!
> It is the cause. Yet I'll not shed her blood,
> Nor scar that whiter skin of hers than snow,
> And smooth as monumental alabaster,
> Yet she must die, else she'll betray more men.
> Put out the light, and then put out the light. [5. 2. 1–7]
> Thou cunning'st pattern of excelling nature, [5. 2. 11]
> It is a sword of Spain, the ice brook's temper;— [5.2.253]
> I kiss'd thee, ere I kill'd thee. No way but this—
> Killing myself, to die upon a kiss. [5. 2. 358–59]

No doubt she marked as the fancy took her, without any clear understanding of why just these lines should so appeal to her. They tell a curious story, for they are wholly concerned with jealousy, bitter loss, and the killing of a beautiful, false woman.[40]

TWO ✠ THE GEOGRAPHY OF THE
UNCONSCIOUS

A curious myth has grown like bindweed in the criticism
of Emily Dickinson's poetry to the effect that it is *about* almost any subject
except what it is in fact about. An English reviewer once counted the
poems editorially assigned to the "Love" section of early editions and
reported with apparent satisfaction that her work lacked eroticism. There
is, on the contrary, no more erotic poetry in the English language. This
is the secret of its drive, of its febrile energy, of the inexplicable fascination
it has for many baffled readers. Death is eroticized, pain is eroticized,
religion is eroticized. She cannot write about a hummingbird without
turning it into an erotic symbol; and her bees and flowers and butterflies
are innocently, blatantly eroticized, almost but not quite to the point of
comedy. Expressed in a slightly different way, she has but two subjects,
which are in fact one subject—an eroticized death and what might be
called a thanaticized eros.

Much of this symbolism came into consciousness. The poet knew at least
what or whom she was writing about and how far she was diverging into
fantasy and wish fulfillment from the real experience she called "This
pattern—of the Way—" (944). She did indeed create a drama of which
she was by turns the happy or the tragic hero, but always with a basis in
reality; and her uncomfortable awareness of this reality led her to write to
T. W. Higginson in July 1862, "When I state myself, as the Representative
of the Verse—it does not mean—me—but a supposed person" (L268).
Unlike some of her critics and explicators, Higginson would have looked
carefully at the four enclosed poems for an explanation of her uneasy
self-consciousness, and he would have found one suspicious poem. Three
months earlier it had gone to her sister-in-law as a letter-poem beginning,

"Dear Sue, Your—Riches—taught me—poverty!" and ending, "Dear Sue—
You see I remember—Emily—" (L258).

To catch her in a halftruth is not difficult ("the yarns, O! irreverence,"
Higginson would say of her picturesque exaggerations to him); [1] the real
task is to discover those truths of which she herself was unaware. It must
be premised, of course—and in the teeth of some obscurantism—that there
is an unconscious mind to discover. Much weightier is the objection that
every human being's symbolism is unique and cannot be interpreted
without his associations. Still, the analogical faculty has its own severe
limitations, and the symbolisms of the unconscious tend to show a strong
family likeness; the conscious mind can indeed be affronted and wearied
by the sheer idiot monotony of the unconscious. Then the frequent repeti-
tions in Emily Dickinson's poetry, the incessant reworkings of the same
themes, plus suggestions in her letters and in her reading, go far toward
supplying the necessary associations.

Like other lyric poets, she uses much oral imagery—but uses it, as she
does her colors, jewels, and similar clusters, with an extravagance and an
intensity far in excess of her models. This oral imagery, like other important image clusters, is virtually confined to her major period. Of several
hundred occurrences of words denoting food, drink, hunger, thirst, and
the like, no more than 15 percent are in handwriting later than 1866; such
words as *berry, famine, hunger, hungry, drink, drunk, flagon,* and *flask*
do not manage to cross the gap; and *thirst, eat, feed, breakfast, drunken,*
liquor, and *nectar* appear once only in later years. On one occasion she
describes "Fame" as a "fickle food," and elsewhere she says of some
generalized book lover, "He ate and drank the precious Words" (1659,
1587); but as a rule her oral symbols apply to affection or, more exactly, to
romantic love.

In her loveless girlhood, says an 1863 poem, she eased her "famine" at
her "Lexicon" and drank the "dry Wine" of "Logarithm" (728). Then
came the "one more" of her letter to Higginson, and twice she was the
"Debauchee of Dews" and once "the little Tippler / Leaning against the
—Sun—" (128, 214). After 1860 she was never again so blissful. The food
may "exterminate," reads a reproachful poem of 1864, but the "hunger—
does not cease—" (904). She is the beggar lad accosting the lady with a
"timid cry for 'Bread,'" the little "Bird" singing to earn the lady's
"Crumb," the schoolboy "Homesick for steadfast Honey" (717, 880, 319).
But after 1860 the lady rarely "feeds Her little Bird," who falls fainting on
her yellow knee, "crumbless and afar" (941). Only in imagination can
Emily still "banquet" on the other's "Countenance," and the "single
Crumb" that loads her table is simply her "Consciousness" of the lost
beloved (815). God has given to every other bird a loaf but to her a crumb
she dares not eat—"tho' I starve" (791). Her one "Draught of Life," her

one "Dram of Heaven," has cost her an existence; if she had known the cup would be offered once only, she might have "kept it longer" or "drunk it stronger" (1725, 1720). Sometimes she accuses a "Goblin" of drinking her "Dew" or complains that she has been led to the brink of a well to be tantalized by the sound of its dripping; a poem of different mood, however, says her drought may be destitute but she had the "dew" (430, 490, 1754).

This oral symbolism makes a first striking appearance in a letter to her new friend, Kate Turner, in which the poet paraphrases Matthew 25:35-36 and associates herself with the "hungry, and thirsty" (L203). Between the young widow's departure from Amherst in early March 1859 and her return in August, Emily may have sent her a poem beginning "Have you got a Brook in your little heart" (136), which describes the brook as the source of the poet's "draught of life." In March this "little brook of life" is in spate, with the snowmelt hurrying from the hills and even the bridges letting go; but if it is not recruited, then "later," on some burning noon "in *August*," it may go dry. This ingenious appeal had its successors, for oral symbols abound in the 1859 poetry. "Water, is taught by thirst," and only those who have experienced "sorest need" can truly "comprehend a nectar" or "Flagons, and Cooling Tamarind" (135, 67, 73). The well-fed outsider is told to speak "Reverently, to the Hungry," of his "viands" and her "wines" (119). Beggars like the poet fancy themselves reveling at a savory feast or pressing "thirsty lips to flagons," and yet the sweet brooks babbling in deserts are all too distant for delight (121).

About May 1860 the poet wrote a letter to Mrs. Turner, alluding to a third visit during the winter just past and urging her to make another visit that summer: "Oh: Dew upon the bloom fall yet again a summer's night" (L222). Although the letter expresses strong feeling, it seems quite happy, as does the exceedingly oral poem, "I taste a liquor never brewed" (214). With these exceptions, the scanty oral symbolism of 1860 sounds more intense and painful than that of the previous year. In a mood as foreboding as it is elegiac, Emily opens a box of letters and remembers that these "faded syllables" once "quickened" her "like Wine," or she places herself among the patient "Laureates" who "die of thirst—suspecting / That Brooks in Meadows run!" (169, 167). A late 1860 poem, written in the language of little "Tim," wonders whether the "Ransomed folks" (the loved persons or person) will laugh at her in heaven or scold her for being "hungry" (215). Other 1860 poems allude to an event of so crucial a nature that she describes it as a marriage. She begs this "Eden" to "Come slowly" (211), and, speaking of her "accepted Breath," she says there can be no "Wilderness" or "Desert Noon" where this happiness attends her (195). And in a poem of almost unbearable tension she writes of escaping with her lover from the "Desert" and the "thirst" into the "Tamarind wood," where the "Leopard" poet "breathes—at last!" (209).

The year after her flight into the tamarind wood, Emily Dickinson wrote a poem expressing the most intense agony of loss, 'One Year ago—jots what?" (296). Since it is an important poem, and rich in oral symbolism, it deserves a fairly detailed analysis. She is writing on the "Anniversary" of their "Grace" or "Glory" (their understanding, union, symbolic marriage), and for once she may be quite literal in saying that "Twelve months" have elapsed since they "breathed"—presumably in the tamarind wood. She does not expect such an anniversary again until they meet "in Eternity," when they will "feed upon each other's faces—so— / In doubtful meal, if it be possible / Their Banquet's real—." This poem, like others (190, 643, 1072), hints at the lack of some final consummation. In an oral poem already mentioned, she declares that if she had known the first cup was to be the last she would have "drunk it stronger" (1720). Here she remembers:

> I tasted—careless—then—
> I did not know the Wine
> Came once a World—Did you?
> Oh, had you told me so—
> This Thirst would blister—easier—now—

The rest of the poem, which treats superior experience as superior age, implies that she confronted a more informed, aggressive sexuality.

A few weeks later the poet sent her friend Samuel Bowles the interesting poem, "Victory comes late" (690). In brief, victory is a kind of food, a sweet-tasting "Drop," which an "economical" God tardily bestows on lips too frozen to take it. God's table is spread so high she must dine on tiptoe, yet she wants so little. "Crumbs" and "Cherries" fit such "little mouths," whereas the "Eagle's Golden Breakfast" would be too grand for "Robins" like Emily. May God keep his vow to "Sparrows," / Who of little love— know how to starve!" The fact that she sent this poem to Bowles raises interesting questions. She had seen him in late 1861, and the conversation had reached some degree of intimacy, for at one point she had embarrassed herself by bursting into tears. If the poem is her attempt to respond to his well-meant advice, then the significance lies in the contrast between the little birds and the eagle. She appears to be telling Bowles, politely, that eagle love is much too grand, it "dazzles" the little birds; but in a subsequent packet copy she alters the line to suggest not so much a respectful awe as fear and revulsion: "The Eagle's Golden Breakfast strangles— Them—."

In some three dozen 1862 poems using oral symbolism, there is considerable variety of mood. She may write, as in her 1859 manner, that "Beggars" are best able to define "Banquets" and that "Thirsting—vitalizes Wine"; or, with a change of mood, she may declare that the starving attach "Undue Significance" to "Food," that "Distance" alone makes it appear

"Savory" (313, 439). The second theme is developed in an 1862 poem beginning "I had been hungry, all the Years" (579), which appears to reflect on a moment of near consummation, presumably in the summer of 1860. It is her "Noon" to dine, the climactic hour of life and of love. Trembling, she approaches the "Table," touches the "Curious Wine," looks unbelievingly at the "ample Bread," so different from the "Crumb" shared with the "Birds"—and finds she has lost her appetite. Yet, addressing the "Lady" who has shown her a "Summer...Illegitimate," she begs the "Crumb" of a smile just large enough to stow a "Robin's Larder" (651). And poem 612 says a "Gnat" would have starved on the "Food" of love dealt out to her, nor has she had the gnat's privilege of flying away to "seek a Dinner for myself."

Some poems with oral symbolism have already been cited from the remaining years of her major period. There is no great difference except in an increased willingness to admit that her position is hopeless. "Deprived of other Banquet," she "entertained" herself and by "slender addings" produced a "Loaf" almost large enough for herself and her robin alter ego (773). As often as her "lot displays / Too hungry to be borne," she simply pretends she is what she wants to be (801). Yet there is evidence that the poet did retain some slight hope as late as 1865. If the symbols of hunger and thirst well-nigh vanish after that date, the explanation seems to lie in the final, irrevocable loss of the desperately beloved; the hunger itself did not disappear. In late 1872, she wrote to her cousin Louise Norcross: "How short it takes to go, dear, but afterward to come so many weary years—and yet 'tis done as cool as a general trifle. Affection is like bread, unnoticed till we starve, and then we dream of it, and sing of it, and paint it, when every urchin in the street has more than he can eat" (L379).

A few months later she wrote the poem, "Art thou the thing I wanted?" (1282), aimed, it would seem, at Abby Wood Bliss, fiercely repudiating the old school friend who had given her a scanty, disappointing affection. In June 1877 the former Kate Scott Turner, now widowed a second time, returned to Amherst; and with customary ambivalence Emily wrote, "The Banquet of Abstemiousness / Defaces [var., surpasses] that of Wine—" (1430).

2

Frequently the oral symbolism associates the poet with creatures that can be thought of as sucking, pecking, biting, and swallowing. Five poems identify her fairly closely with a robin or a sparrow eating cherries, crumbs, or "insufficient loaves." At other times she is among the unnamed birds sharing a crumb or picking up the farmer's reluctant crumbs. Elsewhere she must sing to earn her crumb, or she is the little bird the lady rarely feeds. Again, she is the wandering bird who entreats a berry of "Nature." She may also be among the "blushing birds" drinking at the little brook of life that floods in March 1859 and almost runs dry the following August. With exaggerated violence, she is the "Starved Maelstrom" lapping at navies, the "Vulture" devouring the "Broods in lonely Valleys," the "Tiger eased" by a "Crumb of Blood"; or the need for affection can be "a sweet wolf...that demands its food" (872, 1824). A more frequent identification is with creatures that feed by sucking, that is, with butterflies, bees, and hummingbirds.

Her favorite reading contained plenty of sucking images; they have been a staple of lyric poets time out of mind. "Where the bee sucks, there suck I," sings the sprite Ariel;[2] and in the Song of Solomon, which she knew thoroughly, the lover feeds among the lilies of the beloved's body.[3] Elizabeth Browning was notably fond of this imagery and quite explicit in her wording. Lines from her poem, "A Dead Rose," might almost be the source of her disciple's bee-rose symbolism: "The bee that once did suck thee,... And swoon in thee for joy, till scarce alive—." Elsewhere Mrs. Browning speaks of a lily into which one looked "As deep as a bee had sucked."[4]

Commonly, Emily Dickinson is the bee and the beloved friend the flower, but the roles are sometimes reversed, especially in the earlier poems. According to an 1859 poem, she wishes she were a rose, adding that she would be satisfied to "subdue the Bumblebee"; and a few months later she is identified with the little "Heart's Ease," or pansy, who is trying to persuade the "Coward Bumble Bee" to pay her a visit (138, 176). In another poem of this period, "The Flower must not blame the Bee" (206), she playfully associates herself with the bee and the loved friend with the flower. Later in 1860, the far more serious "Did the Harebell loose her girdle" describes the poet as a beleaguered flower or a pearl-moated Eden refusing to admit the impetuous bee-earl (213). Another poem of this period, written under the same joyous but half-pained tension, says that her lips, unused to this "Eden," must sip its "Jessamines" slowly and bashfully, just as the "fainting Bee" comes late to his flower,

Round her chamber hums—
Counts his nectars—
Enters—and is lost in Balms. [211]

A few months later, the lover has withdrawn and the poetry is anguished. A poem of powerful feeling, written in late 1861 or early 1862, identified the poet with a bee, "Long Dungeoned from his Rose," who escapes into a brief delirium of "Liberty," "Noon," and "Paradise"; and a later poem, with overtones of 'Calvary," "Auto da Fe," and "Judgment," declares that the bee's misery is summed up in "separation from His Rose" (512, 620).

An 1863 poem, "Precious to Me—She still shall be—" (727), degrades the poet to an unappetizing "Milliner's flower," from which the loved bee-woman turns away to buzz at large in "Summer's Everlasting Dower." This symbolism carries over into poems that appear unconnected with any particular experience. In the poem "We—Bee and I—live by the quaffing—," Emily and the "Bee" are boys, or perhaps bees, together. Do they "get drunk" or "beat" their "Wife?" she asks, answering with apparent reluctance, "I—never wed—" (230). If only she could "ride indefinite" like the "Meadow Bee," says poem 661, and "flirt all Day with Buttercups." Elsewhere she identifies warmly with the "Bee" that "hangs all Noon in the Buttercup" (956).

In some poems the butterfly is interchangeable with the bee, as in poem 176 urging a return visit by the "Coward Bumble Bee" or delaying "Butterfly." A more striking example is an 1863 poem, " 'Twould ease—a Butterfly— / Elate—a Bee," which declares that as "Blossom" Emily would rather be the other woman's "moment / Than a Bee's Eternity—" (682). In a very early poem, a butterfly coming to lie on the breast of a rose has the ghostly beginning of a personal identification (35). But in spite of this and other references to breast, honey, liquor, and the like, her flower and insect poems appear less clearly oral than Mrs. Browning's examples. A hummingbird literally sips nectar, but the descent of the poet's ruby-throated symbol more nearly resembles a sexual assault than a babe at the breast (1463). The harebell's reluctance to "loose her girdle" does not involve a breast image; and the bee-poet bashfully sips "Jessamines," only to go fainting but blissful *into* the flower's "chamber."

Mrs. Browning's Aurora Leigh, hastening toward Italy, wonders whether her loved hills can feel the urgency and yearning of her soul, "As sleeping mothers feel the sucking babe / And smile?" [5] Emily Dickinson did not need to be taught that hills and mountains could symbolize women, and more specifically, female breasts. As early as the fall of 1851, she dressed her hills in "blue mantillas" (L63), and she continued to dress and undress them for years, now in "purple frocks" or "long white nightgowns" (L228), now in "bonnets" (124, 318), now in a mist of laces that "just reveal the surge" (210). A poem beginning "Sweet Mountains—Ye tell Me no lie" (722) salutes the neighboring hills as protective, maternal deities, "Strong Madonnas" worshiped by their "Wayward Nun—beneath the hill." The "Alps" that bar her way to a feminine *"Italy"* are also feminine—a replication of symbols often found within a poem of hers—for they are described as "siren Alps" that "neglect their Curtains," simultaneously threatening and alluring her (80).

The frozen or rejecting breast is the subject of several mountain poems. This snowy breast does not always appear hostile. Her tall friend, the "Himmaleh," has been "known to stoop" to the low "Daisy," amazed that such a doll as Emily dares grow on the slopes of her snow-covered peaks or "Tents"; and in another poem the bonneted (snow-capped) Alps look down in friendly fashion on the humble "Daisy" at their feet (481, 124). But the peak of Teneriffe, clad in "Mail of ices," does not appear to be in a stooping mood, and the poet can only plead, as she has done in still another poem to Sue, "I'm kneeling—still—" (666). Elsewhere the frozen breast is implied in a statement that the other's "Hight" "Involves Alpine / Requirements / And Services of Snow" (914). Years later, about June 1877, the poet wrote that she was "Unworthy" of the other woman's breast (1414). It may be questioned, however, whether the various mountains are consistently breast images. Like the bee-rose imagery, they sometimes migrate to other regions of bodily geography. The version of the Teneriffe poem that Sue received has undergone a significant alteration; instead of the original "eye of granite and ear of steel," it now has a stronger and more specific "Thigh of Granite—and thew of Steel—." [6]

3

Another mixed group of symbols centers in another bodily area; these symbols are characterized by a high degree of activity and even violence—at times virtually an orgasmic violence. For example, the poet writes that the lover's "fire" came to her "small Hearth" and all her "House aglow / Did fan and rock" with an explosion of light—of "Sunrise" and of "Sky" (638). As "Loaded Gun," she goes with her "Owner" to "hunt the Doe" in a terrain of "Sovreign Woods" and "Mountains" with a "Valley" below; and when she smiles (that is, fires), the "cordial light" erupts from this gun-woman like a "Vesuvian face" letting its pleasure through. Her "Yellow Eye" and "emphatic Thumb" make her a deadly foe to her master's enemies, but at night she stands guard rather than lay herself—with a return to breast imagery—on the "Eider-Duck's / Deep Pillow" (754). [7] In a volcano poem, describing something like an orgasmic pain, she interprets her "Solemn—Torrid—Symbol" as "lips that never lie," as "hissing Corals" that "part—and shut," while whole "Cities" "ooze" or "melt" away (601). These lips obviously do not belong to the same part of the anatomy as those that sip "Jessamines." Another volcano poem, undated but clearly written during these years of agonized suffering, says the "Grass" grows on the slopes of her volcano and it looks a "meditative spot," but "How red the Fire rocks below—" (1677)!

A curious and frequent symbol is that of the bare foot. Sometimes it is an apparent euphemism for nakedness, as in the letter to Kate Turner: "We are barefoot and cold" (L203). Years later, in drafting a letter of 20 June 1877, at a time when Kate was making her long-delayed visit to Sue Dickinson next door, the poet wrote on the back of her draft: "I feel Barefoot all over as the Boys say—" (L506). This sense of *barefoot,* like the remembered childhood delight of going without shoes, can be pleasurable. The word turns mournful when she uses it to symbolize a severe but mysterious deprivation. Probably on the same evening as her first letter to Kate, she also wrote excitedly to Mrs. Holland that they "must all stand barefoot before [God's] jasper doors!" (L204). About the same time, in a mournful poem beginning "A poor—torn heart—a tattered heart" (78), she imagines that this "dusty heart" is taken up to heaven where there are "sandals for the Barefoot—." In another poem of the same year, "the shining Courtiers," presumably the angels, smile kindly at lads like Emily walking "barefoot / Upon their golden floor!" (117). But a letter written in December 1860 makes shivering comment on "gentlemen and ladies who go barefoot," which suggests that her own inner climate is turning bitter (L228). And about the same time, she wrote a disturbed poem, "What is—'Paradise'" (215), asking whether "they wear 'new shoes'—in 'Eden,'" whether she will have to "walk the 'Jasper'—barefoot—." A curious poem written in late 1861 or early 1862 begins "Is Bliss then, such Abyss, / I must not put my foot amiss / For fear I spoil my shoe?" (340). In an 1863 poem she is the beggar lad who hopes to stay his "Trudging feet" in the next world, "The Barefoot time forgotten—so— / The Sleet—the bitter Wind—" (717).

In Thackeray's *The Newcomes,* which Emily probably read as a serial in *Harper's* during 1854–55, there is a startlingly clear illustration of the foot-shoe symbol. Meditating on his unhappy marriage to Rosey, Clive Newcome thinks drearily: "They were not made to mate with one another. That was the truth; the shoe was a very pretty little shoe, but Clive's foot was too big for it." [8] Not, of course, that Thackeray understood the sexual meaning of his symbol or that Emily derived her symbol from him. His "foot" is more narrowly phallic, whereas her shivering "bare foot" often appears to be the whole phallicized body longing to return to the condition of prenatal warmth and security.

The foot is the usual locus of temptation. In late 1861 she copies into packet 8 a poem beginning "A Pit—but Heaven over it—" (1712), in which she "dare not ask" her feet, lest they drop her into the abyss. A few weeks later she sent Bowles "Title Divine" (1072); then, fearing he might interpret it as a confession of sexual relations with some unnamed person, she wrote a short note begging him not to doubt her chastity, her "Snow," adding that the enclosed poem would reassure him if he ever wavered about a "foot" like hers. This poem, "Through the strait pass of suffering," says the martyrs keep their faces on God even though their "feet" may be on "Temptation" (L251, 792). But another poem says that the "better Melody" of Eden's brooks occasioned "Eve's great surrender . . . the feet— that would—not—fly" (503). In poem 346 the "Groping feet" of the poet as "Bird" appear to miss their hold. In another poem the "little Brig" of her hopes is overtaken by a storm, its "white foot" trips, and it goes under (723). In an early poem, written while filled with hope, she is sure that only those who have "climbed the weary league" have a "foot" to explore Pizzaro's "purple territories," that is, the symbolic region of love's wealth (73).

The persistence with which she concentrates on her "foot" or "feet" is curious and perhaps unique to her poetry. When she talks of foot and shoe, bliss and abyss, a male poet might have a curious but baffling sense of familiarity, as of a thing not quite right, and again when he reads of a balloon whose "Liquid Feet go softly out" on a "Sea of Blonde," but the balloon is indubitably female and indubitably Emily:

> The gilded Creature strains—and spins—
> Trips frantic in a Tree—
> Tears open her imperial Veins—
> And tumbles in the Sea— [700]

One poem begins "Frigid and sweet Her parting Face," and Emily's pursuing "Feet" are "Frigid and fleet" (1318); but like the "Groping feet" that pursue the "Phantom Queen" of an earlier poem, they are doomed to failure. And still she follows, crossing three rivers, a hill, two deserts. "The Sea comes last—Step merry feet," but Death has preceded her and usurped her "Premium" (1664).

A kindred symbolism involves the hand, and especially the finger. She uses the latter image with particular sensitivity to the end of 1865, but only twice afterward. The more general term *hand,* as might be expected, occurs more frequently though not in proportion to the number of lines in post-1865 writing; and the word *foot/feet* is also infrequent after 1865. It is as if her whole body were almost painfully sensitized throughout her major period but scarcely at all in later years. With some justice she wrote afterward that she had died.

In several poems the wind is given a hand and fingers and is quite clearly eroticized. There is "that old measure in the Boughs" which the wind makes, "working like a Hand, / Whose fingers Comb the Sky," scattering down "tufts of Tune"; or the "Wind with fingers" goes across the "June," shaking "Petals from a Rose" (321, 409). From its "Fingers" comes a music like tunes in glass; or it runs its fingers in creases through the meadow grass; or with its hands it kneads or rocks the grass (436, 516, 824). Wind and eros are interchangeable, as in poem 297, where love is described as "Private" like the "Woods," "Phraseless" like the "Breeze," yet capable of stirring the "proudest Trees." The wind has been endowed with the poet's own sensitivity.

Perhaps the earliest figurative use of the hand/finger image appears in a letter of May 1852 to Susan Gilbert, then teaching in Baltimore. Anxiously looking toward Sue's return, Emily assures her that "every bud that blooms, does but remind me more of that garden *unseen,* awaiting the hand that tills it. Dear Susie, when you come, how many boundless blossoms among those silent beds!" (L92). Between persons of the same sex the roles shift readily back and forth, and now Emily's hands and now the friend's appear to control the poem. In a quatrain accompanying a pair of knitted garters, the latter are amusingly personified and equipped with their maker's own hands: "When Katie kneels, their loving hands still clasp her pious knee—" (222). In the spring 1860 letter to this friend, she writes: "I touch your hand—my cheek your cheek—I stroke your vanished hair" (L222); and a poem of 1862 or 1863 closes the eyes of the friend, now in effect dead to Emily, salutes the "Quick—Sweet Mouth," then strokes the "Unnumbered Satin" of her hair and fondles her slim fingers (758). A packet 8 poem, written in late fall 1861, apparently describes this same tall, queenlike friend, with special attention to her slender, delicate fingers: "so slight— / They would elate a Sprite" (283). This friend may also figure in an undated poem of intense feeling describing a night scene, apparently a bedroom scene:

Her hand was whiter than the sperm
That feeds the sacred light. [1722]

A poem of late 1861 or early 1862 appears to visualize the friend as among the loved dead; these "Women—plucked away / From our familiar Lifetime—" are also, in variants, plucked from "our familiar gazing" and "our familiar fingers—" (499). A poem in late handwriting, possibly as late as 1877, speaks of "A pencil in an Idol's [dainty] Hand," dooming a "Devotee ... To Crucifix or Block" (1375); but a poem of the same period, which apparently reflects the excitement of a visit from the long-absent "Witch," says the "Hand" that "fondled" the poet's embers in their days of "Fire" can make them live again (1383).

A poem written about 1862, but almost certainly recalling a momentary impulse of the preceding fall, begins "I—Years had been—from Home—" and uses the other's house-body as its primary symbol. The poet stands before the "Awful Door," fits her trembling "Hand" to the "Latch," then cautiously moves her "fingers off" and flees in panic (609).[9] In two poems the beloved is a "Gem" or a "Pearl" that slips through the poet's "fingers" (245, 299). She pleads for "More Hands—to hold" and clutches at their last hours with "greedy hands"; drowning, she thrusts her "Hands" above water to proclaim her steadfast love; drowned, she has eyes "still begging raised—And hands beseeching—thrown!" (263, 322, 537, 201). According to another poem, her fingers are the most vital part of her, the last to die; even her "Feet kept drowsing—drowsing," but her "fingers were awake—" (692). Fingers are also a surprising feature of death, that is, of love's death, for the behavior of this "ghastly Fright" is the frigid replica of the lover's; she feels it salute her "with long fingers— / Caress—her freezing hair— / Sip, Goblin, from the very lips / The lover—hovered o'er—" (512).

Minor images having possible phallic significance, like the pebble and the nest-hunting bird, will be discussed in another context. Here it should be pointed out that poem 913 uses what appears to be castration symbolism; the "Bud," "Stem," "Foot," and brave "Root" of her early hopes are all one and are cut down as one by the confident "Worm." Another apparent castration poem describes the effect of "Frost" (the agonizing rejection she suffered) on the garden-self. If the "Garden [var., Landscape] keep the Gash," if the "wilted [var., Blackened] countenance" fails to "correct [var. efface] the crease" or "counteract the stain," then her injury is mortal (951). In other poems she has been "stabbed" even while she "sued ... forgiveness," or she is the "Bird" stabbed even while she built in the lover's bosom, and her *"little life ... Is leaking—red"* from this mortal wound (497, 238, 236). She has been "Struck," "Maimed," "Robbed," all her bodily "Mansion" torn, yet she continued to "love the Cause that slew Me" (925). She has been lashed by a "Whip" and like a magnanimous bird sings to the "Stone" of which she died (1304). The beloved friend, a "Sceptic Thomas," is invited to split the "Lark" to find its music, "Loose the Flood ... Gush after Gush ... Scarlet Experiment" (861). This "Thomas" poem, in 1864 handwriting, has an obvious connection with Master letter 233, written about midsummer 1861, in which she describes herself as a bird shot by a bullet and asks whether "Thomas' faith" requires another drop from the "gash that stains your Daisy's bosom." A last and most interesting castration symbol is blindness, which the poet herself treated as talion for the offense of voyeurism, although she probably did not understand the connection with her subsequent photophobia.

4

A western lady undresses herself, removing gold garters (knitted for her by the poet), fresh dimities, and purple petticoat, then holds her expiring "Candle eastward across oceans, until its flickering light catches all of the "Bosporus," "Ball of Mast," "Dome," and "Window Pane," in a radiance that is as subtle and mysterious as it is intense (716). The poem is a great success, although any analysis limited to the conscious level would find nothing more than a juvenile conceit in a sentimentalized landscape scene. As a later discussion will show, the success springs in good part from the point of view. The poet herself dwells in the East, whether the dessicated East of the Transjordanian desert or the fabulous Orient of the poetic mind, and she looks toward the West, which is the beloved's quarter. The viewpoint throughout is subtly, quite unconsciously, but passionately voyeuristic, and it is the strength of the poem—and of many another poem.

The intensity of this seeing can hardly be imagined, let alone comprehended. She is almost one concentrated hungry eye, and indeed she finds

"Luxury" in simply remembering the "Luxury" of banqueting on the beloved "Countenance" (815). An 1861 poem, "What would I give to see his face?" offers to exchange various wealths for "*One hour*—of her Sovereign's face!" (247). More sadly she writes, "You see I cannot see...Too vague—the face / My own—so patient—covets" (253). A poem beginning "Not in this World to see his face" (418) tries to find comfort in a heavenly reunion but ends with the disconsolate admission that she preferred the lost earthly paradise. The poem, "I live with Him—I see His face" (463), in spite of its exultant note, appears to depend upon the strength of an imagination that conjures up the lover's face in defiance of distance or estrangement. As she says elsewhere, "What I see not, I better see" (939), describing a dream in which the beloved's face is brilliantly illumined and the dreamer arises and does it "distinguished Grace" until the return of daylight and the end of "perfectness."

Some of these poems employ masculine pronouns, while others use direct address or neuter pronouns or still other types of evasion. For example, the poem "Like Eyes that looked on Wastes" (458) has the line "So looked the face I looked upon— / So looked itself—on Me," but the concluding admission that "Neither would be a Queen / Without the Other" betrays the fact that both are women. Another "face-see" poem, "They put Us far apart" (474), is so ingeniously worded as to avoid sexual identity. A mysterious "They"—the world or the world's law—has put "Us" apart, taken away "our" eyes, "thwarted Us" with guns—but " 'I see Thee' each" responds, and though put into dungeons, "Our Souls" see just as well. Summoned to execution, "We" are still able "to see"; and at the end "Not either" notices death:

> Each other's Face—was all the Disc
> Each other's setting—saw—

Or the "face-see" poem uses examples or generalities: "Deformed Men" (herself) "ponder Grace" (the exquisite beloved), and the "Lost" and "Blind" poet would deem it wealth to see "Day's face" (355). Or she uses direct address, as in "I see thee better—in the Dark," where her love functions as a "Light," a "Prism" directed upon the beloved, or as a "Miner's Lamp" (for she is tunneling toward the other); but best of all she sees her friend "in the Grave," its little panels all aglow with the light she has "held so high, for Thee—" (611). In a final example employing direct address, the lamps are brought in once more, presumably to illumine the face that is the conscious object of this intense and painful seeing, in an imagined life beyond the grave:

> At last, the Lamps upon thy side
> The rest of Life to *see!* [174]

"A single Screw of Flesh" begins with an awed comment on the slenderness of the flesh that retains the deified beloved this "side the Vail." The line, "Once witnessed of the Gauze," suggests that the soul of the beloved manifested itself to her, but as her "eyes just turned to see," it was smuggled past her sight, not into death, for the "single Screw" still holds, but into eternal separation (263). The poem, "I envy Seas, whereon He rides" (498), is a desperate appeal to see; she envies the very hills that gaze on the beloved's journey. How easily everything else can *see* what is as utterly forbidden to her as heaven! The dreadful wrong done to Moses, as to her, was to tantalize by letting him "see—the Canaan" but never enter it (597). Yet, when she once had the opportunity, she half shrunk from the "Glory" she had "importuned to see" (694). Years later the old longing stirred again, and in a letter of late 1872 to Louise Norcross, recalling this history of pain, she writes of the bread of affection for which she has starved, then adds: "Longing, it may be, is the gift no other gift supplies" (L379). A poem of the same period, "Longing is like the Seed / That wrestles in the Ground," voices an almost detached hope that at some hour and in some clime this seed of longing will "see the Sun!" (1255).

During 1859-60 Emily doubtless wrote a number of poems (probably more than the dates of copying indicate) expressing a strong desire to see her absent friend. The blindness poems began sharply on the breach of their intimacy, and from that time the blindness and seeing poems proceeded together, one reinforcing the other. Almost certainly she received on 1 April 1861, the day after Easter Sunday, that letter from a "dainty" hand which sent this devotee to crucifix and block (" 'The first of April,' 'Today, Yesterday, and Forever,' " moans letter 801, as if overpowered by a ghastly coincidence). A few days later she wrote poem 236, describing her injury as *"Blindness—on the Dawn"* and as a hideous wound from which she was bleeding to death. "Before I got my eye put out," begins poem 327, she liked "to see" just as much as did "other Creatures, that have Eyes— / And know no other way—." In a sense she is blaming God for depriving her of that simple organ of pleasure possessed by other creatures, who are simple things too and have no other way of getting pleasure. But if someone should tell her that she could have the "sky," the "Meadows," the "Mountains," all the "Forests," and as much of noon as she could take between her "finite eyes," this news would strike her dead. It is safer to guess, just to put her soul on the "Window pane" (perhaps the pane illumined by the candle of the western lady) where others, unafraid of the "Sun," are accustomed to "put their eyes." Her blindness, in short, is the consequence of the cruel treatment she has received—but, in some curious way, has deserved. Other items in the poem—mountains, forests, meadows, and so on—represent aspects of the faithless beloved.

More soberly and sadly, she blamed not the lover but the structure of the world and the judgment of God. "Renunciation," that "piercing Virtue," is a "putting out of Eyes" just at the moment of sunrise, lest the earthly "Day" outshine "Day's Great Progenitor" (745), as in other poems she emphatically said it would and did. Sometimes it is not her eyes but the lamp or the light of the world that is put out. Science predicts and "bows" in "Eclipses," but this one came without warning, and it is God's fault: "Jehovah's Watch—is wrong" (415). About this time she wrote to her new friend Higginson that the rest of the family "address an Eclipse, every morning—whom they call their 'Father'" (L261). "Good Night! Which put the candle out?" demands poem 259, then suggests strongly that the other person "Extinguished" it. A poem discriminating between fear and despair says the despairing mind is smooth, motionless, "Contented"—like the eye of a bust that "knows it cannot see" (305). Elsewhere, in a fantasy of suicide, she feels as if her "Mind were going blind," and she touches a "Trigger" and wanders out of life (1062).

The period before this brief but illuminating love can also be described as blindness. In a poem beginning "Let Us play Yesterday," she recalls her "Egg-life," her loveless days "at school," before the transfiguring love with its "Cunning Reds of Morning" made the "Blind—leap—" (728). This last line is a conflation of Isaiah 35:5–6: "Then the eyes of the blind shall be opened, and the ears of the deaf shall be unstopped. Then shall the lame man leap as an hart, and the tongue of the dumb sing; for in the wilderness shall waters break out, and streams in the desert." Not only is all the quotation implicit in her line—singing, so to speak, within that line—but it describes precisely how she viewed her brief experience of love.

Among the literary sources of her blindness poems, *Samson Agonistes* deserves special notice. So closely did she study Milton's tragedy of the strong man betrayed into blindness and captivity that she often seemed identified with Samson. Her darknesses, eclipses, lost days, and blazing noons appear to draw upon these lines:

> O dark, dark, dark, amid the blaze of noon,
> Irrecoverably dark, total Eclipse
> Without all hope of day!

Samson cries that he is "Betray'd, Captiv'd, and both my eyes put out"; [10] and she complains of "Treason" (438, 851, 1410) and remembers "Before I got my eye put out," and "Darkness . . . put out her eye," and the "putting out of Eyes" just on sunrise (327, 768, 745). Such lines as these,

> To live a life half dead, a living death,
> And buried; but O yet more miserable!
> My self, my Sepulcher, a moving Grave,

recall poem after poem in which she bemoans her living death. For example, poem 858, "This Chasm, Sweet, upon my life," describes the gulf into which "Sunrise" and "Day" have dropped, within whose "gaping sides" she lies as in a tomb, and yet a tomb that is "turbulent," that she carries with her. Samson complains that he is

Buried, yet not exempt
By priviledge of death and burial
From worst of other evils, pains and wrongs,

and she writes of "The privilege to die," "Death's privilege," "Thy privilege of dying," or of the "Things that Death will buy . . . Room— / Escape from Circumstances—" (536, 640, 1153, 382). And she would have appropriated to herself the bitter reproach of the Chorus:

Thou art become (O worst imprisonment!)
The Dungeon of thy self . . .[11]

Eyeless in Gaza, poet and strong man lamented the treachery of the beloved woman.

5

A determination to keep the poet no less virginal in mind than in body has placed her male editors, biographers, and critics in a dilemma they have been slow to appreciate. Higginson began it with his reluctance to publish "Wild Nights—Wild Nights!" ("lest the malignant read into it more than that virgin recluse ever dreamed of putting there"), and his successors have gratefully followed his lead.[12] But even if the passionate attachment that engrossed her during 1859–60 had been wholly an affair of the brain, no more licentious place could have been found for carrying on a love affair. The satisfied body is incomparably more chaste than the unsatisfied mind; or, as Emily Dickinson observed in one formula after another, "The Banquet of Abstemiousness surpasses that of Wine"! Her unconscious mind dwelt obsessively on certain deprivations, and the images plucked from that unconscious mind betrayed her obsessiveness in clusters of genital symbolism pointing to a vaginal-uterine regression.

There is no need to enter into a detailed analysis of the poet's love-hate relationship with her mother—a mythicized relationship having probably little to do with the qualities of the actual Mrs. Dickinson. Whatever mother substitutes the poet acquired along the way, the primary referent of the symbols remains the mother. This may be illustrated by a poem with the following first stanza:

I had not minded—Walls—
Were Universe—one Rock—
And far I heard his silver Call
The other side the Block— [398]

The "silver Call," which is not a symbol but a recollection, is associated with Romeo's "How silver-sweet sound lovers' tongues by night" and with the title Emily gave to Kate Turner's copy of poem 83, "Whistling under My Window." There is overwhelming evidence, in poems, in letters to Kate, in Master letter 233, that this friend did come calling, quite possibly whistling under Emily's second-story window, and that they went walking (sometimes with the dog Carlo, it would seem, and sometimes not) through the Dickinson meadows and around the frog pond and on occasion as far as the mill. But the Walls, the Universe, the Rock, the Block—these are the mother to whom she can never return, and they are at the same time the barriers that prevent her.

In the second stanza, she imagines how it would be to tunnel into this block or rock or universe (in poem 611 she carries a "Miner's Lamp"), until her "Groove" pushes through into the other's groove, and she can at last *see*. Shortly after her mother's death, she wrote to Mrs. Holland (L792): "We were never intimate Mother and children while she was our Mother—but Mines in the same Ground meet by tunnelling." (A line or two below she is still speaking with an undercurrent of grief for the lost mother: "The Port of Peace has many Coves, though the main entrance cease—.") The figure is the same, even to the doubling of the tunnels or, in the poem, the grooves. In the near-literal sense, both women have "tunnels" or "grooves," but the urgency of the symbol is toward tunneling into the other person—a symbolized regression to the womb.

In the remaining lines she is stopped by a series of trivial barriers—hair, filament, cobweb, straw:

A limit like the Vail
Unto the Lady's face—
But every Mesh—a Citadel—
And Dragons—in the Crease— [398]

Except for the dragons, these remaining defenses—hair, filament, cobweb, straw, veil—are not only light and trifling like the first-mentioned hair, they *are* hair, although it must be added that, for this poet, hair is no trifle. In 1860 she writes to her friend, "I touch your hand—my cheek your cheek—I stroke your vanished hair" (L222), and in poem 758 she talks of touching her hair: "This—We stroked— / Unnumbered satin—." Finally, there is an undated poem that appears to recall the same circumstances: "Her face was in a bed of hair / Like flowers in a plot—" (1722). Other details—the whiteness of the beloved hand, the tenderness of the beloved tongue, the sacredness of the illuminating lamp—suggest the intimacy of the bedroom at night, but all of these tend to fade away and be lost in the effulgence of the unbound hair. It is a fair inference that the erotic strength of this hair derives from a displacement upward.

So far as conscious knowledge went, of course, Emily Dickinson was writing about a real face and a real veil. She was accustomed to seeing her friend's face half-concealed beneath a veil—a widow's black veil, in fact, and hence a potent reminder of the dead rival—but this black veil and this dragon had predecessors. In early 1852 she wondered what would become of her when some "bold Dragon" should bear Susan Gilbert away "to live in his high mountain" (L70). At that time she appeared to have no suspicion that the dragon would be her brother Austin. Behind these successors, however, and convoking and ordering their appearance, loom the small child's mother and father.

It is a coincidence, though a startling one, that in early 1859 she called her domineering father the "Reptile," specifically though playfully identifying him with the old serpent and dragon Satan (beneath her joking manner there would have been a real resentment of the humiliation he had inflicted on her). Speaking of the emotional starvation of her childhood, she says she had been as powerless to remove the claw of hunger as to "make a Dragon—move—" (612). Again, her "Heavenly Father," who often appears to be only her earthly father enlarged, leads his "Chosen Child" away from love by "Claw of Dragon" (1021). These are curious poems, whether or not they bear any relation to "I had not minded—Walls—." In poem 1021 the father is the (plural) dragon in the "Crease" who bars her return to the mother. That it is an abridged primal scene may partly account for the intensity of her wish to see, an intensity already noticed in dozens of poems. In late 1863, shortly after she learned of Kate Turner's engagement to John Anthon, she began to have trouble with her eyes, an apparent photophobia that would give her at least two painful years.

Certain images recur incessantly in the poetry, but fragmented, disconnected, scattered broadcast through myriad short poems, so that their larger meaning is lost. Only when they are fitted together like some huge puzzle does the design become apparent. Then it is possible to see that such disparate images as garden, landscape, and face are interchangeable, that they form part of a complex that includes such images as angle, crease, furrow, well, or sea, and grass, moss, sedge, or hair, and that in conjunction they explicate each other.

When the young poet describes "a brighter garden / Where not a frost has been" and urges her brother, "Into *my* garden come!" (2) even the biographers are able to see an unconscious sexual imagery, although they overlook stronger language of the same period in letters to the beloved Sue about the "garden unseen, awaiting the hand that tills it," and the "many boundless blossoms among those silent beds" or about Emily longing for the return of her "absent One" and "training the stems to my flowers" in anticipation of Sue (letters 92, 102). The motif of this last letter is picked up some nine years later in a poem beginning "I tend my flowers for thee— / Bright Absentee!" (339) in which the poet as "Daisy" draped in modest gray calyx fixes an apparently voyeuristic attention on the undraping of several handsome female flowers, including a cactus that "splits her Beard / To show her throat," that is, a throatlike female opening surrounded by hair.[13] In late 1854 she described a dream about walking with her friend Elizabeth Holland "in the most wonderful garden, and helping you pick —roses," adding that she hoped to repeat the dream and impatiently counted the "hours 'tween me and the darkness, and the dream of you and the roses, and the basket never full" (L175). An 1862 poem, "Ourselves were wed one summer—dear—" (631), makes an unhappy contrast between her fate and that of some other woman: "Your Garden led the Bloom, / For mine—in Frosts—was sown—"; and a poem noticed earlier in this chapter describes the frost-blighting of the poet's "Garden" (or "Landscape" in words suggesting a symbolic castration—"Gash," "crease," "stain" (951). And the beloved woman's "face," in its "bed of hair," is like "flowers in a plot." On occasion, and probably without the poet's conscious knowledge, this garden appears to be genital.

There can be no hesitancy about the meaning of "natures face," occurring as it does in the highly sexual context of her 1880 letter to Otis Lord. The dream she relates to him (including, as it happens, a transparent wish for his death) betrays her curiosity about his sex but rejects the opportunity to "unveil" him. Turning next to the difficulties of their actual interview, she asks how she can respond to his lovemaking when she has never seen his "natures face" (L645). Obviously she knew the meaning of her symbol here, although she probably did not understand the genital significance of her much earlier "Vesuvian face" or of the volcano with "lips" of "hissing Corals" (754, 601). There must also be some doubt that she fully understood the symbolism of an 1864 poem lamenting her failure to pluck the red rose of love. This red rose (identified with the friend in letter 203) "bloomed and dropt, a Single Noon"—the symbolic hour of climax—but the poet, unaware that this was the "single Flower of the Earth," stood hesitating while "Great Nature's Face / Passed infinite by Me—" (978). In still another poem, which states that the lover proposed some special intimacy, she at first draws back— " 'Twas face to face with Nature— forced"—and then changes her mind too late (643). Of the many poems that express her desire to see the beloved face—the goal of her intense and incessant longing—it is probable that several gain heat and strength from a latent sexual meaning. Almost certainly this is true of the poems about the lady's face behind the veil or in the bed of hair. It is true of the poem about the western lady who undressed herself.

The word "Landscape" in poem 951 is a variant for "Garden" and appears to share the latter's covert meaning elsewhere. Of course, it might be thought to connote the breast, since the poet apparently never used it without recalling the final stanza of the Isaac Watts hymn that had awed her since childhood, describing the earthly pilgrim as a Moses who climbs Mount Nebo to look westward toward the Promised Land.

In his discussion of the significance of mountains for morals, religions, and art, Ruskin centers his attention upon the burial of Moses rather than on the "denial of the permission to enter the Promised Land," but he does allow himself one description which, if not erotically tinged in his own unconscious mind, would certainly lend itself to eroticism in the mind of another. Of course, Emily Dickinson was already aware of the possibility of erotic symbolism in the idea of Canaan as a "land flowing with milk and honey"—a conception surreptitiously entertained by other Puritans as well—but Ruskin's description must have added its own peculiar color to that "stately landscape" (168) of her heart's desire. Moses looks westward —and it is a single glimpse—toward "the fair hills of Judah, and the soft plains and banks of Jordan, purple in the evening light as with the blood of redemption, and fading in their distant fulness into mysteries of promise and of love." [14] Ruskin did not appear to have the maternal breast in mind. Neither, probably, did the Amherst poet.

The poet's identification of herself with Jacob at the ford of Jabbok (an identification so meaningful to her that she persisted in it to the last days of her life, in letter 1042) calls for notice here. Apparently it began with a poem of early 1859, "A little East of Jordan" (59), written perhaps during that first two-month stay of Sue's old school friend, Kate Turner. The insistence on the cardinal point, which is not given in the biblical account, suggests strongly that the Angel has come from the West, from Canaan, and that the extorted blessing is a promise to allow the poet to cross over Jordan and enter Canaan. The repetition of the words Jordan and Canaan and the identity of the quests made a fusion of Jacob and Moses as natural in Emily's mind as in the Bible, where both men saw God "face to face." A poem written in early 1860, during her short-lived period of happiness, may be said to have a combined hero, a Jacob-Moses, who talks of being kept out of Canaan but looks with some complacency at the "stately landscape" on the other side (168). This landscape is what Jacob wrestles for and what Moses sees, later and more bitterly, "in Vision—and in Veto" (528).

In poem 59 the "Gymnast" Jacob wrestles with the angelic "Stranger" "Till morning touching mountain—." Now, there are no mountains in the biblical account, which says only "until the breaking of the day." These nonbiblical mountains have entered, as if compulsively, perhaps in unconscious association with very similar language, "Until the day break," twice repeated in mountainous context in the Song of Solomon. The latter's "mountains of Bether," "mountain of myrrh," and "hill of frankincense," on which the beloved is urged to be a roe or a young hart till the day breaks, are mountains the lover climbs or aspires to climb, like the

"Chimborazo" Emily wanted to scale (453). And as soon as the angelic visitor agrees to bless aspiring Jacob, "Light swung the silver fleeces" either "beyond" or "among" these nonbiblical "Hills." Two years later, in a poem beginning "If I'm lost—now—," Emily remembers a happier day when the "Jasper Gates / Blazed open—suddenly" on her "awkward—gazing face" and (pluralized) "Angels" touched her "with their fleeces / Almost as if they care—" (256). Since this angelic fleece is hair, it may be assumed that the "'Peniel' Hills" were likewise covered with a fleece of hair. Finally, this highly eroticized hair appears to recur in an 1864 poem summing up her unlucky experience in love as "Finding," "loss," and "Expedition for / the 'Golden Fleece,'" with the wry conclusion that all of it, including poet-Jason and the "Golden Fleece," proved to be a delusion and sham (870).

Another important component of her landscape symbol appears to be the word *angle*. Although the angle will be treated later as one element in her odd assemblage of geometrical figures, it is clearly more than that. Angle or inverted triangle, it is a recognized female symbol of universal occurrence, and Emily Dickinson appears to have used the word in this sense without ever knowing why it evoked its particular associations. Her initial angle, in an 1861 poem concentrating on "That Angle in the floor" where the lovers separated and all their "Sinew tore" (293), deepens in meaning with every fresh occurrence, until even the word "Sinew" begins to look like an unconscious carry-over from the Jacob story. Another interesting poem, which describes the death of a young soldier as the turning of a metaphorical angle, has only the most superficial connection with the real Civil War soldier of the editor's careful note. The poet betrays her special interest in a conviction that the dead youth *wanted* to die so that he could go up, shining with "Victory," to "look at" the mother who had died in his little-boyhood. She imagines how slowly the seasons must have passed for him, "Till Bullets clipt an Angle," enabling him to pass "quickly round"; and in her mind's eye she sees the "Woman and her Boy" pass proudly across the sky (596). Now this could never have been the wish of any live Belchertown, Massachusetts, youth, but it was very much the obsession of an Emily Dickinson, who would have tunneled through a universe to reach the mother surrogate. She is the "Boy," the little soldier of this poem as so often elsewhere, and the "Angle" appears to be feminine.

A curious "angle" poem, which reads at first like a philosophical reflection on changing values, is actually shot through and through with anger and suffering. She tries to persuade herself that some lost and beloved "Thing," once "so towering high" that she "could not grasp its segment" (angle), was not really worth her toil. In a startling synecdoche, she then reduces the lost beloved to the distinctive sexual organ (betraying her own agonizing self-contempt as well) and declares that her "Cordillera" has proved to be a mere "furrow," her "Appenine" but a "Knoll," and she is luck to be deprived of it, since she might otherwise have waked "in a Gnat's embrace," her giant gone (534)! The desperate and bitter awkwardness of this "waking in a Gnat's embrace" suggests an attempt to deal with an actual memory; but the segment / angle, furrow, knoll, and mountains are features in a symbolic landscape related to the "landscape" of many another poem.

From her bed, according to poem 375, as often as she wakes she contemplates the "Angle of a Landscape" filled with naturalistic details so selected and arranged as to make a troubling, ominous, altogether unnatural impression. First of all, this "Angle" seems to be visible only in association with "an ample Crack," itself described in terms of curious dread as "Like a Venetian—waiting—." After this mysterious beginning, there is a temporary sense of relief in learning that the angle of landscape that "Accosts" her "open eye" is no more than a slanting "Bough of Apples," the "Pattern of a Chimney," the "Forehead of a Hill," very occasionally a "Vane's Forefinger," whereupon the feeling of uneasiness resumes and continues to the icy stasis at the close: "These—never stir at all." Taken together, the various items appear to hint at a subterranean connection with that "Angle" in which their "Sinew tore," and though the poem cannot be unriddled in detail, the fact that these items recur together in other poems suggests that they are related in the depths of her unconsciousness.

Apparently her view once comprised a nearer, moving figure, for poem 375 ends with the otherwise mystifying statement that seasons pass but nothing interrupts the motionless tableau she sees on awaking. This conjecture is strengthened by another poem of this period, "It's thoughts—and just One Heart," which begs for

A Landscape—not so great
To suffocate the Eye—
A Hill—perhaps—
Perhaps the profile of a Mill

and ends by yearning for the second "Heart," which apparently once shared the room with her (495).

These several poems have a curious connection with another 1862 poem beginning

Forget! The lady with the Amulet
Forget she wore it at her Heart [438]

This is the erstwhile friend who knows how to forget, and the poet is the "Amulet" that once nestled at the lady's heart, perhaps in "the Queen's place" of letter 233. Lines promising to serve the lady as faithfully as the "little Rill" that cools the "Forehead of the Hill" or fills the sea or goes "to turn the Mill" may recall an actual excursion, perhaps a stroll to the mill, but they also describe the lady. The "Forehead of a Hill" is one of the objects seen in poem 375; and in poem 495 she views from the bedroom, as *"luxuries,"* a "Hill" and the "profile of a Mill." Although this last is described as a windmill, other references in her poetry, as in her letters, are to the local water mill, which was one of her earliest childhood memories and a favored goal of schoolgirl walks. Emily herself is a water wheel whose "dripping feet / Go round and round" (10), or she expects to be a mill wheel with "belts and bands of gold" and to "whizz triumphant on the new stream" of heaven (L182). In a belated poem, not consciously associated with any person, she describes a tiny mill wheel "in the grass" turning a freshet of dew—Mother Nature in her most intimate aspect (1097).

6

In her comments on the "Tim" poem, Theodora Ward calls attention to the fact that the poet and her boy-self have fixed their longing eyes on a "cozy heaven, with 'Cottages—But, Oh, so high!'" And she relates this image to that of an 1862 poem beginning "I went to Heaven—/ 'Twas a small Town" (374).[15] At times, the cottage-house-room figure is explicitly identified with a person, as in a poem beginning "On that dear Frame the Years had worn," which appears to note the signs of age in a beloved friend (Mrs. Holland, perhaps), who is nevertheless as "precious" to the poet as the "House" in which "We first experienced Light" (940). Here the generalizing "We" may be intended to get over the awkward fact that she had an intense dislike for the mother whose place the loved friend is described as filling.

In several poems, the house image quite clearly represents the lost beloved. If she could crawl between the "Arms of the Wind," says poem 1103, she would hasten to "an adjoining Zone ... ascertain the House" and whether the soul of this house-body is at home, then hold the "Wick" of her own soul to the other's light; or, alternatively, she herself assumes the role of the fire bringer and begs to be allowed to enter the other's house with an apron full of "sticks / To make your Cottage gay" (366). Elsewhere, she may attribute the initiative to the beloved, whose "fire" comes to the poet's "small Hearth" and sets all her "House aglow," fanning and rocking with "sudden light," with "Sunrise" (638). In a more bitter mood she complains that this earthly paradise did not materialize, that the "Sunset stopped on Cottages" precisely at the moment when the "Morning" or "Sunrise" of love was to begin (950). According to another poem, the lonely and desolate poet once saw "A Door just opened—to a House," disclosing an "instant's Width of Warmth," then closing irrevocably (953).

A remarkable poem, written in 1862, describes how she returns to a

"Home" from which she has long been absent but dares not open the door lest a strange new face stare vacantly into hers and ask her business ("My Business—just a Life I left— / Was such—still dwelling there?"). She fumbles at her nerve, scans the windows, fits her trembling hand to the latch, then withdraws it and flees the "House" gaspingly, like a thief, without ever daring to ask her crucial question, that is, whether the lost beloved, reencountered after hyperbolic years of estrangement, still retains any love for the despairing poet (609). Although the poem probably recalls an impulsive moment during the October 1861 visit of Kate Turner, it merits comparison with a similar poem endorsed "Sue" and apparently pleading with her. The poet imagines herself, just like Jesus, standing on tiptoe at the door of the house-body trying to look in and "spy the lady's soul." Not until Jesus gives up will she also stop patiently waiting "upon the steps" and "knocking low" at Sue's heart (317).

The "cozy heaven" of Mrs. Ward's description can be abundantly illustrated in poems and in letters. The heavenly "Mansions" of poem 127 are to be "warm" and "snugly built," and the peculiarly warm, soft, small "Heaven" of poem 374 is "Lit—with a Ruby— / Lathed—with Down" and associated with the mothlike, with Mechlin lace, with "Gossamer" and "Eider." It sounds, in fact, like a cradle, a nest, a womb, or like the following passage from a letter to young Susan Gilbert written about February 1852: "Oh Susie, I would nestle close to your warm heart, and never hear the wind blow, or the storm beat, again. Is there any room there for me, or shall I wander away all homeless and alone?" (L74). Shortly afterward, following a visit to Sue's house, she writes that "when the latch was lifted and the oaken door was closed, why, Susie, I realized as never I did before, how much a *single cottage* held that was dear to me" (L77). A few months earlier, at a Jenny Lind concert she did not much like or understand, she was nevertheless deeply stirred by the song, "Give me my thatched cottage" (L46). In her first preserved letter to Sue, written shortly after both girls reached their twentieth birthday, she makes a soft, warm heaven out of Sue's bedroom: "your little 'Columbarium is lined with warmth and softness'" (L38). The words are borrowed from Longfellow's *Kavanagh,* a book she especially cherished, it would seem, for its account of two girls who were "in love with each other." [16] Now that Sue's sister Martha has returned from Michigan and resumed the place of special confidence and intimacy that for a short while belonged to Emily, the latter writes with melancholy to Abiah Root and paints a warm picture of Abiah and her friend Abby Wood sleeping together and holding hands (L39).

A related symbol is the nest, with the conscious meaning of a loved friend's heart or breast. An 1858 poem says that an unknown woman, very likely Sue, has forgotten the "nest," has abandoned the poet's "bosom," leaving a coffin instead, and is now breathing "God's old fashioned vows" into a more modern ear (39). In an 1859 poem, "Wren" Emily is looking about for a "Nest" and wondering whether she may be aspiring too high (143). This poem seems to anticipate an 1862 poem, already noticed, about the boy "Bobolink" whose nesting tree has been "Clove to the Root" (755). Finally, a prose example that once more involves Sue deserves to be mentioned. A few months after the birth of her first child, Sue complained of being tired of "making *bibs* for her bird—her ring-dove," to which her sister-in-law promptly replied with "a crumb—for the 'Ring dove'—and a spray for *his Nest,* a little while ago—*just*—'*Sue*'" (L238). The spray of flowers is a gift for Sue, whose bosom is the baby's "Nest," and yet the poet appears to reflect, half jealously, on that earlier nest, the womb.

The relatively few tents appear to have the same range of significance as houses. Just as the dead may inhabit "a Hut of Stone" or a (pregnant) "House that seemed / A Swelling of the Ground" or heavily ironical "Sweet—safe—Houses," so they may be described as "Tribes of Eclipse— in Tents of Marble" (654, 712, 457, 216). Less macabre but no less tragic, the poet has "known a Heaven, like a Tent," to pick up its stakes and vanish, leaving her to stare after it very much as the schoolboy stares, bewildered, after the lost bee (243, 319). Although both poems use the word "Heaven," neither the tent nor the bee has any more religious significance than the lost amethyst, the lost nesting site, the lost "Birdling," the phantom meadow, the vanished rainbow, or any of myriad objects symbolizing the lost beloved (245, 755, 39, 20, 257). The technique of the jeweler's loupe is never more misapplied than when it is focused nearsightedly on some three-stanza segment of Emily Dickinson's total poem.

The longed-for heaven can be a well, on the brink of which she suffers the agonies of Tantalus, permitted to hear it drip but forbidden to drink (490). A less tortured poem concentrates wistfully on the beauty of "Droughtless Wells," environed by "Mosses," where "Pebble—safely plays—," but this picture of achieved happiness is a fantasy, a description of what she desired and might have enjoyed under different circumstances. "Pebble" is after all not playing in the well. The second stanza centers attention on the one beloved well, fathoms deep, with a bejeweled belt inlaid with emerald and diamonds. If she were rich she would buy a "Bucket," for she is often thirsty and is too high up to reach the water with her lips. In Revelation she has read of a land where people "thirst no more" and therefore must have "Buckets," but she shrinks away from heavenly grandeur and says her small earthly well is "Dearer to understand" (460). It should be pointed out that the poem rationalizes the bucket as the means of getting into the well, but on the unconscious level, bucket and well are identical, that is, the womb to which she wishes to return.

The "Pebble," it has been suggested, is herself. In a poem that imagines the happy abandonment of home, wealth, and station in favor of the "Stranger," she says she dropped her fate, "a timid Pebble— / In thy bolder Sea—" (966). In an 1861 poem, written probably about the time she began to think of adopting white dresses as a symbol of dedicated seclusion, she imagines herself in bridal white and, in language that associates this poem closely with the preceding example, says it is a "timid thing—to drop a life— / Into the mystic [var. purple] well—" (271). Timidity often appears in the poems on any approach to eroticism. It is timid to drop a life, she drops a timid pebble, and the pebble that plays *safely* in the well is obviously a timid one. As a wren, she goes about in "timid" search for a nest (143). Her highest ambition is to "Dwell timidly" with the beloved; and the two lovers try "timidly" to expound the alphabet of love to each other (275, 568). As beggar lad, she approaches the "Lady" with a "timid cry for 'Bread' " (717). According to a variant preserved by Mabel Loomis Todd, the "mighty room" that witnessed some crucial turn in the love affair was at first called a "timid room" (1767).[17] Finally, the beloved woman whose "face was in a bed of hair" speaks to the poet with a "tongue more timid" than the tune in the leaves (1722).

A complex and puzzling history surrounds a poem beginning "What mystery pervades a well!" (1400). The surviving fragments in the poet's handwriting seem to be of the years 1871 and 1877, but the original six-stanza poem transcribed by Mrs. Todd may very well belong to the symbol-rich years 1859–65. In this longer version, the poet muses on the limitless depths to which the water descends and confesses that, to her, looking at the water's surface, its "lid [var., lip] of glass," is like looking into the face of an abyss. She wonders how the grass can "stand so close and look so bold" upon these awesome depths. Pondering the relationships of her symbols, she remembers that the sedge stands beside the floorless sea and does not betray any "timidity." Sea and well are manifestly the same thing (vagina and uterus), just as the sedge, the grass, and the "Mosses" (pubic hair) of an earlier deep-dug well are identical with each other and closely connected to the well-sea. The fifth stanza opens with the line, "But nature is a stranger yet" (an allusion to the awe of looking into the "abyss's face," that is, into "Great Nature's Face," as in poem 978). A partial draft of 1877, which begins at this line, replaces "nature" with "Susan"—"But Susan is a stranger yet"—and talks of the difficulty of scaling her "Haunted House." Although Emily often adapted her poems to quite different situations and people, it is nonetheless suggestive that she associated one well-abyss poem with Susan.

One last well poem deserves notice. It begins "Of Death I try to think like this— / The Well in which they lay us" (1558). And the erotic symbol becomes the death symbol it has all along threatened to become. This development is more complicated than can be easily explained. The Well of Death, she tries to persuade herself, may be like a "Brook" (and here surfaces her latent fear of "Jordan's stream and death's cold flood" from Isaac Watts's "The Heaveny Canaan") that menaces us only to add zest to the search for the "Flower Hesperian"; and she remembers straying in childhood beside a "Brook that seemed a Sea," then bravely leaping it to clutch the alluring "Purple Flower" beyond. Now purple is her death color (98, 117, 171, 234) and is appropriately associated with the West, the region of death, but it is also love's color: "Purple" is the "Color of a Queen" (776). A number of poems suggest that her love-death symbol was further complicated and intensified by the fact that the beloved actually lived westward from Massachusetts.

The most striking aspect of this symbolism is its radical ambivalence. Although the poet longs for a quite earthly Canaan, her symbol derives from the morbid context of Watts's hymn and seems always threatening to return to death. Wells and seas or houses, rooms, and tents represent erotic passion and the very person of the beloved, but with a change of mood they become graveyards and tombs. The color purple royalizes both love and death, and the love-hungry bee inevitably merges with the goblin-bee Death that "will not state—it's sting" (511). A startling example of this ambivalence occurs in an 1860 letter to the cherished new friend, Kate Turner. Recalling past friendships that ended painfully, the poet writes, "Why did you enter, sister, since you must depart? Had not its heart been torn enough but *you* must rend your shred? Oh! our Condor Kate! Come from your crags again!" (L222). And the beloved friend is metamorphosed into a death symbol, the devouring vulture. There is no mistake or accident here. In the deep unconscious of the excited poet the beloved is indeed a vulture that rends flesh, just such a one as appears in a horror poem written several months prior to their meeting:

Fierce from the Crag above us
The hungry Vulture screamed— [9]

And in the back of the poet's mind would be sounding these cruel lines from a part of the Bible she knew well, Job 39:28–30: "She dwelleth and abideth on the rock, upon the crag of the rock, and the strong place. From thence she seeketh the prey, and her eyes behold afar off.... And where the slain are, there is she."

It cannot have been easy to be the best friend of an Emily Dickinson. Not only is the friend seen as a deadly threat, the poet herself can be still more deadly. From the beginning she buries Sue with a persistence that should have earned that young woman higher marks for a generous forbearance than hostile biographers have been willing to allow her. Sue Dickinson had a great deal to endure. In an overwrought letter of April 1852, Emily shows some faint suspicion of this: "Do I repine, is it all murmuring, or am I sad and lone, and cannot, cannot, help it?" She is afraid her feelings are wrong and that God will punish her by taking Sue away: "and when *you* are gone, then I'm gone—and we're 'neath one willow tree" (L85). A week or two before the formal engagement of her brother and Sue, but after Austin had told her his plans, she wrote painfully that she had been .

looking toward "the golden West, and the great, silent Eternity, for ever folded there," which would soon "open it's everlasting arms" and gather her and Sue in (L103). For years she struggled blindly to keep an emotional grip on Sue, and to some extent she succeeded; such parasitism cannot have been good for the relationship between the young husband and wife. A few months after their marriage, Emily scissored from the local paper of 12 December 1856 an advertisement showing two tombstones and put it among her keepsakes. A year later she may have been too glumly morose to take any part in Sue and Austin's reception for Ralph Waldo Emerson, a man she admired. By late September 1858, however, she was sufficiently recovered to "bury" Sue once more in an almost jocose style: "I'll keep you in a casket—I'll bury you in the garden—and keep a bird to watch the spot—perhaps my pillow's safer—Try my bosom last— That's nearest of them all, and I should hear a foot the quickest, should I hear a foot—" (L194). The tone is now growing morbid, and indeed she goes on to mention tears. This idea of a joint burial, the dead Sue on the bosom of the dead Emily, is repeated in a poem of that period that addresses Sue by her nickname "Dollie." After describing her own sad, early death, the poet continues:

So when you are tired—
Or perplexed—or cold—
Trust the loving promise
Underneath the mould,
Cry "it's I," "take Dollie,"
And I will enfold! [51]

As late as 1865, such feelings as these appear to remain lively—if *lively* is quite the right word. In a poem beginning "Here, where the Daisies fit my Head" (the daisy being her personal symbol because of its countrified commonness and its associations with the graveyard), she says that to this grave she will be willing to confide her "Flower," presumably the magnificent, cultivated rose of many poems, and then they will not be "separate, Herself and Me," but will "constitute" a "single Bloom" (1037). This is probably the same friend whom she "buries" with morbid pleasure in the 1862 poem beginning "These—saw Visions—" (758).

The beloved friend may be thought of as dead or dying or simply mortal. A poem beginning "Promise This—When You Be Dying—" (648) urges that Emily be summoned on that important day and permitted to hear the beloved's "latest Sighing," to "Belt" the other's eyes ("Not with Coins" but with kisses), and afterward to hover protectively over the grave. It is a fairly morbid performance. An even more curious exercise, surviving in an 1862 four-stanza poem ("I see thee better—in the Dark") and in an undated variant of the last two stanzas (1666, "I see thee clearer for the Grave"), is set in the grave itself.

If these several poems, and the letters to Sue, may be thought to hover on the border of necrophilia, one last poem is clearly over the border. The two opening stanzas are frantic and appalling;

If I may have it, when it's dead,
I'll be contented—so—
If just as soon as Breath is out
It shall belong to me—

Until they lock it in the Grave
'Tis Bliss I cannot weigh—
For tho' they lock Thee in the Grave
Myself—can own the key—

These are outdone by the last stanza, which is the rationale for all these necrophilic poems:

Forgive me, if the Grave come slow—
For Coveting to look at Thee—
Forgive me, if to stroke thy frost
Outvisions Paradise! [577]

7

From first acquaintance to perhaps the end of her life, Emily Dickinson associated the loved friend with frogs. On the primitive level the frog is a ubiquitous female symbol, though it may not seem necessary to look to the unconscious for an association that letters and poems prove to be a deliberate one. In late spring 1860, Emily writes joyfully that summer is returning, "and 'Frogs' sincerer than our own splash in their Maker's pools—" (L222). Some months later, apparently in early January 1861, she writes: "It is too late for 'Frogs,' or which pleases me better, dear—not quite early enough! The pools were full of you for a brief period, but that brief period blew away, leaving me with many stems, and but a few foliage!" (L209). The "you" of which the pools were full appears to be the friend as water lily (in poem 923, mentioned in the previous chapter, the poet describes herself as a boy drowning in anguish while the pond spreads its indifferent "Lilies / Bold above the Boy," and letters of that period witness strong associations with lilies). Consciously she would not select so grotesque an image as the frog to represent the beautiful and beloved friend; but whenever the frog comes to mind, the friend appears to be in the near neighborhood.

In late fall 1861, she assembled in packet 8 a number of poems immediately inspired, or recalled, by the fact that the now-estranged friend was once more in the house next door. Among these is the only surviving copy

of her "frog" poem, "I'm Nobody! Who are you?" (288), which goes on
to say how very "dreary," how "public," how "like a Frog," to keep telling your name to an "admiring Bog!" Not a subtle poem or an important
one, it was exactly the kind of poetic joke that would delight her friend.
As for the apparent hint that Kate also was shy and retiring, the poet chose
to think so, and in a lively letter of February 1859 to Mrs. Holland, she
pictured the two friends fleeing from unexpected company and "clinging
fast like culprit mice," "so scared" were they (L202), and in a poem two
years later remembered that the friend might wear a "Bonnet like a
Duke—/ And yet a Wren's Peruke / Were not so shy / Of Goer by—"
(283). Even Kate seemed to fancy the picture at times, though she had
little of the hostility and fear that walled in the unhappy poet.

The frog poem has a plausible source in Charles Mackay's "Little Nobody," which appeared in the *Springfield Daily Republican* of 23 January
1858. Emily may have written her own wittier version not long afterward.
There is evidence that some of her poems existed in work-sheet drafts or
were sent off in fair copy several months or even years before they were
entered in packets, and this is a likely instance. What better explanation of
the twice-quoted "Frogs" than that Emily wanted to remind Kate of this
poem? It may well have been among those poems that made the new
friend impulsively call her "great."

Mrs. Turner paid her first visit to Amherst shortly after New Year's
Day 1859; but as Mrs. Bianchi slyly observed, her Aunt Emily had been
acquainted with the handsome young "clergyman" long before they met.[18]
In other words, Emily had been accustomed to hear Sue talk about her
Cooperstown friend and had read some of Kate's letters and knew that
she was as bookish as Sue and a still more avid reader of poetry. On a
cold, blustery January day, soon after Kate's arrival, Emily apparently
brought out the poems she had lately begun to assemble and showed them
to the new friend. They were upstairs in the southwest bedroom, the
"mighty room" of the poetry, and the poet would remember that she
was wearing a Merino shawl against the cold and standing at her west
window, presumably awaiting the verdict (768). Perhaps within the hour,
surely no later than the following morning, she wrote an impulsive letter
to sixteen-year-old Louise Norcross, to whom she was not in the habit of
writing but who would serve as outlet for her excitement: "It's a great
thing to be 'great,' Loo" (L199). And in the handwriting of early 1863,
when Kate was once more visiting Amherst, poem 738 begins "You said
that I 'was Great'—one Day—," then jokes somewhat grotesquely about
a difference in heights, as if the tall friend had teased her about her size;
and in fact Master letter 248 records just such a joke: "Wonder wastes my
pound, you said I had no size to spare—."

Without genius or any ambition for herself, young Mrs. Turner performed the admirable function of reflecting the genius of others. She was

an effective reader (the quality of her voice seems to be described in poem 283, "A Mien to move a Queen"), and she apparently displayed this talent quite early in her first visit to Amherst. She would seem to be that "fairy surprise" of a fine reader to whom the poet alluded, somewhat mysteriously, in her excited letter to young Louise Norcross. As to what she read, there is a slight bit of evidence that on this occasion or at a later visit she was invited to read that scene from *Henry V* in which the blunt and homely monarch declares to *his* Kate:

> By mine honor in true English, I love thee, Kate; by which honor I dare not swear thou lovest me; yet my blood begins to flatter me that thou dost, notwithstanding the poor and untempering effect of my visage.... My comfort is that old age, that ill layer-up of beauty, can do no more spoil upon my face. Thou hast me, if thou hast me, at the worst; and thou shalt wear me, if thou wear me, better and better; and therefore ... take me by the hand, and say, "Harry of England, I am thine!" which word thou shalt no sooner bless mine ear withal but I will tell thee aloud, "England is thine, Ireland is thine, France is thine, and Henry Plantagenet is thine." [5.2.229-47]

There seems to be no other explanation of the hitherto inexplicable fact that in Master letter 233 Emily declares, "the love of the Plantagenet is my only apology," or of her trick of putting French tags into some of her poems to Kate. Without command of any language except her own, she might have been impressed by the excellent French of her new friend. The 1861 poem, "Many a phrase has the English language," ends with the lines:

Say it again, Saxon! [var., English language]
Hush—Only to me! [276]

as if the other person had sometimes teased her by speaking the magic words in French.

Apparently this first visit of nearly two months ended about 2 March, when Kate left Amherst to visit friends in Boston. That night Emily wrote her a letter, headed "Amherst," in which such phrases as "Sweet at my door this March night" and "Will you still come?" are to be taken, not as anticipating, but rather as recalling some pledge of friendship. Kate herself is gone, after spending the night of 1 March with Emily in her room. In the words of this letter, "*Kate* [has been] gathered in March!" She is "a small bouquet," indeed a single "*Rose,*" which the poet has "worn upon the breast"; "So I rise, wearing her—so I sleep, holding,—Sleep at last with her fast in my hand and wake bearing my flower" (L203). The situation resembles that of an 1862 poem, "Her sweet Weight on my Heart a Night" (518), but of course there were to be other nights.

A letter to Mrs. Holland, written perhaps in the same hour as the one to Kate, testifies to the emotional intensity of this new relationship. The poet must "stand barefoot," as in the letter to Kate; and with a recollection of the young widow's invariable black, she invents a metaphor for Mrs. Holland who will "doff [her] weeds for a Bride's Attire" to welcome Dr. Holland's return. Emily has been "told that fasting gives to food marvelous Aroma, but by birth a Bachelor, disavow Cuisine." She feels an *"impatience"* for that heaven where alone she hopes never to be parted from the beloved, yet she wants to "touch" her friend and is fearful of "attentions from the Angels" of death. Her sister Lavinia being absent, "in Boston," she is "somewhat afraid at night"—indeed is deeply afraid and confesses, half jokingly, to a tension and an anxiety so great that she sees the furniture moving in the dim light of the room (L204).

Kate returned to Amherst in August 1859, and being always a tireless walker and particularly fond of strolling along country lanes with a woman friend on her arm, she must soon have enlisted the homebound Emily in excursions to the mill or to some local hill or stream, as the poems suggest.[19] According to a hint in Master letter 233, there was a favorite walk across the Dickinson meadows to the pond, which in August would be full of frogs and of native water lilies. Perhaps the frog poem originated at this time. The following spring Emily suggests that the season of "Frogs" and of their pleasant outings is coming around again (L222). But this letter, which is otherwise peculiarly happy, strikes one anxious note: "There is a subject dear—on which we never touch, Ignorance of its pageantries does not deter me—I, too, went out to meet the 'Dust' early in the morning, I, too in Daisy mounds possess hid treasure—therefore I guard you more—You did not tell me you had once been a 'Millionaire.'" The subject is death (covertly, Campbell Turner's death), and since Emily had no more obsessive topic, it must have been Kate who imposed the taboo. Now Emily had known about the dead husband long before she met Kate, and the knowledge strangely excited her. What she could not be sure of was her comparative standing. In effect, she was begging for assurance that her friend preferred her; and Kate maintained an awesome, a terrifying silence (maintained it until she read the *Poems* in 1891 and for the first time began to speak of the long-dead husband, distractedly, painfully, as if she did in fact connect these two early loves).[20] According to the poems, Emily looked forward with one part of her mind to an immortal union with her friend; and in master letter 233 she would write, "I used to think when I died—I could see you—so I died as fast as I could—." After the intimate relationship was broken off in the spring of 1861, she was driven to confess her jealous suffering, her inability to forget "that sorrow and frost [the dead Campbell] are nearer than I—." And a curious sentence toward the close of this summer 1861 letter shows her complaining once more that Kate would never lay that particular ghost in Emily's mind: "you did'nt come to me 'in white' nor ever told me why" (L233).

In late 1861 Sue Dickinson wrote to her sister-in-law: "If you have suffered this past Summer I am sorry, [but] ... If a nightingale sings with her breast against a thorn, why not *we*?" Now a man might be totally insensitive to the emotional currents behind the purdah curtain, but a woman could not fail to sense that atmosphere, and Sue Dickinson was the intimate friend of both women. She encouraged Emily to go on with her poetry and enlisted Bowles's help in what seemed meant as a pleasant surprise, getting "Safe in their Alabaster Chambers" (216) into the *Springfield Republican* of 1 March 1862. She may also have persuaded Bowles and Josiah Holland to make those editorial overtures that Emily, with justifiable anger, refused that winter (L261). The barbarous butchery the *Republican* of 4 May 1861 had inflicted on "I taste a liquor never brewed" (214) could have left her with little dependence on Bowles's good faith and no respect for his taste.[21]

After Kate's visit in late 1861, after the inclusion of the "frog" poem of happier days in the 1861 packet 8, there was a winter of silence, broken in late April 1862 by Kate's surprising "fire" letter. Emily's reply, as analysis has shown, concealed a bitter anger and hurt beneath an almost impenetrable cloud of allusion (L317). But in a letter to Mary Bowles, written almost certainly within the same hour, she gave way to her anguish about a Katie, forever lost, under cover of sympathizing with Mary, whose husband was away for the summer. When the "Best" has gone, she began, everything else seemed of no consequence, for the "Heart wants what it wants—or else it does not care—." Through the dim haze of suffering, she caught a momentary glimpse of Mary's surprise, perhaps distaste, for she went on to confess humbly that she could not help writing like this. The truth was she had exhausted her restraint in the tight-lipped letter to Katie and was reduced to sobbing: "Not to see what we love, is very terrible—and talking—does'nt ease it—and nothing does—but just itself." Thinking of the hair she had caressed, the face of her terrible concentration, she wrote that the "Eyes and Hair, we chose—are all there are—to us—." And finally, amid references to the warm spring day, the gardening, Sue's baby in his cart, came this revealing but possibly unconscious association: "The Frogs sing sweet—today—They have such pretty—lazy—times—how nice, to be a Frog!" (L262). The frog of her early poem does not "sing sweet" or have "pretty—lazy—times." It is bloated with self-importance, like the "Corporation" of Master letter 233 that was going to heaven and putting Emily out of love with the next world. But the frog that is peculiar to Kate has all along had its peculiar attractiveness. In desiring "to be a Frog," the poet desires to be enclosed, safe, irresponsible, "lazy," lapped warmly in the womb.

Did the two women write again after their exchange of April 1862? There is no record that they did, but of course Kate received many more letters than she kept, and of course Emily always knew what her lost friend was doing. There was never any breach of friendship between Kate and Sue, and the latter kept Emily informed. In the early spring of 1863 the lost friend was once more in Amherst. She had recently become engaged to John Anthon, a pleasant young man from a well-known New York family, slightly younger than herself; but—as Emily would learn in due course—she seemed curiously reluctant to conclude the marriage and in the fall of 1864 persuaded her father that her state of mind necessitated a fairly long and expensive trip abroad.[22] With her friends, the Edward Clarks and their son, Alfred Corning Clark, she traveled in Europe for six months and was not at all anxious to return. There is no evidence that she wrote to Emily from Europe, yet a poem of this period describes a "Rigor" in the poet's life, relieved only by the knowledge that another person bore its "Duplicate / In other Continent" (1022).[23]

Although Kate returned to New York in May 1865, her marriage was to be delayed another year. By early 1866, however, she had apparently fixed on a wedding day, for Sue saw a need to give Emily fresh distraction. She smuggled another poem to Bowles, "A narrow Fellow in the Grass" (986), which appeared in the *Republican* of 14 February 1866. Far from being appreciative, Emily wrote angrily: "it was robbed of me" (L316). At about the same time, she gave her sister-in-law a poem written originally in the painful winter of 1861–62, "Title divine—is mine" (1072). The chastened Sue could hardly fail to recognize this poem as Emily's comment on the approaching marriage: "it was robbed of me." In the same period, a poem went off to Kate's intimate friend Gertrude Vanderbilt, with whom Emily had had a slight and probably jealous acquaintance in late 1861. Apparently she wrote the poem in 1864 to commemorate Mrs. Vanderbilt's recovery from a dangerous gunshot wound, but since it can be read as an elegy on the death of love, it may have seemed even more appropriate in 1866:

Than [death's] old Arrow is a Shot
Delivered straighter to the Heart
The leaving Love behind [831]

8

A curious parallel may be observed between the years 1856 and 1866. On 1 July 1856 Susan Gilbert married Austin Dickinson in Geneva, New York, an event of painful significance to the young woman who was both jealous friend and devoted sister. The poetry Emily had begun writing under Sue's influence now ceased, if it had not already come to an end after the Judas-like betrayal Sue's engagement represented to her. The few letters of early 1856 betray signs of fatigue and discouragement, and no letters survive that can be placed with any certainty between the wedding and sometime in 1858—perhaps because none were written.

In the last months of 1858, Emily began to write poems again and an increasing number of letters, and from early 1859 through 1864 she wrote poetry at a prodigal rate. Even in the year 1865, when she was in Boston for many months and forbidden to use her eyes, she produced almost as many lines as survive in 1860 handwriting. Then came an abrupt decline. Only 307 lines can be provisionally assigned to 1866, and of these some 240 occur in record copies of packet 35, carefully finished for the most part and likely to be months or years later than their first working out. A mere 64 lines survive in 1867 handwriting, and though there would be slight increases later on, she would never again exceed 300 lines in any year except 1872, (339), 1873 (468), 1874 (361), and 1877 (333). These figures contrast markedly with the totals of her major period: 1859 (1,151), 1860 (825), 1861 (1,283), 1862 (5,534), 1863 (1,704), 1864 (1,688), and 1865 (752).

Still more surprising is the abrupt decline in imagery. Again and again certain clusters of images—colors, gems, place-names, bodily imagery, and the like—march up to the year 1866 and then vanish as into a profound gulf—to reemerge, if at all, a subdued and diminished and scattered band. Here too the abundant evidence that she often reworked the poetry of her major period suggests that poems in late handwriting but in the old mode may actually have originated on the other side of the gulf.

Her correspondence suffered an equally striking decline. During the first seven or eight months of 1866 there are five letters and one brief note. After August there can be no certainty that she wrote another letter until sometime in 1868. A letter to Mrs. Holland is provisionally dated late November 1866, and an excerpt from a letter to Louise Norcross is still more uncertainly dated "1866?" In 1867 a mere two-line note survives, and 1868 is only a little less barren. Once again her life dims beneath a cloud of fatigue and discouragement. Three of the packet 35 poems, in 1866 handwriting, sound the valedictory note with special plangency: "We learn in the Retreating," "Ended, ere it begun," and "Of the Heart that goes in, and closes the Door" (1083, 1088, 1098). A poem written a few months later says the owner of a "Diamond" may grow indifferent to his "Gem," but if the diamond is for sale, a lover too poor to buy may "sight and sigh" and go almost "mad" with "fear" because another person is buying (1108). Surely it is no coincidence that on 30 August 1866, after long delay, Catherine Scott Turner married John Hone Anthon in Cooperstown, New York.

In the poet's later period, the most productive years were 1872–74. To be sure, a slow but identifiable rise had set in after the nadir of 1867, but the marked increase in late 1872 and the two following years may reflect an excited, even painful awareness of a tragic reversal in the life of her friend. "Somewhere upon the general Earth," says poem 1231, is the "Magic" that once "consecrated" the poet, but the magician has become vaguely remote, unlocated; and in late 1872 Emily did not in fact know where her friend was, only that she was somewhere in Europe going from one famous doctor to another in the vain hope of saving her husband's life. Kate had left New York on 16 October 1872 in too much haste and distress to think of anyone outside her family, but her mother had written to Sue, who of course informed Emily; and the stages of their friend's tragedy, as Sue reported them over the next two years, appeared to keep the poet in an uneasy stir, reviving old feelings and making them available once more to the poetry.

A letter to Louise Norcross, mentioned earlier, witnesses to her uneasiness in late 1872. After an excerpt made by the Norcross cousins, Emily speaks of the bread of affection for which she has starved, describes "Longing" as the "gift no other gift supplies," and ends by warning that "No bird resumes its egg" (L379). Very likely she was now reviewing old poetry, for poem 728, written some ten years earlier, speaks of the "Egg-life" and then asks poignantly, "Can the Lark resume the Shell—." A poem in a late 1872 packet, "Longing is like the Seed" (1255), may have suggested, instead of being suggested by, the related line in the letter to Louise and may have been composed years earlier. Another poem in this late 1872 packet is demonstrably a redaction of an 1862 poem, "I Years had been from Home" (609). One can but speculate on the number of times she revised old work and then destroyed the earlier drafts. A third packet 36 poem, "To disappear enhances" (1209), may well have originated in the early period of loss it recalls. Still other poems of late 1872—for example, "The Sea said 'Come' to the Brook" and "Now I knew I lost her" (1210, 1219)—are early in theme and perhaps also in their original composition. Several poems in the 1873 handwriting give a similar impression of being revisions of earlier work, particularly "Because that you are going," "While I was fearing it—it came," and "The most pathetic thing I do / Is play I hear from you," in which she tenderly salutes as "Goliah" the tall friend who had teased her about her height (1260, 1277, 1290).

This poetic revival was apparently cut short by the sudden death of Edward Dickinson on 16 June 1874. All 1874 poems that can be dated by inclusion in letters do in fact precede her father's death. Indeed, it is hard to believe she would have assuaged her grief for him by composing such a poem as "Frigid and sweet Her parting Face" (1318), which recalls the long-ago day when the beloved woman rejected the life of "Penury" which a "Home" together would have entailed for two penniless women (with no cousinly duke of Wellington to place them on the civil pension list, like the famed Llangollen ladies in whom Kate would take so absorbed an interest).[24] Still other poems dealing with the lost beloved were probably written prior to mid-June, if they were not in fact revisions of still older work: "Delight's Despair at setting," "I cannot want it more," "Not with a Club, the Heart is broken," and "Elizabeth told Essex" (1299, 1301, 1304, 1321). Another love poem. "Go slow, my soul, to feed thyself / Upon his rare approach" (1297), went to her cousins with a specific reference to the date: "Infinite March is here, and I 'hered' a bluebird." The poem itself is without any March association in word or image, and the final lines, with their telltale "Redemption," clearly identify the subject: "Go boldly—for thou paid'st his price / Redemption—for a Kiss—." No doubt the date reminded the poet, ever sensitive to anniversaries, that March was the beloved's birth month and the bluebird her totem.

Few poems, it may be assumed, were written in the latter half of 1874, and the 1875 total ebbed to a scant 181 lines. But the year 1876 shows a significant rise, and the following year brings her poetic activity to its last crest, much of it centering on Kate's long-delayed return to Amherst in June 1877. Emily at first hesitated to see her friend. After her death, says poem 1410, she would not "murmur" if those she loved "below" should learn why she had "shunned" them. To divulge her secret would rest her own heart, but it would "ravage" theirs. "Why, Katie," the poem concludes, "Treason" could speak, but her own voice would be lost in tears. The poem was never sent; she did see her friend and was profoundly moved by this fresh and, as it proved, final interview. The now-widowed Kate Anthon, a sad and lonely woman, may have come looking for a renewal of their old companionship, but the meeting would have convinced her, without ever broaching the possibility, that her old friend was now too hopelessly crippled to leave her prison. For her part, Emily had the satisfaction of seeing her friend weep (1426). But the most interesting effect of this interview was a renewal of her intense fear of the grave. It can be seen in a letter to Higginson, written in June while Kate was apparently still next door, begging him as a former clergyman to reassure her about a life after death. When Bowles visited Amherst a day or two after Kate left, Emily granted him the unusual privilege of an interview and begged him also for reassurance about immortality. What she sought was evidence in the smiles, words, or gestures of a dying person that he had caught a glimpse of the next world (the following January she would be particularly distressed to learn that Bowles himself had died reluctant and despairing, with no hopeful gleams from the beyond). Bowles answered her urgent inquiry by letter, a portion of which has lain unrecognized in George Merriam's biography of him:

> It was very sweet to see you at last. I hope I may oftener come face to face with you. I have little spare strength or time for writing and so testifying to my remembrances, and you are very good to like me so much and to say such sweet and encouraging things to me....
>
> I spoke to you of "Warrington's " revelations of immortality at the close. They were greatly impressive to me. Here is the record. You may like to read it, even from an enemy.[25] (The enclosures described how the dying man's uncertainty changed, "as the end drew near, into the serenest assurance, and his mental vision was filled with the fa-

miliar figures and faces of those who, having gone before, seemed to revisit and welcome him.")

On 10 December 1877 (the poet's own birthday) came the death of an old friend, Elizabeth Lord, wife of Mr. Dickinson's friend Judge Otis Phillips Lord. The poet and her sister enjoyed a pleasant relationship with the Lords, and Lavinia, at least, was on visiting terms with them. After Mrs. Lord's death, Emily doubtless wrote her usual feeling letters, with their usual covert inquiries into possible deathbed evidence of immortality. Some months later the sixty-six-year-old widower decided that the poet could supply the warmth and domestic convenience so sadly missed after the death of his wife. Emily herself was now forty-seven and not likely to do better; and the surviving drafts of her letters show that his attentions did flatter and goad her into a last desperate effort to prove her womanhood. She only proved that the "Eagle's Golden Breakfast" still strangled her.

In *The Other Victorians,* Steven Marcus has assembled convincing evidence that the average Victorian male (who still exists and writes biographies of Emily Dickinson) not only tolerated but frequently demanded virtual frigidity in his womenfolk. His coadjutor was the average Victorian female. Elizabeth Gaskell, whose life of Charlotte Brontë both Emily and her sister-in-law much admired, quoted with emphatic approval from a letter demonstrating Charlotte's hysterical frigidity toward a man who had proposed to her: "Friendship—gratitude—esteem—I have; but each moment he came near me, and that I could see his eyes fastened on me, my veins ran ice. Now that he is away, I feel far more gently toward him; it is only close by that I grow rigid, stiffening with a strange mixture of apprehension and anger, which nothing softens but his retreat, and a perfect subduing of his manner." [26] If such behavior was demanded of "nice" women, including apparently that nice married woman Elizabeth Gaskell, one can only speculate on the excessive, the hysterical shrinking Emily Dickinson must have betrayed to cause the judge such pained perplexity at their infrequent meetings. To add to his bewilderment, she reproduced in her letters the narcissistic passion of a Brontë novel. He must have decided, like the naive Austin courting Susan Gilbert, that her "true feelings" came out only in her correspondence.[27]

An 1878 draft, written near the beginning of their courtship, employs metaphors that are quite interesting and sexually charged. Apparently he had been pleading for an early marriage, and she now assured him that the "Stile" was God's and must not be crossed until it seemed right to her, when she herself would "lift the Bars, and lay you in the Moss—" (L562). "You showed me the word," she added, but here she was misleading or forgetful; years earlier she had written of female "Moss" in association with a well she wanted to enter or from which she drew back in terror. She now regretted that she must send him away "hungry"; unhappily, he wanted the "divine Crust and that would doom the Bread." Next, she essayed two lines of a poem (identifiable with a transcript made by Mrs. Todd), and a curious and betraying effort it is. She begins, "Oh, honey of an hour," as if she were once more the bee eager to rifle the flower's chamber, then in midpoem confusedly reorients herself and ends as an "unfrequented flower" (1734). Late at night she hears a whistling boy who reminds her of the judge, and it is apparently the same boy who went to her friend Kate in poem 83, with a title intended for that friend alone, "Whistling under My Window." In short, a number of the old images and symbols reappear in these letters to Lord, but she can no longer handle them as richly or freshly as in her major period.

There is an interesting prose fragment, undatable but in handwriting of these years, which must have been intended as a paragraph in some letter to Lord:

> Don't you think you could understand if you perhaps tried
> The Rafters of the Apocalypse must not be too bare
> Of the sweet Adjacency that Exalts by humbling I never knew
> When Questions are not needed for answers [PF31]

The opening line, like sentences in her identified letters to Lord, seems to be another plea for understanding of her lack of physical response. The "Apocalypse" of the next line is the glorious marriage of the future—the remote future, it would seem, for the preparations must not be scamped. The "Rafters" are from the Song of Solomon 1:17 ("The beams of our house are cedar, and our rafters of fir"), and these several allusions appear to mean that the house of love must be slowly and carefully built. The third line, translated with bare literalness, says she has never had sexual relations, but in allusiveness it is heavily and even viciously charged. "Adjacent" (to use the form that appears in her poetry) is of the rarest occurrence in poetic vocabularies. Shakespeare, however, uses it twice, both times in erotic context and in plays Emily especially admired, *Romeo and Juliet* and *Antony and Cleopatra*. The verse that most probably lingered in her unconsciousness was Mercutio's taunting allusion to Rosaline's "quivering thigh, And the demesnes that there adjacent lie." This "sweet Adjacency" (sexual intercourse) "Exalts by humbling." But why "humbling"? And are they both to be humbled, or is it more particularly the woman who will be humbled? Whatever Judge Lord's assumptions, it could not have escaped the poet's notice that men in general believed they humbled woman. As a child of the Puritans, she read the Bible and, like other Puritan children, acquired in horrified secrecy much raw knowledge that would normally be forbidden her. She knew that the Old Testament repeatedly used the expression "to defile" or "to humble" a woman as meaning to have sexual intercourse with her, whether enforced or free. By the choice of a word the poet may have told more than she intended, betraying a deep, unconscious anger as furious as the archetypal Lilith's in the tales of Hebrew scholars.[28]

Mixed with her dread of his sex, there was also an understandable curiosity, illustrated in a letter of about 1880. She had been wondering, she said, what their sexual relations would be like. She often dreamed of him at night and just lately had had a dream in which he was dead and she had been asked to unveil a statue of him but had refused to do to the dead man what she had never done to him in life. In actuality, Lord had visited her the day before, and she remembered that their hour together had been beautiful, but obviously it had had its awkward moments—even periods of constrained silence. "Diviner Edens," she now proposed calling them. "Therefore Love is so speechless—," she explained, but added immediately, "Seems to withold Darling"—and the uncomfortable truth was out. She denied the "seemed," often feared she had been only too frank, but— "How could I long to give who never saw your natures face—" (L645).

This tragicomedy of "The Statue and the Bust" continued for six years, that is, until his death, by which she was grieved, to be sure, and not a little relieved. Such poetry as she wrote during these six years—and there is not much of it—is either trivial or curiously still and cold, as if her courtship had forced her into a confrontation with the terrible, riddling depths of herself. After his health failed, she wrote a poem beginning, "Still own thee—still thou art / What surgeons call alive— / But slipping— slipping I perceive /To thy reportless Grave." And in a stasis of icy detachment she asked herself what questions she should put to him, what answer wrest from him, before he should "exude away / In the recallless sea" (1633).

In August 1880, not long after her uncomfortable hour with Lord, she put another question—or perhaps hesitated on the verge of putting it—to an older and more trusted friend than her elderly suitor. Her question dealt, or would have dealt, with that fantasy which had devoured her life. The first reference to this dread secret occurs in a packet 8 poem, "Rearrange a 'Wife's' affection!" (1737), written presumably in the fall of 1861. Her "Secret" is "Big," but it is *"bandaged"* and will never get away from its "Weary Keeper" until she leads it through the grave to the beloved. In a poem of the next year, "A Secret told" (381), she is afraid it will escape her, after all, and reminds herself how much better it is to be afraid of the secret than to fear it and the person she told it to. Another poem of that year, "Only God—detect the Sorrow [var., Possess the Secret]," affirms that the "Jehovahs—are no Babblers" (626). "Nature and God," according to an 1864 poem, know her so intimately as to startle her, but she trusts them to keep her "Secret" as inviolate as "Mercury's affair" (835). A copy to Bowles may have been intended as a subtle plea not to guess at what she had so nearly betrayed in the winter of 1861–62. Since so much was known to Sue, and through her to Bowles, with whom Sue was on confidential terms, it may be wondered what secret Emily thought she still had. Years later, tongue edged with malice, Sue Dickinson told her daughter that the friends' "partings overheard were like those of desperate final sundered souls." [29]

Possibly the secret was the terrifying discovery of the sexual basis to this attachment, with some extravagant promise to renounce happiness in this life for the hope of fulfillment in the next. The poems repeatedly say so, and Emily's behavior supports such an interpretation. After her friend's engagement in the spring of 1863, of course, there remained little reason for hoping, and she dealt with the situation partly by a realistic acceptance and partly by distancing and transforming it into literature. Still, it continued to hurt her and to shut her away from a hostile world. In 1864 and 1865 she made pseudo-escapes to Boston to have her eyes treated, although there was little a doctor could do for an eye disease so manifestly psychosomatic. Her father and her sister thought she was malingering, and she did have a desperate need to get away from her family and into the congenial society of the young Norcross cousins, her only trusted confidantes. These two ventures were succeeded by years of self-imprisonment in her father's house.

In 1878, when the newly widowed Judge Lord offered her his hand, she tried to take it but could not. He pressed her and she suffered under the pressure. They settled down to a weekly exchange of letters, and he visited her once or twice a year; and with each visit, with each letter, the pressure mounted. A curious bit of evidence in a manuscript of about 1878 hints at a covert resistance on her part. The poem, "I thought the Train would never come" (1449), addresses the expected visitor as her "Provoking Lover" and appears to be a sentimental trifle designed for enclosure in a letter to Lord. Below the poem, however, she has practiced writing her signature—"E Dick E Emily D D Dickinson E Dickinson"—surely the betrayal of a stubborn reluctance to surrender her identity. The night following his visit of early August 1880 she dreamed wishfully of his death.

Perhaps a day or two after this visit, she received another caller. Years later she would remember that she was in her little conservatory and that her sister, hearing the visitor inquire of the maid, remarked in surprise that the "Gentleman with the deep voice" wanted to see Emily. Going alone into the family parlor, the poet saw rise before her, "like an Apparition," the man whom she called her "closest earthly friend" (L765)— not Judge Lord but the Reverend Charles Wadsworth. She had seen him once before, about March 1860, and apparently on no other occasion. There is evidence, however, that she had read something of his that interested her—no doubt a strong affirmation of faith in immortal life—and had initiated a correspondence with him about 1858, just as she had done or would do with other strangers. Shy in person, she was bold enough on paper. In 1860 Wadsworth happened to be visiting an old friend in North-ampton and found it easy to work in a brief call on his unknown cor-respondent in neighboring Amherst. Possibly she wrote to him two or three times a year, as she did to Higginson, and then more often and with greater urgency for some years after her father died. The nature of her dependence shows that he was of crucial importance to her in weathering the crisis of Edward Dickinson's death. In the Wadsworth family there would linger a plausible tradition that her letters were an anxiety-ridden appeal for reassurance about immortality.

Although a successful clergyman, Wadsworth was a much less attractive human being than her friends Bowles and Higginson, being a racist and a bigot, a writer of dull sermons, a harsh father who had alienated his daughter and his older son. Still, there must have been much sweetness in his manner with Emily to give him such influence over her. Then, too, only a bigot would have carried the conviction, speaking as if from Mount Sinai, to assuage her terror of the grave for even a few minutes. It is at least curious that after his death she sought out another racist and bigot, Washington Gladden, to receive her pitiful inquiry: "Is immortality true?" (L752a).

"Why did you not tell me you were coming, so I could have it to hope for?" she now asks Wadsworth.

"Because I did not know it myself," he said quietly. "I stepped from my Pulpit to the Train" (L766).

She asked how long it had taken him, and he answered jokingly, "Twenty years" (L1040). At some point in the conversation he remarked that he was "liable at any time to die," and in fact he died less than two years later. But for some reason Emily paid little attention to so gloomy a forecast—"thought it no omen" (L766)—perhaps because she was nerving herself to open her own problem to him. Should there be an immortal life, would she be found worthy to share in it? She was "spotted" (964). Could she be sure that God would pardon her?

Within the last few months, she had written another poem about her dread mystery, " 'Secrets' is a daily word" (1385). This word, she says, may be "Muffled" or "Mortised" (just as the secret of her 1861 poem is said to be "*bandaged*"), and then it "resists surmise"; "Murmured," it ap-parently ceases to be. But though she seems tempted to murmur the secret and rid herself of some indescribable burden, the remaining lines carry it stoically to the end. "Dungeoned in the Human Breast," these secrets are guarded by a "Grate inviolate." They are not simply dungeoned but "stapled" there and will emerge once only, "dumb" or "armed," to the "Sepulchre." Having roughed out her poem, she then turned the sheet over and wrote on the back: "Let me go for the Day breaketh." Perhaps she has reversed the roles of her early poem and is now pleading with the dark Jacob of her obsession to set her free.

How much of this she hinted to Wadsworth cannot be guessed. But something she must have said—some question about the fate of those who carry secrets into the sepulcher—for he "seemed almost overpowered by a spasm of gloom." Startled, she said, "You are troubled." He answered, shivering, "My life is full of dark secrets—," and perhaps it eased her fear to know that the man whom she counted on to assist her "in another World" (L776) had his own dark secrets.

They talked more easily now of his son Willie, the only member of his family she ever heard him mention. This boy of eleven was the Benjamin of Wadsworth's old age and clearly his greatest pride. With a smile, the father declared that if Willie should "find a gold watch in the street he would not pick it up, so unsullied was he" (L1039). Writing afterward to Wadsworth's friend, she would repeatedly mention this boy Willie, "whom, forgive me the arrogance, he told me was like me—" (L776). In some curious way, it gratified her to be identified with Willie, to become Wadsworth's "Boy" too.

On this warm August evening, she was moved to speak of frogs. Consciously she may not have remembered the long-ago walks in an August twilight with the friend whom she would always associate with frogs. Unconsciously the association was there. In August 1880, the house next door had as its guest young Harry Bartlett, Kate's beloved nephew, whose birth in the spring of 1860 had been the "prettiest of pleas" delaying her return to Amherst.[30] Lavinia Dickinson, who kept up with events next door, reported to her sister that Kate's nephew was visiting Sue and nineteen-year-old Ned. The old tenderness flaming up, Emily wrote once more of the woman whom she also linked with snowy peaks:

> Of whom so dear
> The name to hear
> Illumines with a Glow
> As intimate—as fugitive
> As Sunset on the snow— [1504]

Then, troubled by this rush of tenderness at a time when she had been trying earnestly to love Lord, she turned the sheet and wrote on the back:

> I do not care—why should I care and yet I fear I'm caring
> To rock a fretting [crying, wailing] Truth to sleep—
> Is short [no, frail, poor] security
> The terror it will wake persistent as perdition
> Is harder than to face the frank adversity—
> There is an awful yes in every constitution [PF79]

In the pleasant August twilight she called Wadsworth's attention to the frogs croaking in the distant pond. They were her "Dogs," she said. Once more the father thought of his Willie and said, "the Frogs were his little friends." Then, with a last smile, he rose to go. She too was smiling, briefly secure in the faith that she was Wadsworth's boy Willie who had frogs for his friends. Above the August dusk the snow-crowned peak of the mind's eye caught the last radiance of a dying sun.

THREE ✤ THE JEWEL IMAGERY

In early 1862, perhaps shortly before she asked Higginson for a serious evaluation of her work, the poet gave her sister-in-law a letter-poem headed "Dear Sue, Your—Riches—taught me—poverty!" (L258). This extravagant contrast between Sue Dickinson's opulent personality and the poet's "poverty" includes some interesting lines:

Of "Mines"—I little know—myself—
But just the *names*—of *Gems*—
The *Colors*—of the *Commonest*—

They call fresh attention to what appears to be her most important poetic stratagem—the deliberate, wholly conscious search for usable clusters of imagery to incorporate into her work. A brief survey of her jewel imagery suggests that it forms such a cluster and that further examination will throw light on her poetic technique as well as contribute to an understanding of the individual poems.

Much detail can be gathered from tables 1 and 2. Comparison with other poets, for example, shows that she had considerable precedent for using jewel imagery and that the practice was especially strong in the work of such fellow Victorians as Tennyson and Robert Browning, nor did it die out in the work of modern poets like W. B. Yeats and Wallace Stevens. Except for Keats, whose approximately fifteen thousand lines are roughly commensurate with her approximately twenty thousand shorter lines, she outgoes all her models; and Keats does not have her variety. It is strikingly evident that her poetry contains as many instances of jewel words as the Bible or the entire lyric and dramatic works of Shakespeare, and that she uses jewels more frequently than Milton or the neoclassic poets. If the percentages of jewel words in the total wordage of the individual poets were to be compared, she would appear even more begemmed than such lapidaries as Browning and Tennyson. Merely as ornament, jewel words would seem to be a significant element in her poetic vocabulary.

The variety of jewel names is also significant. Her gems and precious organic substances, amber, coral, and pearl, form a close parallel with the biblical list, and certain key words suggest a special indebtedness to the twenty-first chapter of Revelation. In her poetry and her correspondence, she uses nine of the twelve foundation jewels of the heavenly city—jasper, sapphire, emerald, chrysolite, beryl, topaz, chrysoprase, jacinth, and amethyst—finding unmanageable only the chalcedony, the sardonyx, and the sard. She does use the onyx and may have known that some authorities identify the sardonyx of Revelation with the onyx of the high priest's breastplate in Exodus 28:20 and 39:13. The only nonbiblical jewels she employs are the opal, the garnet, and the rather doubtful hyacinth, and her 1847 Webster's dictionary identified the garnet with "the carbuncle of the ancients," hence with a biblical jewel, and the hyacinth with the biblical jacinth. Table 1 indicates that this poetic employment of biblical jewels first became popular in the Victorian age.

"In none of the allusions to precious stones made by Shakespeare," says George F. Kunz in a study of Shakespeare's jewel usage, "is there any indication that he had in mind any of the biblical passages treating of gems." [1] This is true even of a striking passage in *Othello* ("If heaven would make me such another world / Of one entire and perfect chrysolite"), for the chrysolite was well known and extravagantly valued in Shakespeare's day.[2] A biblical influence upon Milton can be shown, particularly in a description of the Almighty's chariot, which draws hints from the first chapter of Ezekiel and the fourth of Revelation, but he omits a number of the sacred jewels and does not point conspicuously toward any of the richly jeweled passages of the Bible.[3] The neoclassic and romantic poets neglected the sacred jewels, as did Emerson and, in his earlier work, even so typical a Victorian as Tennyson. The latter's one definite employment of the heavenly jewels, in his rather wooden "Columbus," came too late to have any influence on Emily Dickinson. Table 1 shows that Robert Browning used nearly all the foundation jewels, but it is not certain that Emily had an early acquaintance with any of his works except, very probably, *Men and Women,* where the instances are few and scattered.

A study of Table 2 and of the particular letters and poems on which it is based shows that Emily Dickinson's jewel imagery prior to 1858 was scanty and conventional—"teeth like pearls" (L15); "pearls" gathered by plighted maidens (L93); "baskets of pearls" (L77); "baskets made of pearl" (L175); a look worthy of a "pearl" (L180); "Little *Emerald Mack*," the Irish washwoman (L85); and so on. Perhaps to thank a friend for a gift book, she produced an apparent acrostic on the name of Poe—"the pearl, and then the onyx, and then the emerald stone" (L171).[4] No new gems appeared in her letters, and none at all in her few poems, until late 1858.

Table 1. Jewel Incidence in the Work of Selected Poets

	Dickinson	Bible	Shakespeare	Milton	Dryden	Pope	Wordsworth	Byron	Keats	Emerson	Tennyson	R. Browning	E. Browning	Yeats	Stevens
Agate	1	4	5	1	1	0	1	1	0	1	2	3	1	1	2
Amber	23	3	6	7	6	6	2	6	10	4	6	6	6	3	2
Amethyst	6	3	0	0	0	0	0	0	4	0	1	2	4	2	1
Beryl	5	8	0	2	0	0	0	0	0	1	1	2	0	1	0
Carbuncle	0	4	5	2	1	0	0	0	0	1	0	0	0	0	0
Chalcedony	0	1	0	0	0	0	0	0	0	0	1	0	1	0	0
Chrysolite	2	1	1	1	0	0	0	0	0	0	1	1	0	2	0
Chrysoprase	2	1	0	0	0	0	0	0	0	0	1	1	2	2	0
Coral	2	2	7	2	4	1	2	7	8	1	0	7	2	1	6
Crystal	3	5	20	17	24	9	37	13	36	4	4	31	24	1	22
Diamond	14	4	22	7	8	10	6	6	20	9	55	31	6	0	17
Emerald	12	6	2	1	3	1	7	7	5	0	12	4	1	1	11
Garnet	3	0	0	0	0	0	0	0	0	0	2	1	0	0	0
Jacinth	[1]	2	0	0	0	0	0	0	0	0	1	1	0	0	0
Jasper	2	7	0	3	0	0	0	2	2	0	2	3	6	0	1
Jet	0	0	4	1	3	1	1	6	6	1	2	6	0	1	1
Lapis lazuli	0	0	0	0	0	0	0	0	0	0	0	4	0	3	4
Onyx	1	11	0	0	0	0	0	0	0	0	0	0	0	1	0
Opal	5	0	2	1	0	0	0	0	1	2	1	4	4	1	4
Pearl	31	10	41	11	18	3	16	17	40	10	34	71	8	25	8
Ruby	8	6	10	4	6	2	3	1	6	4	13	17	2	6	7
Sapphire	4	12	3	7	3	0	3	3	7	0	5	9	2	0	4
Sard	0	4	0	0	0	0	0	0	0	0	1	1	0	0	0
Sardonyx	0	1	0	0	0	0	0	0	0	0	2	0	0	1	0
Topaz	3	5	0	1	0	0	0	0	0	0	2	5	2	0	2
Turquoise	0	0	1	0	0	0	0	0	0	0	2	3	0	0	10
Others*	1	4	0	0	0	0	0	1	0	0	0	0	0	1	1
Totals	128	104	129	68	77	33	78	70	145	38	151	213	71	53	103

* Dickinson, 1 hyacinth; Bible, 2 bdellium, 2 ligure; Byron, 1 cornelian; Yeats, 1 chrysoberyl; Stevens, 1 cornelian.

Note: Number in brackets refers to gem name in a letter.

Table 2. Emily Dickinson's Gems

	Before 1858	1858	1859	1860	1861	1862	1863	1864	1865	1867–85	Totals
Agate										1	1
Amber			1		2	11	6			3	23
Amethyst			2	1	1					2	6
Beryl				1		1	2			1	5
Chrysolite		1						1			2
Chrysoprase								1		1	2
Coral						2				[1]	2[1]
Crystal						2	1				3
Diamond			1		2	7	3			2[1]	14[1]
Emerald	[2]		1		1	4	1			4[3]	12[5]
Garnet					1	2				1	3
Hyacinth								1			1
Jacinth									[1]		[1]
Jasper			[2]	1					1		2[2]
Onyx	[1]	1							[1]		1[2]
Opal				1	1	2				1	5
Pearl	[8]	1	2	2	1[2]	16		1[1]	1	[4]	31[15]
Ruby				1	1	6	7			[2]	8[2]
Sapphire				1	1	1	1			[1]	4[1]
Topaz			[1]		1	1[2]	1			[3]	3[3]
	[11]	3	6[3]	8	13[2]	55[2]	22	4[1]	1[2]	16[12]	128[33]

Note: Numbers in brackets refer to gem names in letters (exclusive of poems enclosed).

Since her letters tend to echo her poetic concerns and are treated here as an extension of her poetry, it may be assumed that she had not yet discovered the possibilities of a jewel imagery or the particular attractions of the jewel chapter of Revelation.[5]

In the latter half of 1858, when she apparently transcribed such earlier poetry as she thought worth keeping and began to write new poems, she showed a marked interest in Revelation. To her absent sister-in-law, on 26 September, she wrote of the "seal" being opened and of the angels that "fall on their faces," and to her friend Elizabeth Holland, about 6 November, she spoke of the "bright chirographies of the 'Lamb's Book'" (letters 194, 196).[6] Perhaps in late September, she wrote her poem 24 about stars swinging "their cups of Chrysolite"—inspired, it may be, by a poem in the October *Atlantic* called "The Cup," which describes a symbolic goblet with "Edges of Chrysolite." In October appeared Longfellow's *Courtship of Miles Standish,* and since she was an admirer of Longfellow, she may shortly have been reading these lines:

Slowly as out of the heavens, with apocalyptical splendors,
Sank the City of God, in the vision of John the Apostle,
So, with its cloudy walls of chrysolite, jasper, and sapphire,
Sank the broad red sun, and over its turrets uplifted
Glimmered the golden reed of the angel who measured the city.[7]

But Longfellow had already read, admired, and caught his idea from—and so, probably, had Emily Dickinson—popular Elizabeth Browning's amazingly popular *Aurora Leigh,* which uses imagery from Revelation at a number of strategic points and closes with these lines:

"Jasper first," I said,
"And second, sapphire; third, chalcedony;
The rest in order, ... last, an amethyst."

One need not believe with John Ruskin (in a work Emily Dickinson read at this time) that *Aurora Leigh* was "the greatest poem which the century has produced in any language," or with Hippolyte Taine that it was an epic worthy of comparison with the work of Homer, but the existence of such opinions helps explain the multiplication of heavenly jewels in the next several years.[8] The pages of the *Atlantic Monthly,* for example, grew as begemmed as the Gaikwar of Baroda. Oliver Wendell Holmes's "Autocrat" sees a river lying "as smooth as a sheet of beryl-green silk." A poem already mentioned, "The Cup," glitters with amethyst, emerald, jasper, and chrysolite. In June 1859 the editors notice a work by Augusta Browne Garrett entitled *The Precious Stones of the Heavenly Foundation, with Illustrations Selected in Prose and Verse* (a series of bad poems and dull sermonets stretched on the framework of the twelve jewels). An article of the following month entitled "Rock, Tree, and

Man" makes an observation on "the ruby, the emerald, the topaz, the amethyst, chalcedony, carnelian, jasper, agate, and garnet, and all the beautiful varieties of rock crystal." Harriet Prescott's suspense story, "Circumstance," which Emily Dickinson complained "followed me, in the Dark—so I avoided her—" (L261), interrupts the horrors to describe "the holy Jerusalem...with its splendid battlements and gates of pearl, and its foundations, the eleventh a jacinth, the twelfth an amethyst—with its great white throne, and the rainbow round about it, in sight like unto an emerald." [9]

The jewel fever was at its height in 1859, a year during which Emily Dickinson worked the heavenly amethyst and the emerald into three poems and a topaz and two jaspers into her surviving letters, together with other references to the New Jerusalem.[10] A letter of 2 March 1859 to her friend Mrs. Holland exclaims at the idea of any complacency "when we must all stand barefoot before [the Father's] jasper doors!" (L204). A letter written a few months later to her friends Samuel and Mary Bowles seems to reflect the excitement of a recent discussion of Mrs. Browning's popular book:

Tonight looks like "Jerusalem." I think Jerusalem must be like Sue's Drawing Room, when we are talking and laughing there, and you and Mrs Bowles are by. I hope we may all behave so as to reach Jerusalem.
...
    You shall find us all at the gate, if you come in a hundred years, just as we stood that day.
    If it become of "Jasper," previously, you will not object, so that we lean there still, looking after you. [L189] [11]

Perhaps on this same summer day of 1859 the poet wrote again to Mrs. Holland: Wicked as she is, she has been reading her Bible and has found the promise of a land "where friends should 'go no more out'; and there were 'no tears,'" and she wishes they were both there tonight, with the "hundred and forty and four thousand" chatting pleasantly beside them.[12] On the other hand, she has been having a wonderful time on earth of late—"and if God had been here this summer, and seen the things I have seen—I guess that He would think His Paradise superfluous (L185).[13] The wonderful summer continuing into the fall, she wrote to Bowles after another of his brief visits: "Friends are gems—infrequent. Potosi is a care, Sir. I guard it reverently, for I could not afford to be poor now, after affluence" (L205). Writing to Mrs. Bowles in early December, she observed that since the recent storms, "the days turn Topaz, like a lady's pin" (L212). Years later she spoke to Mrs. Bowles of an occasion when she had talked with Bowles about "his Gem chapter" (L536), an interest in Revelation 21 apparently stimulated by his enthusiasm for *Aurora Leigh*.

About May 1860 she wrote to her friend Kate Turner, somewhat in the vein of her letter-poem to Sue: "You did not tell me you had once been a 'Millionaire.' Did my sister think that opulence could be mistaken?— Some trinket will remain—some babbling plate or jewel!" (L222). Five foundation stones appear in four poems of that year, and in 1861 six heavenly stones decorate as many poems. The year 1862, which witnessed her greatest poetic production, has three emerald poems, a beryl, a sapphire, and a topaz. In a letter of 12 January 1862 she tells Bowles that the "Moon rides like a Girl—through a Topaz Town" (L247), and to another friend she writes in late April that the cat mistakes dandelions for "*Topaz* mice" (L317). In the October 1862 *Atlantic,* Henry David Thoreau protests in one of his last essays against this fad of using precious stones as color names: "What do we know of sapphire, amethyst, emerald, ruby, amber, and the like—most of us who take these names in vain? Leave these precious words to cabinet-keepers, virtuosos, and maids-of-honor,—to the Nabobs, Begums, and Chobdars of Hindostan, or whatever else." [14] There may be a self-conscious echo of his words in her poem 722, written perhaps late in 1862 or early in 1863, with its expressed fear that she may at times "fail—or feign, / Or take the Royal names in vain—." But though she admired Thoreau and doubtless read his "Autumnal Tints," she would not necessarily adopt his opinions and may even have picked up her new color words "umber" and "gamboge" from the very list Thoreau dismissed with contempt as derived from "obscure foreign localities." The sharp decline in her foundation jewels after 1862, with their virtual disappearance after 1865, simply follows the curve of other image clusters.

If the emerald is omitted as being too well known to be specific, it will be observed that her remaining foundation jewels occur twenty-six times in poems and letters during the period 1858–65 and only five times during the succeeding years. The conclusion seems clear: like Harriet Prescott and Longfellow and many others in the late 1850s, she was charmed by Mrs. Browning's poetic use of the heavenly jewels, adopted them for her own poetry, and after some five or six years laid them by. Except for emerald and amethyst, the heavenly jewels have no roots in her symbolism and are significant largely because they show her responsiveness to contemporary enthusiasms and, being traced back to the joint influence of Longfellow and Elizabeth Browning, can be used to correlate letters and poems. She employed other jewel names—a remaining 113 instances in letters and poems—and had other sources than the twenty-first chapter of Revelation.

According to her niece, Martha Dickinson Bianchi, the poet and her sister had "a good deal of old-fashioned jewelry ... garnet brooches and sleeve-buttons ... foreign corals and cameos," some of which Lavinia Dickinson continued to wear, although Mrs. Bianchi remembers the poet as having ceased to wear any jewelry except a white and gold cameo pin, a gold watch, and a ring or two.[15] The recollection appears to be accurate.

In a letter of summer 1882 the poet suggested to T. W. Higginson that his baby might "pin her Apron or her Shoe" with an enclosed trinket which she had just received, adding, "but I never wear Jewels—" (L767).

Mrs. Bianchi's account of her aunt's jewelry has a special interest. Although coral is named in the Bible and garnet is identified with the biblical carbuncle, such an origin would not explain the strongly personal realization of these jewels in the poet's work. Unlike the merely ornamental heavenly gems, her garnet and coral flame angrily in their poems and pulse red as heart's blood, which in a sense they are. Their color is still more significant than their personal associations. Garnet and coral, together with ruby, make up her red gems, and for Emily Dickinson the color red consistently symbolizes love, life, intense vitality, and intense suffering.

The first coral occurs in a poem of early 1862, "I tend my flowers for thee— / Bright Absentee!" (339). As both gardener and flower *draped* in modest gray calyx, "Daisy" looks on enthralled at the *undraping* of other, less common flower females, roses breaking open, carnations tipping spice for bees, a fuschia ripping her "Coral Seams," a cactus splitting "her Beard / To show her throat." [16] This curiously voyeuristic scene, which has been examined earlier along with other unconscious garden symbolism, serves here to throw a rather surprising light on the flower woman's "Coral Seams." The second coral poem, "A still—Volcano—Life—" (601), written, or at least copied, somewhat later in 1862, employs the tragic side of her symbolic red and gives startling novelty to the coral lips of poetic tradition by identifying them with the crater of an erupting volcano:

The Solemn—Torrid—Symbol—
The lips that never lie—
Whose hissing Corals part—and shut—
And Cities—ooze away—

Her red garnet is associated with a volcano in a poem that comes suspiciously short and late. A four-line stanza in the handwriting of 1869, it is a clean pencil copy and looks like the surviving stanza of a longer poem written at a time when volcanoes, Etna, Naples, and symbolic jewels were very much a part of her working vocabulary, that is, about 1862. In its present form, it is no more than a rhymed proverb, "Security is loud," with a most implausible example. The figure itself is a striking one—the mountain basking and purring like a great sleepy cat, then suddenly baring a bloody fang; but for Emily Dickinson, as for Naples, not security but only terror would have erupted with that fiery "Garnet Tooth" (1146). Everywhere in her poetry the tooth is an image of terror.

One other poem with garnets takes us back to late 1861 or early 1862, and it is a love poem. She sent a copy of it at this early period to her friend Bowles and another copy to Sue Dickinson about 1866, just at the close of her major period of creativity. According to this poem she has had an experience comparable to marriage, but "without the Sign," "Royal—all but the Crown," "Betrothed" but "without the swoon"—in short, without that sexual embrace that joins golden flesh to golden flesh and garnet blood to garnet blood (1072).

Last of her red gems, the ruby is the most various of the three and the most difficult to read. In at least six of the eight ruby poems, the color is basic to its meaning and sometimes is virtually all that meaning, as in an early and slight poem that describes the morning sky hurrying into some "Ruby Trowsers"—the sole occurrence of male attire, it would seem, in her manifold dressings and undressings, although ruby trousers are perhaps still more suggestive of an odalisque (204).[17] Poem 223, pleading for a smile, offers diamonds from her fingers, "Rubies—like the Evening Blood," "Topaz—like the star," and declares that her offer would be " 'a Bargain' for a *Jew!*"—presumably such a Jew as Shylock. The very similar poem 247, written about the same time and entered in the same packet, promises "Shylock" fantastic wealths in the form of bobolinks, bees, and assorted flowers if he will sign a bond to grant her one hour of her lover's face. These poems in the handwriting of late 1861 have enough in common with poem 304, written (or perhaps only copied) in 1862 handwriting, as to be clearly the product of one inspiration. Poem 304 describes the sudden apparition of a dawn like "Hindered Rubies" or, reflecting the violence of her volcano poems, like the light that a "Sudden Musket—spills—." The sunrise shakes itself abroad like "Breadths of Topaz" packed up for the night and now unrolled (a copy of this poem is addressed "Sue," who may be at least partially identified with the "Lady" who unrolls the bolt of topaz sunshine). Dawn being now complete, the orchard sparkles "like a Jew." Neither in this poem nor in poem 223 does the ruby depart appreciably from its descriptive role; it is the red of dawn and evening light or of blood.

In poems 400 and 466 the ruby functions as value with little or no hint of color. How could she care for pearls, asks poem 466, when she owns the sea, or for "Brooches," when the "Emperor"-lover is pelting her with "Rubies"? In poem 400 she is once more deprived of love and desperately anxious to reach her lover—"to tell Him I am true!" She will pay a boy in diamonds to carry her message, and if it is too large for him, he is to hire another boy and pay him in solid gold, or if the latter hesitates, then in "Rubies," for her message must be delivered. Here the extravagance of tone implies that the "Rubies" are heart's blood.

Somewhat apart from these sunrise and love poems is the description of a visit to a fantasy heaven, a "small Town— / Lit—with a Ruby— / Lathed—with Down—." There is a Talmudic story that Noah's ark was lit only by precious stones or, according to one version, by a single great ruby; and she would have found a mention of this story in James T. Fields's article, "Diamonds and Pearls," in the March 1861 *Atlantic*. With its warm red glow, its downy lining, its soft gossamer and eider, her intimate little heaven may well share the symbolism of the protective ark (374).

The rather difficult poem 583, "A Toad, can die of Light—," appears to contrast the death that annihilates all distinction, and therefore all meaning or value, with the life that makes possible a limitless discrimination and choice and hence value. In death, what advantage has man over toad, earl over midge? But life is different, runs the next stanza, and therefore one should "measure Wine— / Naked of Flask—Naked of Cask— / Bare Rhine—," a directive which at first seems to annihilate distinctions all over again. "Which Ruby's mine?" she demands in the final line. Perhaps it is only by stripping off the containers and getting down to the "Naked," the "Bare," that one arrives at fundamental discriminations. Ruby, wine, and Rhine are assuredly one and the same, and they represent, jointly or severally, that other trinity of life, love, and suffering; but in other respects the poem remains cloudy.

One last ruby poem, sent with a flower to her cousin Eudocia Flynt in July 1862, describes the flower as a plush and velvet cup containing "Depths of Ruby" and begs the recipient to play that her lip is a "Humming-Bird— / And sipped just Me—" (334). In her diary Mrs. Flynt recorded its arrival with five exclamation marks, a suggestion that she considered the poem somewhat overdone. The real surprise is that no copy seems to have gone to Sue Dickinson, for it was Sue that the poet would have been most likely to associate with the hummingbird. During that period the *Atlantic* was a veritable aviary, and both women read the magazine pretty carefully. One article in particular, entitled "The Humming-Bird" and published in the June 1860 *Atlantic,* would infallibly have attracted the attention of the poet and her sister-in-law. It is in the form of a letter between two women friends.

"What bright-winged thought of yours," the writer asks her dear Estelle, "sent him so straight to me, across that wide space of sea and land? Did he dart like a sunbeam all the way?" She calls the bird her friend's "special messenger...darting to our oriel, my Orient...all the intense life of the tropics condensed into this one live jewel,—the glance of the sun on emerald and rubies." He is "Our knight of the ruby throat...with busy birring sound, like Neighbor Clark's spinning wheel...[and with] the long slender bodkin you lent him": "Now, just now, he darts into my room, coquets with my basket of flowers, 'a kiss, a touch, and then away.' ...You did well to trust this most passionate pilgrim with your secret; the room is radiant with it. Slow-flying doves may well draw the car of Venus; but this arrow tipped with flame darts before, to tell of its coming." And she closes her letter with the words "Your own Susan, Susy, Sue. P.S. 'May our friendship never moult a feather!'"[18]

In late 1861 Sue Dickinson sent a note to her sister-in-law, in which she spoke of some flowers, apparently a gift from the latter's conservatory: "The flowers are sweet and bright and look as if they would kiss one—ah, they expect a humming-bird—" (L238). In the circumstances of their friendship, attenuated but by no means broken off, these words were almost tantalizing. In late 1861 or early 1862 Emily Dickinson wrote a confused poem about a hummingbird, "Within my Garden, rides a bird" (500), and shortly afterward wrote poem 334 and sent a copy to Mrs. Flynt but not to her sister-in-law; and she must have composed at least a work-sheet draft of "A Route of Evanescence" (1463), a poem that survives in fair copies of 1879 and later.

No diamond poem exists in handwriting earlier than 1861, but a number appear to date from the publication of Fields's article in the *Atlantic Monthly*.[19] The most important of these (621) does not actually name the jewel but employs symbol within symbol within symbol like a series of Chinese boxes; the last box encloses the diamond. Although the basic meaning is clear enough, the poem gains in richness with a knowledge of her reading. In early March 1861, she wrote to her Norcross cousins that she had forwarded "Loo's note" as requested, adding, " 'Is there nothing else,' as the clerk says?" (L230). Already she must have been working at poem 621, "I asked no other thing," for the "Mighty Merchant," to whom she offers "Being" in payment of her heart's desire, sneeringly repeats "Brazil?" twirls a button of his coat, and asks indifferently, "But— Madam—is there nothing else— / That We can show—Today?" And beneath the symbolic "Brazil" glitters another symbol, the magnificent Star of the South (even the name is appropriate, the South being her symbolic region of love and the star symbolizing the beloved) described in Fields's article:

> The *Star of the South* ... the largest diamond yet obtained from Brazil ... is owned by the King of Portugal. It weighed originally two hundred and fifty-four carats, but was trimmed down to one hundred and twenty-five. The grandfather of the present king had a hole bored in it, and liked to strut about on gala-days with the gem suspended around his neck. This magnificent jewel was found by three banished miners, who were seeking for gold during their exile. A great drought had laid dry the bed of a river, and there they discovered this lustrous wonder.[20]

Commonly her diamond represents value, as the diamonds to pay the boy messenger of poem 400; the diamonds "jumbled on" in poem 460, which describes the beloved as a begemmed and droughtless well; the diamonds that have become a legend in poem 397, the diamonds she offers with rubies and topaz for "just a single smile" in poem 223; or the diamond in "far—Bolivian Ground" of poem 395, which appears to be a conflation of the mythic wealths of "Brazil" and "Potosi." In poem 427 the diamonds for which she is diving and which she proposes to string "in fine Necklace," wear on her "Hem," and bear on her breast at "Court" are the very person of the beloved. The diamond of a letter of September 1871, which deplores the absence of Sue Dickinson and concludes with the assurance that "the Lock is firm upon your Diamond Door," clearly connotes value and perhaps strength and impregnability as well (L364). Again, the "Duties Diamond" of poem 700 can only be duties of the highest consequence, and the curious "Whip of Diamond" of poem 665 is no doubt intended to suggest value, although one cannot dismiss its cutting quality. Minor exceptions are the snowflake diamonds from "Polar Caskets" (375), which evoke the sparkling brilliance of the stone, and the hard and cutting "Tongues of Diamond" that revile her in poem 753.

After an absence of four years, the diamond appeared again, and for the last time (except for the 1871 letter to Sue), in two 1867 work-sheet drafts. Poem 1110 asks whether the diamond, if it grew as common as the dandelion, would be treated as some other thing or person or experience has been treated. Poem 1108 suggests that a diamond in possession does come to seem as common as the dandelion; but if one sighted it in a "Seller's Shrine," how one would long for it and sigh over one's poverty and be "mad" with "fear" lest "any other" should buy it. Both poems appear to reflect cloudily and inartistically on the same experience.

According to Ruskin, the worth of a diamond is "the understanding of the time it must take to look for it," a correlation of value with scarcity that seems to inform a number of Emily Dickinson's jewel poems; as she wrote to Sue Dickinson, proposing to keep Sue in a "casket," "how much you cost—" (L194). The handwrought article, Ruskin contends, cannot be distinguished from machine work any more readily "than a diamond can be known from paste. Yet exactly as a woman of feeling would not wear false jewels,"[21] so a builder would not use cheap ornament. With some sacrifice of accuracy to alliteration, Emily Dickinson wrote, "We play at Paste— / Till qualified, for Pearl—" (320).

Among poets the pearl is the most precious of precious substances, as a glance at Table 1 will show. Even where the incidence of usage is not high, as in the Bible, the particular occurrences may be so rich in symbolism that they impress beyond all others. The "pearls before swine," the "pearl of great price," and the twelve gates to the heavenly city that "were twelve pearls; every several gate...of one pearl," are remembered when all other jewels are forgotten.[22] It is the jewel most often and most strikingly honored in the plays of Shakespeare. A diamond may be a mere object of merchandise ("A diamond gone, cost me two thousand ducats!" cries the distracted Shylock), but Ariel's "Those are pearls that were his eyes" belongs to another realm of poetry. "I see thee compass'd with thy kingdom's pearl," says Macduff, hailing his young king in words that may have occasioned Emily Dickinson's "their People Pearl" (457). To the question whether Helen of Troy is worth keeping, Troilus replies: "She is a pearl, / Whose price hath launch'd above a thousand ships." Of the desired Cressida he speaks no less extravagantly: "Her bed is India; there she lies, a pearl"; and the space between them he calls "the wild and wandering flood." Most memorable to Emily Dickinson, who especially valued *Othello,* would have been the Moor's agonized account of himself as "one whose hand, / Like the base Indian, threw a pearl away / Richer than all his tribe." [23] Besides the forty-one Shakespearean pearls, she would have known the pearls of Milton and of Keats and at least some of the seventy-one pearls of Robert Browning. Of Tennyson's pearls she would doubtless have remembered best the line from *In Memoriam:* "When Time hath sunder'd shell from pearl." [24] Popular literature would have rained down showers of pearls, for it was a jewel especially dear to the Victorians.

The aura of sentiment, folklore, and myth surrounding the pearl is probably greater than that of all other jewels combined. On the side of sentiment, the pearl comes directly from nature unaltered by man and can be thought of as natural and simple like a flower; the French marguerite is both pearl and daisy. In the region of myth, Aphrodite arises from the foam of the sea and drifts landward on her shell—the Great Mother, the Venus Genetrix to whom Caesar dedicated a buckler of the pearls that are sacred to her. Of the two magnificent eardrops worn by Cleopatra at her feast for Mark Antony, the pearl that was *not* dissolved (in vinegar, according to Pliny, but more romantically in wine) "was cut in half to make earrings for the Venus of the Pantheon." [25] Divested of its more obvious sexuality, the pearl was appropriated to the Christian Queen of Heaven, and it became the custom to dedicate famous single pearls and ropes of pearls to the Virgin and in paintings to embroider her robes with pearls. Unpierced, it is called the virgin pearl, and from time immemorial the qualities of purity and chastity, customarily associated with maidenhood, have been attached to it.

Not surprisingly, the most sexually charged of Emily Dickinson's jewels is the pearl—and from at least as early as the girlhood days when she first began to think of writing poetry. In a letter to Susan Gilbert that dwells somewhat emotionally upon the possibility of marriage for either of them, she imagines how dull their lives must seem to "the plighted maiden, whose days are fed with gold, and who gathers pearls every evening," although the letter as a whole suggests that the prospect is more frightening than desirable (L93). Some weeks earlier, she thanks Sue for sending her a letter with "golden thoughts, and feelings so like gems" that she is sure she "*gathered* them in whole baskets of pearls!" (L77). This figure of the pearl basket recurs in a letter to her admired friend, Elizabeth Holland. The girl has had a dream of walking with her friend in a wonderful garden and of helping her pick roses, and she longs for darkness and sleep and another such "dream of you and the roses, and the basket never full," characteristically adding that she looks forward to the heavenly life in which they will "gather flowers of gold in baskets made of pearl" (L175). In an 1860 poem, the symbolic pearl baskets are symbolic "Tankards scooped in Pearl" from which she drinks intoxicating happiness (214).

In another 1860 poem, the pearl figures clearly and consciously as the outer defense works of virginity; the importunate lover is urged not to attempt the "moat of pearl" (213). According to a poem of the next year, however, the "lonesome" ones with whom the poet identifies are now outside the Garden of Eden and vainly striving to climb the barrier, here called a "purple Moat" (262). Many years later, the barrier moat has become a stile, and behind this stile the poet is once more entrenched against an importunate lover, as in letter 562 to Otis P. Lord.

In a quite early poem, she hopes the "Father in the skies" will lift her "Over the stile of 'Pearl' " (70), and here the barrier appears to be no more than a rather arch version of the pearly gates of the heavenly city and is religious, if anything. Congratulating young Bowles on his coming marriage, however, she makes use of the heavenly pearls to describe the young man's entrance into a quite earthly paradise: "I had feared that the Angel with the Sword would dissuade you from Eden, but rejoice that it only ushered you. 'Every several Gate is of one Pearl' " (L864). In a last example that seems to fit this pattern, she is wearing her "Sod Gown," traveling with appropriately pale horses and carriage, her "Baggage a strapped Pearl" (surely that long untried viriginity), and carrying a "Whip of Diamond"—a startling figure, to say the least—as she rides "to meet the Earl" (665).

In a number of poems, the pearls are merely ornamental—dews like pearls (333), flowers that are pearls in an ocean of summer (484), the spider's "Yarn of Pearl" (605), "Threnodies of Pearl" squandered by a bird (634), necklaces of raindrop pearls (794), even a "Wrinkled Pearl" discarded at the close of "Nature's Party" (873). A few poems using the pearl may be described as marriage poems. For example, poem 473 tells how the shy, meek, "Dowerless Girl" prepared herself for the proud new estate of "Bride" by learning to hold her "Brow like an Earl" and to "Prove—like a Pearl—." It is a kind of Tennysonian Dickinson—the simple village maiden preparing herself for her new role as the wife of the eccentric lord of Burleigh.[26] Poem 493, "The World—stands—solemner—to me," is another lord of Burleigh poem but without the picturesque details. This soul that now "bears another's name" is oppressed with the fear of not being good enough "To wear that perfect—pearl— / The Man—upon the Woman—binds—." A third marriage poem, "She rose to His Requirement" (732), insinuates that the wife does miss something in her new life but, like the sea that develops both "Pearl" and "Weed," keeps her dark secret. These marriage poems are puzzling and not very convincing; the studied humility rings false. Much more interesting is a poem that describes an imaginary visit to the sea with details that to some readers have suggested an unconscious eroticism.[27]

In the last months of her life, Emily Dickinson observed to Mabel Loomis Todd that she had never seen the sea—"We correspond, though I never met him" (L1004)—and her statement may be accepted as fact. Not only the fantasy details, like mermaids or frigates with hempen hands, but all details of poem 520 have been invented and hence might be thought more likely to well up from unconscious needs and fears. At the outset the poet stands cockily defiant, eyeing the mermaids that have come up to look at her and the frigates that are trying excitedly to help her. "But no Man moved Me"—until the sea goes over shoe, apron, belt, and bodice, then follows hard on her panicky retreat. She can feel his "Silver Heel" on her "Ancle" and then her "Shoes...overflow with Pearl—." Only when they meet the "Solid Town" does he bow and, with a mighty look at her, withdraw.

A small group of poems concern themselves with the act of diving for the pearl. Poem 7, which uses a number of figures for the heavenly life, calls pearls "the Diver's farthings / Extorted from the Sea," presumably meaning that one dives into the sea of death to obtain the pearl of immortal life. In another early poem, "Her breast is fit for pearls" (84), the poet makes the deprecatory admission that she is "not a 'Diver,'" by which she doubtless means that she has no ornament (no poem?) worthy of the other woman, for she goes on to describe herself as nesting comfortably in her friend's heart. A poem already mentioned, "'Tis little I— could care for Pearls" (466), boasts of a "sea" of love so ample and complete that she is no longer dependent on or concerned about individual pearls. A poem beginning "Removed from Accident of Loss" (424) recalls a time when she had been as unconscious of "Riches," apparently meaning earthly love, as the "Brown Malay" is unconscious of "Pearls in Eastern Waters" already destined for him.

Two final pearl-diving poems, both devoted to the earthly prize, appear to come directly from her reading of Fields's article. In an early 1861 poem, *"One Life* of so much Consequence" (270), she describes a beloved and now-vanished life as *"One Pearl"* so important to her that she would dive for it on the instant even if she knew that "to *take* it" would cost her *"just a life!"* Here she does not boast of owning a sea so ample she can dispense with individual pearls. With the *Atlantic* article fresh in mind, she could envision her human pearl as the great and beautiful Peregrina and discount all the terrible risks of the dive.[28] Never mind that the sea is full of pearls; she knows it, but her own gem remains unblurred, "distinct from all the row" of other gems, *"Intact—in Diadem,"* a description which gives the reader the strange sensation of looking deep into the sea at a glimmering white pearl that not only was never inside an oyster but is already mounted in a regal circlet. More realistically, Shakespeare speaks of a good man living in a poor house as "your pearl in your foul oyster." [29] Emily Dickinson's underseas pearl has doubtless never known an oyster. It is dark uterine water into which she prepares to dive—or rather, at the last moment, dares *not* dive:

> The Malay—took the Pearl—
> Not—I—the Earl—
> I—feared the Sea—too much
> Unsanctified—to touch—

And while she was still praying to be worthy this "Destiny," the "Swarthy fellow" dived, seized her jewel, and afterward wore it on his "Dusky Breast"—a "Negro" who never even dreamed that she wooed the pearl (452). If her lost pearl is indeed the Peregrina (the incomparable, or the pilgrim and stranger—either translation would have pleased her), then the surprising "Negro" is accounted for. Of the "beautiful Peregrina," Fields writes that it was fished up in American waters by a Negro slave, who almost threw the modest bivalve back into the sea but bethought himself, "pulled the shells asunder, and, lo, the rarest of priceless pearls!" [30] The detail about the "Negro" bearing the incomparable pearl on his "Dusky" (unworthy) breast is probably taken from the account of that fatuous king of Portugal who had a hole bored in the magnificent Star of the South. The "Negro" or "Malay" need not be any particular rival but simply the general unworthy who have borne off her prize and now wear it on their sooty breast, when she would have thought a "Vest of Amber" too poor for it.

Or a passage from "The Fire-Worshippers" section of Thomas Moore's *Lalla Rookh* may have caught her attention:

> Bolder than they who dare not dive
> For pearls, but when the sea's at rest,
> Love, in the tempest most alive,
> Hath ever held that pearl the best
> He finds beneath the stormiest water.[31]

Fearless in pursuit of diamonds, Emily approached the pearl with the gravest apprehensions.

Some poems suggest that she is searching for the pearl of great price incorporate in the adored and perfect friend, for, as poem 959 sadly admits, the suspicion has but lately touched her that she is looking "oppositely" for what can only be found in heaven above. One such poem has already been noticed, "We play at Paste—/ Till qualified, for Pearl" (320), a copy of which apparently went to her friend Emily Fowler Ford. A similar poem beginning "Shells from the Coast mistaking" (693) appears to make a somewhat ungenerous contrast between the inferior friends of her girlhood and the true "Pearl" that she has discovered in "After Ages." A poem written perhaps a year earlier laments a loved woman friend—the "Quick—Sweet Mouth" that she now misses so poignantly, the "Unnumbered Satin" of the hair she once stroked, the "Fingers of the Slim Aurora" that she once fondled among her own. As for the feet that once ran to meet her, they, or at least their coverings, are to be "adjusted," translated like Prince Ferdinand's father into something rich and strange—"Pearl—for Stocking—Pearl for Shoe—" (758). Very likely the lost friend is dead to the poet (the line "Not so arrogant—this Noon" sounds like a bit of wishful thinking, of getting one's own back), but in other respects the friend is probably no more dead than the king of Naples. The deaths that Emily Dickinson celebrates are seldom real ones. In one curious poem, "If I may have it, when it's dead" (577), she apologizes for being in such haste to bury the beloved friend—"Forgive me, if to stroke thy frost / Outvisions Paradise!"

Among these pearls of great price, and surely the most interesting, is the one commemorated in the letter-poem to Sue Dickinson with which this chapter began. An editorial note in the variorium edition makes the conjecture that it was meant for a long-dead friend, Ben Newton, but when it was reprinted three years later as a *letter to Sue* the editors conceded that it might have been intended for the person to whom it was addressed. Sue Dickinson would have found nothing in the manuscript that related the poem to anyone except herself and nothing that she did not perfectly recollect as belonging to their joint experience. The poet's intention was to remind her, not to puzzle her.

Before they two met (says the poem)—and that would have been before the winter of 1849–50, by which time the friendship was being forged— the poet had thought herself a "Millionaire" in such small wealth as the friendship of an Abiah Root, a Jane Humphrey, a Ben Newton. Then the admired Sue swam like a new world into her ken (this first stanza adopts Keats's pattern of geographical metaphor, replacing his "realms of gold" and "peak in Darien" with an equally exotic "Buenos Ayre" and "Peru"), whereupon the poet knew herself poor. The second stanza recites her ignorance of mines and gems and diadems—an ignorance so vast that she is only just able to recognize *"the Queen"* (Sue herself in another guise). The third stanza compares Sue with the "India" and "Golconda" of legendary wealth and declares that a daily smile from the beloved friend would be better than a *"Gem";* and the last stanza identifies Sue with the pearl of great price. The following lines are of particular interest:

I'm sure 'tis *"India"*—all day—
To those who look on you—
Without a stint—without a blame—
Might I—but be the Jew!

The confession of a limitation on her claims to Sue is an oblique reminder of that jealousy of her brother so transparently expressed during the days of his courtship. Knowing that Austin was to propose to Sue at the Revere House in Boston on 23 March 1853, she wrote to him the next day that she had repeatedly (and, it would seem, anxiously) "dropped in" on the scene of his proposal (L109); and her congratulatory letter four days later was cool and reserved (L110). Some two weeks later she wrote to him that she had taken *his* place with Sue on Saturday evening, "but I will give it back to you as soon as you get home" (L115). In October 1853 she wrote to Sue, who had just returned from New York, that she would have been with her that evening except for the fact—a grudging concession of her brother's superior right—that *"Somebody loves you more"* (L135). A year later, the knowledge that Austin was starting west to visit his fiancée wrenched from her an anguished "He will see you, Darling! What I cannot do. Oh *could* I!" (L176). As Theodora Ward has pointed out, her relationship with brother and friend had been of such intimacy that "it could not have been easy for her to accept the exclusive nature of their new relation." [32] It was perhaps a little deeper and sadder even than that. When Austin settled down with his bride in the house next door, he insured the lifelong continuance of the dilemma.

During the early years of this friendship, the most enthralling public mystery was the disappearance of Sir John Franklin and his crew on a voyage to discover the Northwest Passage to the Orient. An 1864 poem (851) alluding to Lady Franklin's long-continued search for her husband is a reminder that a possible new route to India was a lively topic in the Victorian mind and therefore in the mind of Emily Dickinson. She and her sister-in-law gave the name "Northwest Passage" to a drafty hallway in the elder Dickinson house where they frequently met and conferred, and in letter and poem the word "India" consistently represents the heart's desire.[33] As late as 1884 the poet would call the marriage of a friend the discovery of "the shortest route to India" (L900). Another lively source of her image might have been some lines from *Don Juan* describing a woman's outward coldness as a "North-West Passage / Unto the glowing India of the soul." [34] But the prime source of her symbolic India would no doubt have been Shakespeare. Sir Toby Belch shows his approval of Maria by calling her his "metal of India." The magnificence the English display on the Field of the Cloth of Gold is said to make "Britain India; every man that stood / Show'd like a mine." Splendor such as this appears to inform the lines in which Emily Dickinson laments the end of love as the loss of "my moment of Brocade— / My—drop—of India" (430). The "drop" could be an intoxicating dram or even a pearl eardrop worthy of a Cleopatra. Although Indian waters were not notably rich in pearl oysters, India was a center of pearl dealing, and the two are linked in a passage from *Troilus and Cressida* already noted: "Her bed is India; there she lies, a pearl." To look at her own pearl of "India," Emily Dickinson cries, "Might I—but be the Jew!" This "Shylock" of caskets and jewels and ducats, whose appearance in three other poems has been noticed, may be a clue to the associations swarming in her mind, for it is to Shylock's daughter Jessica that the scapegrace Lorenzo recalls the bright night on which Troilus "mounted the Troyan walls / And sigh'd his soul toward the Grecian tents, / Where Cressid lay that night." [35]

In the final stanza of the letter-poem to Sue, the poet makes the surprising statement that she allowed the "Pearl" to slip through her fingers while still "a Girl—at School!" It is this puzzle that led George Frisbie Whicher and after him the editor of the variorum *Poems* to conclude that she must be thinking of the dead Ben Newton, even though the poem plainly states that this *"Gold"* still *"exists"*—at a painful distance. Whatever her original feelings may have been—and her comment on Ben Newton's marriage suggests a half-amused surprise that this man should marry or should find anyone willing to marry him (L44)—it was doubtless more plausible to suppose that she would belatedly imagine a romance with Newton rather than a lost opportunity to retain the exclusive devotion of a Susan Gilbert. But the evidence for Sue is there.

After engaging herself to Austin Dickinson, Sue returned to Amherst in a panicky retreat not unknown to other girls in her situation. At this juncture, Emily Dickinson was receiving the confidence of both brother and friend, and her sympathies must have been sorely divided. She wanted to keep Sue for herself, and she may have had the illusion, to which Sue could have contributed, that a broken engagement would restore the original situation. But her loyalty to her brother came to the fore, with perhaps a glimmer of insight into the fantasy nature of her wishes, and she wrote to Austin, " 'Let not your heart be troubled'—so believe in [Sue?], believe also in me!" (L113). On 8 April she wrote to him again, observing that on the previous evening she and Sue had "walked down to the Old Oak Tree [which figured, in some unexplained way, in Austin's courtship], and sat there and talked a long while, principally of you, and ourselves" (L114). In private meetings like these, Susan Gilbert doubtless rearranged her feelings, talked herself into her engagement once more, and left her friend Emily with the permanent illusion of having sacrificed some opportunity.

It is an odd fact that Ben Newton died on 24 March 1853, one day after Susan Gilbert and Austin Dickinson became engaged at the Revere House in Boston. Not surprisingly, these two funerals have been confused by the poet's biographers. There was never any doubt in Emily Dickinson's mind as to which was the more painful to her. On 25 April 1862 she wrote to her new friend, T. W. Higginson: "When a little Girl, I had a friend, who taught me Immortality—but venturing too near, himself—he never returned— Soon after, my Tutor, died—" (L261).[36] The "Tutor" is commonly, and plausibly, identified with Ben Newton. As for the friend who taught her "Immortality (and according to poem 809, "Love is Immortality"), she wrote to her sister-in-law about 1884:

Be Sue—while I am Emily—
Be next—what you have ever been—Infinity— [L912]

FOUR  DRY WINE

Logarithm—had I—for Drink—
'Twas a dry Wine— [728]

In the letter to T. W. Higginson quoted at the end of chapter 3, the poet used the language of the schoolroom to make some personal disclosures:

When a little Girl, I had a friend, who taught me Immortality—but venturing too near, himself—he never returned— Soon after, my Tutor, died—and for several years, my Lexicon—was my only companion. Then I found one more—but he was not contented I be his scholar—so he left the Land. [L261]

Taught, Tutor, Lexicon, scholar: these words are part of that larger school vocabulary that forms so distinctive and pervasive a metaphor, or series of related metaphors, throughout her work. Outvying her Puritan models, she not only views this life as a schooling for the next but even expresses a faith in a process of continuing education, for she expects to go on learning in "the fair schoolroom of the sky" (193). A beautiful spring day is "Heaven's 'Peter Parley,'" which prepared earth's children for "sublimer Recitation" above (65), although in more desperate mood she begs to be allowed to keep her "Primer," her "A—B—C," and let more learned persons graduate to the skies (418).

In one sense the school days are the lonely, studious isolation of her middle twenties. The 1863 poem about the "dry Wine" begins:

Let Us play Yesterday—
I—the Girl at school—
You—and Eternity—the
Untold Tale— [728]

And she speaks of drinking "Logarithm" and of easing her famine at her "Lexicon," words that associate this dreary interim with the five years following the close of her passionate friendship with Susan Gilbert and the death of her "Tutor," Ben Newton, when, as she told Higginson, her "Lexicon" was her only companion. Now comes the "one more" of her letter, who is entreated to be, and apparently for a time is, the poet's instructor in love. In poem 568, beloved and poet are pupils in the same school, where they learn "the Whole of Love," the "Alphabet," "Words," a "Chapter," "the mighty Book," and then, "each to each, a Child," try to "expound" the divine mystery in each other's eyes. But these happy school days come to an end, the beloved rejects the scholar, and the poet puts herself to a new school and asks bitterly to be taught a different lesson:

Knows how to forget!
But—could she teach—it? [433]

This last poem is remarkable largely for the determined and persistent use of school terms, especially those drawn from the sciences. In the 1862 version, she pores over her "Greek" but, remaining a "Dunce," asks the lost beloved to teach her that "Oddest of sciences... How to forget!" Three years later this science has become the "Easiest of Arts" for a quick learner like the faithless beloved, who knows how to make that "Sacrifice for Science" the poet could not learn from "School" or "Globe" or "Logarithm." Perhaps it is in a book, and she can buy it; or it may be like a "Planet," and "Telescopes" will show her; or if it is an invention, then there must be a "Patent." In despair she appeals to God as teacher, "Rabbi of the Wise Book."

The chief sources of her school metaphors were the mathematics and sciences she studied at Amherst Academy and at Mount Holyoke College. No doubt they lent themselves to poetic use more readily than other school subjects. Besides, in his essay "The Poet," Emerson had warmly commended them to the beginning writer, asserting that only the poet knows the true use of "astronomy, chemistry, vegetation, and animation," remarking on "the charm of algebra and the mathematics" as sources of tropes, and urging "a little algebra" instead of the "village symbols" of outworn mysticism.[1] But, apart from Emerson's influence, the multiplication of her scientific terms and certain peculiarities in her use of them are evidence that science itself held a strong fascination for her.

In her early work, it is true, she sometimes adopted conventional attitudes. One of her "prentice" poems makes the usual romantic attack upon science:

"Arcturus" is his other name—
I'd rather call him "Star." [70]

But this is nonsense intended to amuse her sister-in-law, Sue Dickinson, who took a mathematician's interest in astronomy and shared with Emily her almanac, "The Year's Progress for the Sky." Sue's formula for meeting domestic crises, says her daughter Martha, was a philosophical "Why care —with Algol so far away?" [2] In female academies and seminaries, astronomy was a required subject, and the texts employed were by no means elementary; at Mount Holyoke the young poet studied Olmsted's *Compendium of Astronomy,* an abridged edition of the text used at Yale. She must already have had an introduction to the subject, however, for as early as February 1845 she writes to a friend that the latter's *beau idéal* has no doubt been "changed into a star some night while gazing at them, and placed in the constellation Orion between Bellatrix and Betelgeux" (L5), evidence of a better knowledge of the heavens than most fourteen-year-olds possess. Later, there may have been visitors' night at the Amherst College observatory, founded in 1847 and equipped with a small telescope, which was replaced by a much larger and finer instrument in late 1855. About 20 January 1856 she wrote to her friend Mrs. Holland, regarding a family move, that she supposed they "were going to make a 'transit,' as heavenly bodies did" (L182).

An early poem, probably written toward the end of summer 1859, mourns the departure of the beloved friend, who has "dropt as softly as a star" out of her summer evening; and because the poet is

> Less skillful than Le Verriere
> It's sorer to believe! [149]

Although she spelled the name as she doubtless pronounced it, the illustrious Frenchmen was more than a name to her. Somewhere she had read, possibly in O. M. Mitchel's *Planetary and Stellar Worlds,* of the brilliant intellectual feat performed by the young astronomer who argued from the perturbations of Uranus that there must be a new planet outside its orbit and "dared to reach out 1,800,000,000 of miles into unknown regions of space, to *feel* for" this cosmic stranger.[3] Perhaps the poet thinks herself less skillful than the astronomer because he finds a new "star" and she can only lose one.

Some four or five years later, she sent to her friend Samuel Bowles another poem which almost certainly alludes to Leverrier's calculations respecting Mercury, although the astronomer she names is one of the Herschels. According to the poem, Nature and God understand her perfectly yet have never "told" on her:

> My Secret as secure
> As Herschel's private interest
> Or Mercury's affair. [835]

The key word is "Secret." She had good reason to fear that in early 1862, under the same agonizing stress that led her to confide in the completely unknown Higginson, she had given Bowles a clue to the identity of the person she was in love with (letters 250, 251). This poem appears to urge him to be as discreet as God, and it does so in terms of "Mercury's affair." On 12 September 1859, in a paper read to the French Academy of Sciences and widely reported in the United States, Leverrier announced, as the result of inquiry into a marked eccentricity in the orbit of Mercury, that either Newton's law of gravitation could not be rigidly true or the motion of Mercury's perihelion must be accounted for by the disturbing influence of an unknown inner planet.[4] Even in this post-Einsteinian age there is occasional speculation about an intra-Mercurial planet (but now of insignificant size) which Leverrier was once so sure of. As the unknown planet that occasions the perturbations of the known, the beloved "Stranger" of her poetry was appropriately symbolized.

Several poems use astronomical names: for example, in a variant of poem 311 the January snowstorm withdraws, playfully hesitant, then "curls itself in Capricorn / Denying that it was—." A poem to Sue admits the hopelessness of trying to follow "wise Orion," perhaps with the flattering hint that Sue herself is a bright Orion "Dazzlingly decamping" beyond the reach of her admirer (1538). In several poems (23, 82, 282, 851) the legend of the lost Pleiad supplies a metaphor for lost friends or flowers or love. According to poem 851, she will give up seeking the faithless beloved when the "Astronomer" stops looking for "his Pleiad's Face." Two years later she has apparently given up her quest, for poem 1086 contrasts "everlasting Light" with the "Discs" (the face of the beloved conceived as earthly sun) that once satisfied her sight, adding that this earthly sun now seems "dimmer than a Saturn's Bar," words that may recall a glimpse of Saturn's rings through the Amherst College telescope.

The "Disc" of her poems is usually a sun, although, in its underlying sense of a face and in keeping with the ambivalence of all her symbols, it can be Death's "Marble Disc" or "Granite face" (310). In poem 474, both poet and beloved are suns or have sunlike faces, for when they are called upon to die, "Each other's Face—was all the Disc / Each other's setting—saw—." A Disc poem beginning "I make His Crescent fill or lack" declares that the speaker controls the changes of the moon, only to add that she and this moon "hold a Mutual Disc— / And front a Mutual Day" (909). Subsequent "Disk" poems (with change of spelling) abandon the love theme to take up her fear that life after death will be a ghostly existence without "face" or other recognizable feature—"Costumeless Consciousness" (1454). That she was much disturbed by the notion of a bodiless existence appears in such poems as "'And with what body do they come?'" (1492) and "The Spirit lasts—but in what mode—" (1576). The lines "sheen must have a Disk / To be a sun" (1550) appear to be a troubled arguing with this belief.

In some poems the sun represents the warmth and light of love or, more powerfully, a feared though desired sexual passion; again, it may represent the actual person of the beloved. An 1862 poem has a sun-lover who makes sexual overtures and, when these are rejected, withdraws "to Other Wests" and undergoes an interesting transformation into a "furthest Star" and finally a distant "Moon," to whom the poet as sea can now only hopelessly "adjust Her Tides" (643). An 1871 poem sent to her sister-in-law appears to identify Sue Dickinson with the sun and adjures her to "Shine" her best and "Fling up" her "Balls of Gold" (1178), imagery reminiscent of an earlier poem describing the sun as "Juggler of Day," "Kissing her Bonnet to the Meadow" (228).[5]

A related metaphor is the eclipse that blots out the sunlike love.[6] "If *He dissolve*," that is, if the sun-lover is lost to her, then it will be *"Eclipse—* at *Midnight*," the final darkness on a life already dark and problematical (236). In a poem that tries to find some compensation for loss, she says that "Eclipses" at least "imply" the existence of "Suns" (689). "Eclipses be—predicted— / And Science bows them in—," says poem 415, then caustically upbraids the "Jehovah" who has blackened her sky without warning. To Higginson she insists that "God" is "an Eclipse" (L261). Elsewhere she says her experience has been "Murder by degrees," that God has teased her as a cat teases a mouse, letting her half die, then rally "For consciouser Eclipse—" (762). About this time she begins to write with covert hostility that she is "taking lessons in prayer, so to coax God" (L266) or that she is "not reared to prayer" (L280). She was reared in a patriarchal religion, with God an enlarged image of the father, and she viewed this relationship, whether consciously or not, as the ground of their bitter rivalry. But God is a "Telescope," one great unclosing eye fixed on her "Perennial," and she has no hope of escaping him (413). Part joke, part superstitious fear, this poem may embody another recollection of this Amherst College telescope.

A poem of more serious tenor brings her fears down to her society where they belong. Beginning quietly with "I tie my Hat—I crease my Shawl," she speaks of the trivial duties that must be done even though "Existence" has effectually ended. Then she confronts the "Miles on Miles of Nought" (the same "Infinities of Nought" confronted by the two women lovers of poem 458) and the miles of "Action" that will be "sicker far," and her tone heightens perceptibly. Yet she remains in firm control of her poem, choosing figures that, far from exaggerating, seem to understate her dilemma. For the sake of others, she has to "simulate," and it is "stinging work." She has made discoveries about herself she knows would invite the meddling cruelties of "Science" and of "Surgery," and these are eyes "Too Telescopic" to bear without a protective covering (443).[7]

There were happier periods in her life, notably the joyous months from January 1859 to late 1860. Early in 1860 she would write another of her girlishly romantic poems upbraiding the "Savans" for their anxiety to

" 'Classify' " everything. Those who stand like her and Moses gazing across Jordan at the "stately landscape" will think "superfluous / Many Sciences" the "learned Angels" do not bother with in their "scholastic skies!" In the "Belles lettres" of that heaven, may she and (no doubt) the loved friend take their low places as *"Stars"* among the "profound *Galaxies*" at God's "grand 'Right hand'!" (168). The poem sentimentalizes religion in a way not native to her and romantically attacks the scientific discipline that in reality she found quite congenial—and very serviceable as a source of metaphor.

Early and late she used a good many astronomical terms, most often as metaphorical counters in a game of wit. A poor, torn, tattered heart is too engrossed in misery to observe night descend or "Constellations burn" (78). The wind has a "bowing intercourse" with, among other things, "Equinox" and "Asteroid" (1137). One poem speaks of the "Wonderful Rotation" of the earth, and another of the sun's "fair rotation" (6, 839). With nature we are always comfortable, introducing ourselves as easily to "Planets" as to "Flowers," but with human nature our "etiquettes / Embarrassments / And awes" begin (1214). Yet "Nature," which can assign a sun, "cannot enact a Friend"; the one is mere "Astronomy," the other an effect of magic—"Astrology" (1336). Again:

I thought that nature was enough
Till Human nature came
But that the other did absorb
As Parallax [var., Firmament] a Flame. [1286]

In her youth the first successful determinations of stellar parallax were being made, and with them, for the first time, came absolute proof of the awesome distances to the fixed stars. Almost certainly the word *parallax/ firmament* (the latter defined by her 1847 Webster's as "an expanse, a wide extent . . . stretching, extension") is here used to suggest immense distance. If the order of the sense is that flame absorbs parallax (firmament), then she may be saying that the great flame of these human suns annihilates the vast distances between them.[8]

Sometimes she appears to pluck words from astronomy with some of the original flavor still clinging, and then use them in quite other contexts. Words like *perturbation* and *eccentricity* are possibilities. For another example, "To feed upon the Retrograde" is not quite the same thing as to feed upon one's memories (904). Elsewhere she writes:

Crisis is a Hair
Toward which forces creep
Past which forces retrograde [889]

and human tragedy achieves some of the deliberateness of a cosmic event. Even the "Stock's advance and Retrograde" moves to a more stately rhythm than an ordinary rise and fall (1089). A sunset becomes a "Transit in the West / With harrowing Iodine" (673). In lighter vein, an oriole is the brilliant yellow "Meteor of Birds" (1466). For the dead, one is invited to search "Over the Arc of the Bird— / Over the Comet's Chimney—" (949) but pauses instead at the odd figure to wonder whether the comet's *chimney* can be the long, smokelike streamer of its tail, and which of three great comets she may be recalling. Would it be the greatest of these, the 1843 comet, visible in daylight and with a tail sweeping 200 million miles of space, witnessed by a twelve-year-old? Would it be the splendid Donati's comet, which appeared in 1858 in a fiery plume like a bird of paradise? Or did she recall the ominous "war comet," the "Red Avenger," which flashed into the sky of 30 June 1861, in her own most dreadful year, and lightly brushed the earth with its long, luminous tail? [9] Was she thinking, possibly, not of meteors but of this comet and the superstitious fears attending it when she wrote, late in 1861,

> Convulsion—playing round—
> Harmless—as streaks of Meteor—
> Upon a Planet's Bond— [792]

Or had she read somewhere, or heard from her elders, of that spectacular and terrifying cloud of meteors spreading out from the constellation Leo and shooting their rays thick as snowflakes from midnight to dawn of 13 November 1833, while the superstitious tolled the church bells or fell on their knees to await the imminent Judgment? For there were many New Englanders that night who saw "the stars of Heaven," even "the third part of the stars," fall to earth and expected the heavens to part like a scroll; it must have been a tale often told in Emily's youth. These Leonids were to come again in splendor thirty-three years later, and by late 1861 astronomers were looking for evidence that the shower was building toward its climactic reappearance. But Judgment had not fallen in November 1833, nor did it on the night of 30 June 1861, when the earth swept through the great comet's tail, nor would there be anything to fear in the thickening swarm of Leonids that November: "Harmless—as streaks of Meteor— / Upon a Planet's Bond—."

One stanza of a poem surviving in 1874 handwriting, possibly written near the time of the small but brilliant Coggia's comet, suggests nevertheless a last recollection of the great comet of midsummer 1861:

> Enchantment's Perihelion
> Mistaken oft has been
> For the Authentic orbit
> Of its Anterior Sun. [1299]

Although she knew that the planets move on elliptical courses, the modest eccentricity of their orbits would not have given her a striking trope. But she would remember, almost to superstition, the magnificent comet of 1861 sweeping in from the far depths of space on a course to the sun, only to undergo its perihelion passage, within weeks of the destruction of her own hopes, and be carried out into the depths of frigid space once more.[10]

Finally, there is the figure of the summer solstice in four poems of late 1861–65. The best of these is the first, which begins "There came a Day at Summer's full," then describes the ordinariness of that day, "While our two Souls that Solstice passed— / Which maketh all things new" (322). Apparently she wrote the poem in late December 1861, about the time of the winter solstice itself, speaking of a time loved by reindeer, calling it "the Sun's objective," the year's "Finland" (1696). As a symbol she preferred the summer solstice, perhaps because the final parting occurred in summer and she had vivid memories of stifling heat, but surely in good part because only the *summer* solstice could be a tragic turning point. She might write that the lovers had gone beyond the sun's standstill and were transfigured in eternal love, but the very choice of metaphor carried with it the tragic admission that this sun of love was withdrawing southward, and forever. Curiously, Sue Dickinson, who made Algol her symbol of incalculable distance, used the solstice to signify astronomical rarity, saying dryly of her mother-in-law's housekeeping that the parlor rug was changed only at the solstice.[11] Perhaps the poet caught this verbal trick from Sue.

2

To her sister-in-law, Emily Dickinson once sent the lines

Best Witchcraft is Geometry
To a Magician's eye— [1158]

Sue's daughter Martha supposed they were a tribute to her mother's skill in mathematics. Certainly the poet was aware of her sister-in-law's interests and had written long ago to the young Sue teaching in Baltimore that she often fancied her "descending to the schoolroom with a plump Binomial Theorem struggling in your hand which you must dissect and exhibit" (L56). In another early letter to Sue, exaggerating her timidity about attending church alone, Emily smiles at the "geometry" of her circuitous journey: "It would have puzzled Euclid" (L154). She speaks of studying "Algebra, Euclid . . . & reviewing Arithmetic again" to prepare for her admission examinations to the South Hadley seminary (L15). From Mount Holyoke she writes to her brother that she has finished her examinations in Euclid "& without a failure at any time" and compares her relief at having got through four books with his greater relief at having "finished the whole *forever*" (L19). Although her interest could not have been practical and professional, like Sue's, neither could it have been perfunctory or hostile; the scientific language of her poems is drawn overwhelmingly from the twin disciplines of mathematics and astronomy—employed, of course, in her own distinctive way.

It was to be expected that she would frequently add, divide, multiply, and subtract, although it is a curious fact that poets in general avoid the last operation.[12] Of the poets who most influenced her, only Robert Browning subtracts (five times), and not one of them suffers a "sharp Subtraction / From the early Sum" (814). Since it is the one operation involving loss, there would seem to be a temperamental difference. She uses *cipher* three times, as compared with Shakespeare's seven, Wordworth's and Browning's three, and Byron's one, but she alone is a "least Cypherer," who worries about a "Tract ... Set Cypherless—to teach the Eye / The Value of it's Ten" (545). (This poem, " 'Tis One by One—the Father counts," fails by reason of its excess: "peevish Student," "Numerals," "Rule," "Slate and Pencil," "School," "Eternal Rule," and "Urchin's Sum.") She computes, counts, measures, adds up twenty-three sums of various kinds, separates the months like balls to keep their "numbers" from fusing (511), sees the pain-hunched "Figures" of the human clock quiver "out of Decimals / Into Degreeless Noon" (287), remembers poignantly the "Hesitating Fractions" that feared to become a "Whole" (643), finds "Life's sweet calculations" falling coolly on dead ears (735), defines her love for Sue in terms of a good investment that increases by the "minute Per Cents" (1248).

Excited about parting with her beloved friend, she estimates her "prize" in "broken mathematics" and finds it "Vast—in it's fading ratio" (88). On a similar occasion she declares that "Delight is as the Flight— / Or in the Ratio of it," adding, "As the Schools would say—" (257); and another separation from the beloved elicits the anguished cry that every ecstatic instant must be paid for "In keen and quivering ratio" (125). When she declares that love is the "Exponent" of earth, it may be wondered whether she means that love interprets and defines earth or, more grandly, that this is an earth raised to the love power (917). In somber mood, "Mathematics" does not affirm the number of crucifixions (553); and in joyous mood, "mathematics" is equally helpless to define happiness (1668). A poem beginning "Bound—a trouble— / And lives can bear it!" proposed to "Deal with the soul / As with Algebra!" (269). In "Heaven" there will perhaps be "Some new Equation, given—" (301). Some of the problems set by life she will "keep—to solve / Till Algebra is easier— / Or simpler proved—above" (600).

When Emerson recommended algebraic symbolism to the beginning poet, he did not allow for the fact that it is less picturable than Euclid. Emily did what she could with algebra but turned early and more often to geometry. Snakes bisect the brake, hurricanes the human heart; death is the "Bisecting Messenger" of Paradise, and the bride of death is borne away in a "bisected Coach" (11, 928, 1411, 1445). A friend takes "Cobweb attitudes" on a "plane of Gauze!" (105). The coffin, oddly, is a "diminished Plane" (943). The floor of her prison, compared with the pools of boyhood memory, is "a Demurer Circuit—/A Geometric Joy—" (652). Any "Conjecture" regarding life after death is at best an "oblique Belief" (1221). Her pet word, "Circumference," has almost as many varieties of meaning as it has contexts, but in general it appears to mean the sphere of the individual consciousness, also the ecstatic enlargement of this consciousness, also the new or expanded domain, or at times, and almost in the sense of Emerson, the terminus or dread boundary between human and divine.[13] In her fourth letter to Higginson, who had wounded her by polite disparagement of her poetry, she wrote defiantly that she could not stop for his smiling: "My Business is Circumference—" (L268). Possibly she meant that her business was to expand, to give herself up to the *furor poeticus* of that remarkable year. More soberly she may have been saying, "I am striving to unify my life and my poetry." Clearly she was aware that her safety, indeed her sanity, depended on setting bounds to these explosive forces and bringing them under control.

Toward her several "spheres" she appears neutral or even cool. She describes an outward ripening, like that of a peach, "whose forces Spheric wind" (332), and a very similar poem says the smaller lives "hurry to a sphere/And show and end—" (1067). Elsewhere she speaks of the planets as "docile spheres" (128), of the music of "the Spheres" heard on a beautiful day (157), of the grass as a "Sphere of simple Green" (333). Somewhat more picturesque is the geometric figure in the "dry Wine" poem, where she recalls that she was

> Still at the Egg-life—
> Chafing the Shell—
> When you troubled the Ellipse— [728]

"Ellipse" is the appropriate figure, and yet she may also have remembered an article in the April 1860 *Atlantic Monthly,* "The Laws of Beauty," which exalts the ellipse as the most beautiful of geometric forms.

An 1864 poem, so clotted with scientific metaphors as to be almost unreadable, dares one to "Banish Air from Air" or to "Divide Light" or "Odors," affirming that they will reunite like "Cubes in a Drop" or "Pellets of Shape"—presumably an allusion to molecular attraction or crystalline structure, the whole of this confused figure being doubtless intended to describe the properties of a love indivisible and indestructible. And when this love is forced, as by a flame, it only changes into a more active and powerful form: "with a Blonde push/Over your impotence," it flashes into "Steam" (854).

A late poem, which once more appears to contrast the ordinary miracles of physical nature with the transcendent wonder of human love, says it will be easy to find the "Cube of the Rainbow," but the "Arc of a Lover's Conjecture" is beyond discovery (1484). A quite human rainbow appears several times in the work of her major period. An 1861 poem stresses the transiency of "that Bent Stripe" on her "childish Firmament," at a time when she supposed "Rainbows" were common, empty skies the exception (257). Distance is the theme of an 1862 poem; she is no nearer to her lover than children are to the "Rainbow's scarf" (496). "Each Life Converges to some Centre," begins another poem; but to reach that "Centre," that "Goal," that "Brittle Heaven," is as hopeless as to touch a "Rainbow's Raiment" (680). The glories of summer cannot cheat her of her suffering any more than "Rainbows" held before a dying child can hide the "Sepulchre" (574). The grave itself yawns toward her in the form of an arc—"this low Arch of Flesh" through which she must pass into death (616). In short, the arclike curvature of the rainbow love, or beloved, or grave (in the universe of her symbols they are identical) is more significant than beautiful color, remoteness, and transiency; and geometric form associates that rainbow with her symbolic crescent and even her symbolic angle.

Commonly, Emily Dickinson used "crescent" to mean incomplete, young, ungrown; and consciously she may not have intended anything else. In praise of her dead nephew, she insisted that he was no "crescent [but] travelled from the Full—" (L868). According to one of her so-called Master letters, she is older, but the love remains the same, as do the "moon and the crescent" (233). Presumably the poet is the incomplete one, the "crescent," and the beloved friend is the full moon. However, the beloved may undergo phases as well. "When Moon's at full—'Tis Thou—I say—," reads a poem that addresses the beloved as "Ishmael" (an outcast like herself, according to letter 304), and it continues: "When crescent—Thou are worn —I note— / But—there—the Golden Same—" (504). In a disc poem already mentioned, Emily puts this moon through its phases: "I make His Crescent fill or lack" (909). Poem 508, one of her "marriage" poems, uses both arc and crescent to signify her incomplete or maiden phase:

Called to my Full—The Crescent dropped—
Existence's whole Arc, filled up,
With one small Diadem.[14]

A poem beginning "A Bee his Burnished Carriage / Drove boldly to a Rose" describes the rose as withholding "not a Crescent / To his Cupidity" and speaks of their "Moment Consummated" and of the flower's "Rapture" of "Humility" (1339). The imagery is so blatantly sexual that she could only have intended a real bee and a real flower and a quite botanical corolla, but the latent meaning of her crescent is now clear.

Symbolically, the richest of her geometrical figures is the angle. Sometimes it appears to mean a sharp and irreversible turn, as in the poem about the Civil War soldier who misses his dead mother, "Till Bullets clipt an Angle / And He passed quickly round" (596). Speaking of another death, very likely her own, she says that the person who now tries to find her (by analogy with other poems, most probably the too-late-repentant beloved) "must pass the Crystal Angle / That obscure Her face—" (649). Again, "Experience is the Angled Road" that leads precisely opposite to the direction the mind supposed it was taking, thus paradoxically forcing the mind to choose its "Preappointed Pain" (910).

The earliest of these angle poems, and on the surface the most literal, is one that focuses upon "That Angle in the floor" where the beloved turned one way and she the other and all their "Sinew tore" (293). In a poem of the following year, "We see—Comparatively—," she at first appears to be talking philosophically, even generally, about changing attitudes resulting from the growth of experience, but the emotionalism, indeed, the hot anger, of the two final stanzas leaves little doubt that she is writing out of a bitter personal disappointment. She remembers a "Thing" which once towered so high that "We" were unable to grasp its "segment" or "Angle," but in the light of today's "finer Verdict" our Cordilleras and our Apennines have become mere knolls and furrows (534). The use of angle as a variant for segment is indicative of the close symbolic relationship between her angle and the arc-crescent group described earlier. Every time she wakes, according to poem 375, the "Angle of a Landscape," which accosts her through "an ample Crack," proves to be a slanting "Bough of Apples," a chimney, a hill, and occasionally a "Vane's Forefinger," all these curious items in a landscape suggesting some kind of relationship with the "Angle" in which their "Sinew tore." Indeed all these angle poems, including, it would seem, the one about the young soldier who rejoins his dead mother by way of a bullet-clipped "Angle," appear to be strongly if unconsciously eroticized, as has been already observed in chapter 2.

3

Editors and biographers have somewhat hastily assumed that Emily Dickinson was ignorant of the great scientific movements of her day, that her physical seclusion was an intellectual seclusion as well. But if she did not know about Darwinian evolution, and within a few months of the publication of *On the Origin of Species,* then she must have closed her eyes resolutely to three excellent and favorable articles by Asa Gray in the 1860 *Atlantic Monthly.* She rarely alluded to her reading; very early, she described such allusions as pedantic (L23). When she did speak of some current idea, it was likely to be in a riddling and humorous fashion that betrayed little of her thought. Commenting on her failure to secure a few moments of privacy with Mrs. Holland, she abruptly observed to that friend, "Why the Thief ingredient accompanies all Sweetness Darwin does not tell us" (L359). Here Darwin is the type of the great scientist, but implicit in her thought must be the feeling that Darwinian evolution, by undermining the security of belief, has intensified the sweetness of a life "stolen" from the relentless processes of time. To a man like Otis P. Lord, she could indicate more frankly, with greater assurance of being understood and accepted, the effect that Darwin's theories had had on her own religious faith. After a laugh at the neighbor who thought it shocking of Benjamin Butler to "liken himself to his Redeemer," she added trenchantly, "but we thought Darwin had thrown 'the Redeemer' away" (L750).

Although contributions to early issues of the *Atlantic* were published anonymously, Samuel Bowles's *Springfield Republican* often identified the contributors, and Emily Dickinson may have known that the author of the Darwin articles was America's great pioneer botanist, a recommendation in itself. Asa Gray had quite recently attracted national attention with a major scientific breakthrough of his own. His memoir on the botany of Japan and its relationship to that of North America, which prepared him to understand and accept the far-reaching implications of Darwinian theory, appeared in April 1859. Some three and a half years later, T. W. Higginson, an enthusiastic amateur of botany, paid this tribute to Gray's memoir: "Nothing in the demonstrations of Geology seems grander than the light lately thrown by Professor Gray, from the analogies between the flora of Japan and of North America, upon the successive periods of heat which led the wandering flowers along the Arctic lands, and of cold which isolated them once more." [15] Curiously, Emily Dickinson had written a poem in 1860, at a time much closer to the date of Gray's memoir, which begins

As if some little Arctic flower
Upon the polar hem—
Went wandering down the Latitudes [180]

There is no evidence that Higginson ever saw this poem, but the coincidence of language does suggest some common source, perhaps a newspaper or magazine comment on Gray's work. If she knew and used such a comment, this little poem, not otherwise notable, would be another illustration of her practice of analogizing from important developments of her time and thus conferring upon a personal and limited event the grandeur of great intellectual discoveries and stirring historic occasions, very much as she once wrote that she would give up searching for her beloved traitor when Lady Franklin gave up the "Arctic race" (851). Ironically, her poem was written during the last hours of her greatest personal happiness, when

the "little Arctic flower" could still rejoice wonderingly at having blun-
dered into a southern Eden, not dreaming that in a short while the Arctic
cold would envelop her once more.

Botany was the one science in which Emily Dickinson had some com-
petence. As an eleven-year-old girl she writes of studying "Botany" and
notes that her "Plants grow beautifully"; three years later she is again
studying botany and alludes to the herbaria that she and the other girls
are making (letters 3, 6). Botany was one of the subjects studied at Mount
Holyoke, the textbook during her residence being Alphonse Wood's *Class-
Book of Botany*. Her interest may have been further stimulated by the
presence of a distinguished scientist at Amherst College, its president
during several difficult years, Edward Hitchcock, who began as a chemistry teacher, achieved international distinction as a geologist, and to these
interests added the study of botany. Long after his death the poet wrote to
her friend Higginson: "When Flowers annually died and I was a child,
I used to read Dr Hitchcock's Book on the Flowers of North America,"
adding that this comforted her for their absence (L488).

Her intimate knowledge of botany sometimes betrayed her into the
pedantry she was otherwise scrupulous to avoid. A weak early poem refers
rather pretentiously to "Bartsia," "Leontodon," and "Epigea" (142). A
much later poem, describing a sunset in terms of a flower, elaborates the
metaphor far too self-consciously to be successful: Sunset is "Firmamental
Lilac" on the hill, the final plant and "Flower of Occident" bequeathed
by the sun, the West being its "Corolla," the earth its "Calyx," the stars
the "burnished Seeds" of its "Capsules," the whole a "Flora unimpeach-
able" to the "Analysis" of time and unavailable to the "synthesis," the
"research," the "theses" of the "Scientist of Faith" (1241). Poem 339 makes
a far more satisfying use of botanical figures. Love, even a frustrated love,
was a surer inspiration than natural history. Frequently the beloved, or
love itself, appears as the magnificent cultivated rose. In poem 978 love
blooms, but when the poet fails to seize her flower, the "Species" disappears. She herself is the "Brave Black Berry" which struggles to live
despite a thorn in its side (554), and elsewhere she is the "Berry—of a
Mountain Bush" transplanted uncomfortably to the public road (579). She
can momentarily assume the arrogance of power and "strut" upon her
"stem" (290), or she can be the apple whose "stem" the Maker shifts for
a critical look at the "Core" (483). In happier times she, or rather her
hope, was "Bud" stepping gaily from her "Stem" like some tulip or
hyacinth, unaware that a "Worm" was already boring at her "brave"
root (913).

Unlike some of her fellow poets, she is able to distinguish corolla from
calyx and does not confuse stamens with pistils. She notes correctly though
disapprovingly that the botanist with his glass computes the stamens in

order to put the flower in a "Class" (70). Besides naming a considerable number of specific flowers and some trees, her poetry has many buds, pods, capsules, stems, stalks, petals, tubes, berries, three calyxes and three bulbs, two corollas, and one sepal. Some of these botanical names appear to be unique to her poetry, and the whole conception of using such terms, so obviously deliberated and executed, is without parallel in the work of poets who influenced her. Unlike them too, she enjoys the occasional half-playful use of such "school" terms as *entomology, ornithology, orthography, philology, physiognomy,* and *topography.* In a poem speculating on the translation of Enoch, she observes, surely in irony, that the words "God took him" are "Philology" (1342). The soul can fly farther on "Pinions of Disdain" than on "any feather specified in Ornithology" (1431). The sad fate of the two butterflies (herself and the erstwhile beloved) can be seen half-ironically, in a version of about 1877 or 1878, as a "monition to entomology" (533). But these are all late and tend to be comments rather than developed poems.

4

Apparently the young girl enjoyed the chemical experiments she performed at Mount Holyoke. To her brother Austin she wrote that her studies included "Chemistry, Physiology & quarter course in Algebra" (L19). Shortly afterward she told a friend that she was "now studying 'Silliman's Chemistry' & Cutler's Physiology, in both of which I am much interested" (L20), and to Austin she wrote that his welcome letter found her "all engrossed in the history of Sulphuric Acid!" (L22). That particular interest reappeared years later in the lines "Power exists in sulphurets [var., Charcoal]—/ Before it exists in Fire" (952).[16] This metaphor for the explosive manifestation of latent power derives from gunpowder, of which two principal constituents, as her chemistry taught her, are sulfur and charcoal; and the poem amplifies the chemical analogy by the use of such words as "Fuse," "ignition," "Spark," "dormant," and "Elements."

In his *Elements of Chemistry,* Benjamin Silliman describes a number of fairly simple experiments to produce the "beautiful violet vapor," the "splendid violet," of the newly discovered iodine. Of one such operation he writes that "iodine vapor, mingling its fine violet with the white flame of the phosphorus, forms a beautiful experiment."[17] This note of aesthetic appreciation is incessant in his work and was doubtless appealing to a future poet. Emily adopted *iodine* as one of her color words in four poems of 1863–64, and although *this* experiment was not an unqualified success (the common association is with the muddy-red tincture of iodine, not with her beautiful violet vapor), it is an illustration of her incessant search for usable vocabulary. Silliman's text, it may be noted, abounds in words like *acrid, adhesion, analysis, apparatus, ascertain, cohere, condense, corrode, criterion, dilute, diminution, experiment, exude, facilitate, fuse, hypothesis, ignition, process, pungent, pyrites, requisite, saturate, superficies,* and many another that duly reappear in her poetry.

To her list of elements, she added phosphorus as a symbol for light, or warmth, and hence for love. The element mercury receives one mention, for the sun is depicted as sulking "in mercury" (1693). To describe the transformation effected by love, she alludes to the identity of "Carbon in the Coal" and "Carbon in the Gem" (356), information she found in the pages of Silliman. In "Ashes denote that Fire was" (1063), the diamond-love apparently changes back to carbon, or rather, since the process is now chemical instead of physical, it burns to ashes in the heat of its own "Fire"—"consolidates" into "Carbonates" that only the "Chemist" can now identify.

Like carbon and iodine, the element oxygen is unique to her poetry, and like phosphorus it is uniquely associated with love. Love is oxygen because it is that element without which one cannot live. To love is to be alive, to breathe; without love, "removed from Air," she is dead and her "Lungs are stirless," no matter how cunningly she may "simulate the Breath" (272). In summer 1860, while she could still believe that her passion was returned, she wrote of escaping with the beloved from "Desert" and "thirst" into the "Tamarind wood," where "Leopard [herself] breathes— at last!" (209). According to a poem of the next year, the awesome splendor of nature might enable one to live without human love, to disdain "Oxygen" (290); but in the same packet is another poem, obviously written at about the same time, that fiercely enjoins suicide on the laboring lungs:

If your Soul seesaw—
Lift the Flesh door—
The Poltroon wants Oxygen— [292]

Late in life she comments on the "Indebtedness to Oxygen" enjoyed by the "Happy," among whom she does not include herself. Her own fate has been to receive a "Bolt" of "Lightning," a passion of suffering, which she would nevertheless not exchange for an entire life of mere contentment (1581).[18] Two other poems make at least slight drafts upon her school chemistry. Comparing the ocean of her present grief with the drops of former woes, she writes that "They prove One Chemistry—" (660). Elsewhere, belief in the indestructibility of matter, the "Chemical conviction" that the very "Faces of the Atoms" will be preserved, gives her the desperate hope that she will once more see those "Finished Creatures" she has loved (954).

5

Despite a manifest interest in scientific discovery and speculation, Emily Dickinson might not have adopted its vocabulary without the influence of Emerson. One need only turn to his prose works to see where she found a large part of her scientific vocabulary, together with the encouragement to use it.[19] Even a hasty and by no means comprehensive count of the scientific and mathematical terms shared between her poetry and Emerson's chief prose works produces some two hundred examples, including such key words, frequently repeated, as *algebra, analysis, astronomy, chemistry, circumference, classify, electricity, equation, formula, geometry, hypothesis, intrinsic, logarithm, mathematics, microscope, science, solstice, stability, synthesis,* and *telescope.* This language functioned, of course, as reminder and authorization; she had already met the words in the science books of her school years, but it was Emerson who told her that they were the stuff of poetry.

With this important exception, her scientific vocabulary owed little to American literary example. Such poets as Bryant, Poe, and Longfellow had almost nothing that she could, in Emerson's phrase, grind into paint; apparently they did not consider scientific or technical vocabulary suitable for poetry. As would be expected, the older English poets also had no great amount of this special language to offer her, although she may have remembered that "God said, Let Newton be! and all was Light." Newton's prism and the law of gravitation duly entered her verse, and she may have been imitating Pope or James Thomson—or indeed Wordsworth—in using the names of such distinguished scientists as Herschel or Leverrier. There is enough resemblance to the language of Wordsworth to suggest that she read him with some attentiveness. Among the younger romantic poets, Keats and Shelley apparently gave her nothing for science; but Byron's influence is too pervasive to be missed, both in his own work, which she clearly knew well, and by reflection in the work of his disciple Elizabeth Browning.[20] The most detailed resemblance is to Robert Browning, who used a majority of Emily Dickinson's scientific words and used them far more often. Neither he nor his wife, however, had that interest in astronomy or in mathematics that Emily shared with Emerson (and of course with her admired sister-in-law). Again, much of this special vocabulary entered Robert Browning's work too late to have much influence on her. Tennyson had surprisingly little to offer in a large body of work, despite his avowed interest in science. Emerson remains the most important influence and a prime source of this particular vocabulary.

But Emily Dickinson does not sound like an Emerson or a Robert Browning. When every allowance has been made for influence and specific borrowings, there remains a perplexed sense of the difference, the uniqueness, in her employment of this vocabulary. The strong interest in science reflected by her language had consequences of greater importance to the intellect of her poetry than finding an ingenious analogy or a witty turn of speech. In playful mood she might wonder whether the pine at her window was "a 'Fellow / Of the Royal' Infinity" (797), or she might mimic the voice of a high school physiology teacher:

A science—so the Savans say,
"Comparative Anatomy"—
By which a single bone— [100]

There is no lightness, however, in a poem beginning "Crumbling is not an instant's Act," which makes of her slow, disastrous retreat from life a quasiscientific generalization, "Slipping—is Crash's law" (997). And when she calls prayer the "little implement" through which men endeavor to reach an absent God and concludes that "This sums the Apparatus / Comprised in Prayer" (437), the coolly ironic tone owes a considerable debt to the language of the laboratory. This language reappears in the "scrupulous exactness" with which she performs actions to keep her "Senses on" (443), and in the several curious uses of the word *experiment,* as if life itself were a laboratory in which all experience, and especially life's concluding act, must be a trial, a test. "Experiment escorts us last"—that is, the final, the "most profound experiment," "Death's Experiment," which may possibly be "Reversed—in Victory" (1770, 822, 550). Elsewhere, the stabbing wound she has received from the beloved friend is the "Scarlet Experiment" or test of her devotion, just as the remembered beginning of love was her "tenderer Experiment" toward humankind (861, 902). In happier mood, the rebirth of spring becomes a "whole Experiment of Green" (1333).

Repeatedly, she uses technical language to mechanize life. A woman has died, and the mourners have "placed the Hair" and drawn the dead woman's head erect; "then an awful leisure was / Belief to regulate—" (1100). Although she appears to mean an awful leisure for belief to order and reduce to rule, the wording is sufficiently ambiguous to allow also for a leisure in which to reassemble the shattered illusion of belief; in either case the action is mechanical. According to poem 451, the "Central Mood" of human character is the "unvarying Axis / That regulates the Wheel" of the outer self, a wheel that has "Spokes" and kicks up dust. In other poems it is a clockwork self that she describes. Behind the carefully composed clockface of poem 1054, the brain's mechanism is skillfully, anxiously manipulating the pointers. In a better-known poem the clock-poet simply stops, her "Dial life" at an end, nor can the most skillful Geneva craftsman restart the snowy "Pendulum," the bowing puppet, that now dangles stirless (287). According to still another poem, "Existence—some way back— /

Stopped—struck—my ticking—through—" (443). In a moment of agony she pushes "Mechanic feet" (761), or her "Feet, mechanical, go round" (341). The grave is marked by a "mechanic stone" (1396). The window of a death house opens "Abrupt—mechanically," and the mattress is ejected on which "it died," the dead person being now less human than the self-opening window (389). The corpse is an "Agate" unjointable—"Beyond machinery" (1135). Even in optimistic mood this imagery does not make for comfort. Hope is a "strange invention" with a "unique momentum," patented by the heart and operated, it would seem, electrically; it is a perpetual motion machine in "unremitting action," but it never wears out (1392). Elsewhere, one's sanity is protected by the "esoteric belt" of a "revolving reason," a wheel with "cogs" (1717). A four-line poem that appears to reflect on last things begins by speaking of religion and ends

When Cogs—stop—that's Circumference—
The Ultimate—of Wheels [633]

It has been suggested that this "Circumference" marks the boundary between human and divine, or between life and death, but whatever the interpretation, the impression it leaves is an uneasy one.

Emerson declared that he knew at once, "through the poverty or the splendor of his speech," how much any speaker had lived.[21] It is more intimately and insidiously, however, that vocabulary betrays. The young girl who once observed that she must "recite as precise as the laws of the Medes and Persians" or lose her character (L7) grew up to be the woman who must be "precise" or "Precisely" or even "preciser" a total of nineteen times in no very large body of work. Here was a positive need of precision, accuracy, "exactness," "proof," "certainty" (a word repeated twelve times), "evidence"—"This timid life of Evidence / Keeps pleading—'I dont know'" (696).[22]

Still half-enclosed in the body of a decaying faith, she was lured by the promise of a methodology. If one performed an "experiment" and were "accurate" and "precise" and "punctual," there would be "certainty" and "proof"—in lesser things. What of the larger? "'Faith' is a fine invention," she wrote to her friend Samuel Bowles, "When Gentlemen can see— / But Microscopes are prudent / In an Emergency" (185). To an unnamed friend she wrote bitterly that "Thomas' faith in Anatomy, was stronger than his faith in faith" (L233), and though she is here upbraiding her friend for a want of fidelity, her mind dwelt enviously on the superior opportunities of Thomas. One of her stranger performances—it can be traced in her correspondence following the death of any friend or even the friend of a friend—was a quasiscientific effort to gather deathbed evidence of posthumous survival. To the end of her days she remained on the horns of her dilemma, without belief but never able to accept her unbelief. Science worked marvels in this world but had nothing to say

about the next; faith, broken-backed and dying, still made the great promises. She would call its promised Heaven

Untenable to Logic—
But possibly the one— [1293]

This evidence of a strong intellectual, if untrained, interest in science
has importance for biography, but it should not be forgotten that her chief
poetic concern with science was to pillage its vocabulary. Naturally the
failures are more numerous than the triumphs, although even the failures
are rarely banal. At times certain unacknowledged, even unconscious, needs
might appropriate suitable images and use them for purposes that she
herself was far from understanding; still, she knew on the whole surprisingly well what she wanted language to do for her. Unlike Mrs.
Browning, who was not a poet but a moralist and a vendor of ideas,
Emily Dickinson was a deliberate, skillful artist employing words. She
complained that her experience had been a "dry Wine," but dryness was
what she sought. At its best, the wit, tension, and irony, the intellectual
toughness of this vocabulary, saved her poetry from the saccharine simple-
ness of most contemporary verse. The poet who drank logarithm escaped
drowning in sugar syrup.

FIVE EMILY DICKINSON'S PALETTE

Writing to Emily Dickinson in late December 1873, Thomas Wentworth Higginson made a pointed allusion to one of his Christmas presents, a watercolor sketch of field lilies in yellow and scarlet. These were not her favorite colors, he said, and perhaps not his own favorite either, but he thought they both should try to cultivate "these ruddy hues of life." Did she remember Julia Ward Howe's poem "I stake my life upon the red"? [1]

A few weeks earlier, during a lecture trip to Amherst, he had called briefly at the Dickinson house and had received an impression of abnormality so strong as to give him irritated concern. He now recommended a tonic of color with peculiar confidence in its quasimagic effect upon emotional and physical health. That he knew nothing about her real tastes and attitudes is clear from Table 3, which reveals as the most striking characteristic of her color system this very insistence upon red and its different shades, including purple, that she sometimes identified with blood. The way to know her would have been to read her poetry, but her supposed critic saw very few of her poems after the initial outpouring of 1862, often no more than a pair of lines or a stanza that gave little indication of her absorbing interest in color. Yet the symbolic and emotional values she attached to any particular hue, and indeed her whole use of color, are aspects of her work that invite attention.

Even a casual reading of her work makes a kaleidoscopic impression on the mind of the reader. Letters as well as poems give evidence of a marked responsiveness to color and of a synesthesia, perhaps playful, that led the poet to talk of hearing or tasting color. After the passing of a circus, she remarked that she had "tasted life" and could still "feel the red" in her mind although the drums were "out" (L318). Or she might say that the world, "usually so red," took on a "russet tinge" when her sister was unwell (L207). Days were "Topaz" (L212), hills took off "purple frocks" (L228), the sky put on "new Red Gowns—and a Purple Bonnet" (L272). In her poems she wrote that the "Tint" she could not take, the "Color too remote," was always the best (627), and that "Blaze" could never be adequately represented by "Cochineal" or noon by "Mazarin" (581). She spoke of artists, tint, easel (110), of paints, brush, picture, canvas (451), of autumn's pencil (163), of famous painters like Domenichino, Titian, Guido, or Van Dyck (chosen for their well-sounding names, it would seem, since all were treated as frustrated landscape artists). God too is an artist who produced, "drew," the poet (155). Late in life she acknowledged the gift of a painting with the remark, "To the Bugle every color is Red" (L985).

One of the marks of romantic style was a deliberate cultivation of color, as Higginson's letter reminds us, and romantic theorists devoted chapters of mystic speculation to its influence on the soul. A belated romantic herself, Emily Dickinson knew that a poet handled color words as a painter handled colors, and when she decided to become a poet she set about acquiring a serviceable selection of color words as one more element in the vocabulary appropriate to her craft.

Scarcely a dozen examples can be found in the twenty-eight letters surviving between her childhood and her twentieth year, and half of these occur in stereotyped expressions from which the sense of color has all but vanished—golden opportunity, silver cord, golden bowl, golden harps, or golden chain of friends. But of course the list appears scanty only in comparison with later years and is doubtless normal for the intelligent, prose-centered adolescent that Emily Dickinson then was. No scrap of poetry survived from these years, and no friend remembered any poems or any interest in poetry.

In January 1850 the sun flew in splendor and glory out of its purple nest, and a young poet was born (L31). The same letter had other, less striking evidence (little snakes are *green,* the friend wears a quiet *black* gown) that the new poet was striving to envisage a universe of color. Not scientifically or naturalistically, however; despite a very real interest in science as a source of metaphor, the poet was so little the close observer that she would write, "Nature rarer uses Yellow / Than another Hue" (1045). What she was trying to do, and for the first time, was to see her world in the emotional tone of its colors. It is a way of seeing that has nothing to do with noble-metal stereotypes or with simple color identifiers.

Shortly after January 1850, she wrote her first surviving poem and betrayed a mysterious excitement connected with some secret ambition. During the next several years, the evidence multiplied that she was striving to become a poet, and her vocabulary became more and more colorful. In fall 1851 she described an unusual display of northern lights—a beautiful crimson sky and rays of gold-pink shooting out of a sunlike center—and other phrases demonstrated her lively new delight in verbal splashes of color. There were rustling brown leaves, rosy and golden peaches, and her brother's "birthright of purple grapes." Recurring to the purple of the grapes, the poet fancied that not even kingly robes were "a tint more royal" (L53). A few days later she was writing to him of his favorite brown bread, of green jackets, crimson leaves, blue hills, and earth's silver hairs (L58). Still more literary was a reference to the "blue mantillas" of the hills (L63).

The color notation was liveliest in 1851, 1852, and spring 1853, when the poet presumably worked hardest at her new craft; it then abated somewhat more rapidly than the number of her letters. No letters at all have survived from spring 1856 to spring 1858, and probably few were written. Years later, the poet would allude to a period of depression in her middle twenties when she found herself unable to write poetry, and the decline in letters and the more precipitate decline in color words support her statement.

When she broke silence again, about mid-1858, she at first seemed little changed from the girl of the early 1850s. The poems in her 1858 handwriting have the look of poems written in earlier years; but the color distribution of 1859 and afterward differs significantly from that of 1850–56. The reds were of special importance in her 1858 color vocabulary, and they remained high in 1859 and afterward. The strong reemergence of blue and purple in 1859 was also significant, for these colors were associated in her mind with freedom, status, successful love, and happiness. In the same period, the blacks and cool colors declined. These colors are heavily weighted emotionally, and their appearance or nonappearance is significant.

The most important development is her emergence from the profound discouragement of her middle twenties. Lyric poets are so rarely made at twenty-eight, the odds against her were all but overwhelming. Almost certainly the discovery of a new poet model inspired her to resume the writing of poetry about mid-1858. In the early 1860s she would write idolatrous poems to Elizabeth Browning, whom she would revere all her life. Perhaps she had some acquaintance with Mrs. Browning's earlier work, but it was the reading of *Aurora Leigh* that proved decisive. If Aurora Leigh could become a great poet and establish the worth of woman as artist, why not Emily Dickinson? The most important discovery for the color system was the symbolic possibilities of the heavenly city of Revelation as exploited by Mrs. Browning. In the next several years Mrs. Browning's disciple used most of the heavenly jewels as color words. Although her copy of *Aurora Leigh* is dated 1859, the several references to Revelation in letters of late 1858 suggest that she was then reading a borrowed copy, probably Sue Dickinson's. After mid-1858, letters and poems alike were studded with such borrowings or with allusions to the promises of Revelation.

Among her important new color words in 1859 were four borrowed from the jeweled foundations of the New Jerusalem—*jasper, emerald, topaz,* and *amethyst.* Others making a first appearance were *azure, amber, cochineal, damask, Tyrian* as a synonym for *purple,* and *alban* and *snow* as synonyms for *white.* Except for *cochineal* and *alban,* she would have found all these color words in *Aurora Leigh* or in Revelation, Robert Browning's *Men and Women,* and the poems of Keats, to which Mrs. Browning's poem strongly directed her. In 1862 she would tell Higginson that Keats, Revelation, and the two Brownings were her poets, but of course she knew thoroughly the early poems of Emerson and the work of Shakespeare, Pope, and Milton, as also the prose of Ruskin, where she would have found virtually all her color words.

In 1860 she borrowed *sapphire* and *beryl* from the New Jerusalem and added *ruby, russet, ebon,* and *dun.* In 1861 the words *rouge, daffodil,* and *bronze* made their unique appearance. In 1862 she tried out such professional artist's colors as *mazarine* and *gamboge* and in an 1864 poem the color *umber. Garnet, coral, Parian, argent, tawny,* and *livid* are among the 1862 additions. Perhaps in the autumn of that year she experimented with *blood* as a color word, for she wrote that the "hue" of autumn "is Blood" (656), and about the same time she described a sunset of "solid Blood" (658). *Phosphor* or *phosphorus,* a possible borrowing from Keats's *Lamia,* is doubtfully a color word. In an 1862 poem it is associated with fire (422) and in a poem of the next year with the color red (689), but it may mean, as in Keats, a light rather than a color, to which Emily has clearly added the notion of heat. The 1863 innovations were a *hazel* to describe her eyes, a rather startling *iodine* of a rich violet shade, and a *blonde* that became one of her death colors. *Iodine* figured in four poems of the 1863–64 period, then vanished. *Blonde,* which had the same frequency in 1863–64, reappeared twenty years later in a new poem or perhaps in an old poem copied into 1884 handwriting (1624).

As shown by the number of lines per year in the color table, she reached the peak of her production in 1862. The next two years, though high in comparison with any year other than 1862, witness a marked decline, and in 1865 and 1866 the drop is abrupt, with the color words declining still more precipitately. No color words appeared at all in the few 1867–68 poems, and the letters of those years were scanty and equally colorless. It was clearly a period of lessened vitality reminiscent of a similar period ten years earlier. The evidence suggests that from this depression she never really emerged.

More important than statistics of incidence are the uses to which she put her colors, the meanings she attached to them. About half are used, more or less naturalistically, to describe sunrises, sunsets, flowers, birds, the coming of spring, a summer's day, or the like. Purple ships toss on daffodil seas (265); sunset washes the banks of a yellow sea, and purple ships nightly strew opal bales over the landing (266). The morning sky

Table 3. Color Incidence in Dickinson's Work

| | Letters | | Poems | | | | | | | | | | | | |
| | 1850–86 | | 1850–58 | | 1859 | | 1860 | | 1861 | | 1862 | | 1863 | | 1864 | |
	(%)	(no.)	(%)	(no.)	(%)	(no.)	(%)	(no.)	(%)	(no.)	(%)	(no.)	(%)	(no.)	(%)	(no.)
Red	12.2	18	38.5	10	21.1	12	24.3	9	16.7	8	24.5	38	11.1	7	26.5	9
Yellow	20.3	30	11.5	3	15.8	9	5.4	2	22.9	11	22.6	35	25.4	16	17.6	6
Green	14.9	22	23.1	6	7.0	4	5.4	2	4.2	2	7.7	12	4.8	3	2.9	1
Blue	15.5	23	0.0	0	10.5	6	18.9	7	4.2	2	7.7	12	12.7	8	2.9	1
Purple	2.7	4	7.7	2	22.8	13	13.5	5	22.9	11	7.1	11	17.5	11	8.8	3
Brown	6.8	10	11.5	3	1.8	1	10.8	4	2.1	1	5.2	8	1.6	1	8.8	3
Black	9.5	14	0.0	0	3.5	2	8.1	3	4.2	2	3.2	5	3.2	2	5.9	2
Gray-white	18.2	27	3.8	1	17.5	10	13.5	5	18.7	9	20.0	31	23.8	15	26.5	9
Other	0.0	0	3.8	1	0.0	0	0.0	0	4.2	2	1.9	3	0.0	0	0.0	0
Total color words			26		57		37		48		155		63		34	
Total lines			825		1151		825		1283		5534		1704		1688	
Color words per line			0.0315		0.0495		0.0448		0.0374		0.0280		0.0370		0.0201	

Table 3 *continued*

	1865 (%)	(no.)	1866 (%)	(no.)	1867–68 (%)	(no.)	1869–75 (%)	(no.)	1876–77 (%)	(no.)	1878–86 (%)	(no.)	No Date (%)	(no.)
Red	25.0	4	0.0	0		0	28.1	9	25.0	8	23.7	9	23.8	5
Yellow	25.0	4	20.0	1		0	21.9	7	12.5	4	5.3	2	33.3	7
Green	6.2	1	0.0	0		0	12.5	4	6.2	2	13.2	5	0.0	0
Blue	6.2	1	0.0	0		0	9.4	3	15.6	5	7.9	3	0.0	0
Purple	18.8	3	40.0	2		0	12.5	4	3.1	1	15.8	6	28.6	6
Brown	0.0	0	20.0	1		0	0.0	0	12.5	4	10.5	4	0.0	0
Black	0.0	0	0.0	0		0	0.0	0	6.2	2	5.3	2	4.8	1
Gray-white	18.8	3	20.0	1		0	15.6	5	12.5	4	18.4	7	9.5	2
Other	0.0	0	0.0	0		0	0.0	0	6.2	2	0.0	0	0.0	0
Total color words		16		5		0		32		32		38		21
Total lines		752		307		281		1928		632		1652		966
Color words per line		0.0213		0.0163		0		0.0166		0.0506		0.0230		0.0217

Table 4. Color Incidence: Dickinson and Others

	Dickinson (%)	Dickinson (no.)	E. Browning (%)	R. Browning (%)	Emerson (%)	Tennyson (%)	Keats (%)	Byron (%)	Milton (%)	Shakespeare Plays (%)	Other (%)
Red	22.7	128	13.1	17.0	19.0	20.5	10.6	13.7	8.7	11.5	20.1
Yellow	19.0	107	9.6	7.7	11.2	16.7	13.2	10.1	17.8	15.8	12.7
Green	7.4	42	12.4	8.0	11.2	9.7	13.3	7.9	13.6	8.0	6.1
Blue	8.5	48	8.1	4.8	12.0	4.4	8.8	15.4	7.6	3.0	3.3
Purple	13.8	78	5.4	2.6	5.8	4.2	3.2	3.5	5.3	1.9	2.0
Brown	5.3	30	4.7	4.2	4.7	2.6	1.7	3.5	4.5	4.9	1.2
Black	3.7	21	7.0	19.3	7.4	6.0	7.2	17.9	16.3	18.9	16.8
Gray-white	18.1	102	39.0	35.5	27.5	35.9	41.2	27.4	25.0	33.5	37.3
Other	1.4	8	0.8	1.0	1.2	0.1	0.7	0.7	1.1	2.5	0.4
Total color words	564		1,178	2,352	258	1,322	885	1,333	264	1,084	244
Total lines	19,528		32,840	97,526	8,550	37,420	14,839	74,275	17,981	112,396	6,010
Color words per line	0.0289		0.0359	0.0241	0.0302	0.0353	0.0596	0.0179	0.0147	0.0096	0.0406

hurries into ruby trousers (204); the feminine day, undressing, pulls off gold garters and a petticoat of purple (716). Apart from such descriptive uses, her colors have a significance that can be most readily examined in the individual color.

2

For many people, including poets, green is the color of hope, new life, or, at worst, unripe judgment or jealousy. Keats called it "exuberant green" and uses it with exuberance. For Emily Dickinson, green is, quite simply, the "color of the grave" (411). Even where the grave is not named, it is usually lurking in the neighborhood of the color word. The maids who keep their "Seraphic May" on a "remoter green," a "mystic green," are dancing and singing in the kingdom of death (24). If children are playing on still another "green," we learn next moment that "New Weary" are sleeping below (99). The green hills of Yorkshire are associated with Charlotte Brontë's death (148); the death of Aunt Norcross is "in the Green" of the year (995). Blasted by lightning or fire, Nature's "Green People" struggle on with fainter vitality even if "they do not die" (314).

Apparent exceptions are three jewel greens taken from the New Jerusalem: beryl, chrysoprase, and crysolite; but though they are correctly associated with objects naturally green, their color is not so conspicuous a value as their poetic names, and all of them together achieve no more than eight or nine mentions in the poetry. Clearly an exception is *emerald,* a recognizable color word in popular use, which appears at least ten times in the poems. For Emily Dickinson emerald becomes almost the "exuberant green" of Keats.[2] An untidy housewife of a sunset litters the east with "Duds of Emerald" (219), the pine bough is an "Emerald Nest" (161), the wild rose is trimmed or belted with emerald (138), and the wings of the triumphant hummingbird are resonant with emerald (1463). But this word too is always ready to slip into the macabre. During the ominous "Green Chill" of a storm, the poet bars the windows and doors against an "Emerald Ghost" (1593); and the "Emerald Seams" of graveyard grass enclose a "narrow spot" (1183). In a late letter the grave becomes the "emerald recess" (L952).

It was not always so. In early 1850 she writes of attractive little green snakes (L31), and a few weeks later of a wholly figurative "green grove," with branches coming and going, which for some reason is pleasurably exciting to her (L35). This letter may reflect the excitement of her first surviving poem, a long, absurd, half-humorously erotic valentine in which everything is in love with something else—sun and moon, bee and flower, night and day, earth and sky, wind and branches. The recipient is urged to climb a tree boldly and, seizing one of the six maidens perched on the tree, carry her off to the "greenwood" and build a bower for her. Among the six maidens in the tree are the poet herself and a new and admired friend, Susan Gilbert, her future sister-in-law. Elsewhere she repeatedly associates the color green with Sue. In a letter of spring 1852 she plans to send her absent friend some of the new green grass growing beside the doorstep where they "used to sit, and have long fancies" (L85). She imagines herself going through the "green lane" to meet Sue (L94) or Sue tripping on the "green grass" toward her (L96). A painful disagreement between them leaves the poet feeling cold as a stone and silent as a block that had once been a "warm and green" tree with birds dancing in its branches (L172). In January 1855 she remembers that their love for each other began "on a step at the front door, and under the Evergreens" (L177). A few weeks later the knowledge that Sue is coming "makes the grass spring" in her heart (L178). In April 1856, shortly before the marriage of Sue and Austin Dickinson, the poet writes less happily to her cousin John Graves, who in April 1854 slept at the Dickinson house to protect her and Sue during the absence of the other Dickinsons. That earlier April, she says, "got to Heaven *first*," where she hopes to meet it again at God's right hand. In a context that reeks of death, she tries to describe the present April but can only stress the transiency of a world of crumbling "evergreens—and *other* crumbling things" (L184).

Reference to Table 3 shows greens in abundance during 1850–56, and analysis indicates that these greens *are* colors of hope and life. Never again would they be so abundant or so hopeful in letters or poems (the total for the letters during the rest of her life is a mere nine greens or 5.6 percent). It is surely no accident that the greens decline so markedly in later years and that the remaining greens so hover about the graveyard. These are signs of waning hope and of frustrated life. Such a frustration, turning the mind inward toward death, may account for one of the two early instances of a graveyard green. Writing to Abiah Root on 31 December 1850, she says she will make a pilgrimage next spring to the grave of her former school principal, "when the grass is growing green" (L39). But she cannot keep her mind on her dead schoolmaster, who seems to be largely a pretext for the plangent melancholy of this letter. There is some evidence that at this time she thought herself neglected by Sue.

The idea of tending a grave returns powerfully in an 1862 poem which begs the beloved, when dying, to send for the poet. Afterward the poet will insure that the "Jealous Grass" grow greenest and fondest over the beloved dead (648). When her own turn comes, she will journey toward her lover dressed in the "Sod Gown" (665).

3

The ambivalence that bisects the poetry of Emily Dickinson is nowhere more obvious yet subtle, more complex yet simple, than in the color word *blue*. It is one of her personal colors, perhaps because it went well with her reddish-brown hair. In an early letter she tries to decide whether to wear her fawn-colored or her blue dress for the important ceremony of welcoming Susan Gilbert home from Baltimore, and she chooses the blue (L96). A few years later she herself is the little "Heart's Ease" or pansy that, like heaven, will never change her blue (176). But blue is also the color of the beloved. In an early letter the poet imagines herself paddling down the "blue Susquehanna" to meet a girl friend (L69); in an 1860 poem she *becomes* the stream and begs to be absorbed into the "Blue Sea" of another woman (162). As early as fall 1851 blue is associated with the hills seen from her bedroom window, acquiring their attributes of distance, mystery, unapproachableness (722). And these hills are feminine, for they wear "blue mantillas" and hence become protective, maternal deities—an identification that seems natural enough but may have been assisted by these lines from *Aurora Leigh:*

> And now I come, my Italy,
> My own hills! are you 'ware of me, my hills,
> How I burn toward you? do you feel to-night
> The urgency and yearning of my soul,
> As sleeping mothers feel the sucking babe
> And smile? [5. 1266–71]

The April 1856 letter to John Graves makes an early association between blue and Italy. The skies that day are "fairer far than Italy" and "in blue eye" look down on her (L184). Of course she knew and loved the Italy of "Ik Marvel" and other writers of her youth, and the association was strengthened by the reading of George Hillard's *Six Months in Italy* and Mrs. Browning's *Aurora Leigh,* whose heroine longs for "the white walls, the blue hills, my Italy" (1. 232).

Whether azure, mazarine, sapphire, or plain blue, the color is most often and naturally associated with the sky. If the poet is happy, blue connotes warmth, freedom, boundlessness, unlimited power. If unhappy, then it is the color of death or of the cold, frightening, yet alluring veil between this world and the next. Writing to Austin on a "glorious afternoon" of March 1852, she says the sky is "blue and warm," and the sunshine makes gold look dim; it is a day made for "Susie" and them (L80). In a letter to Sue, she regrets that she has no "sweet sunshine to gild" her pages, "nor any bay so blue" (L77). A few weeks later she begs Sue to put the enclosed violets under her pillow and dream of "blue-skies, and home" (L94). In late February 1853 Sue has become "all my blue sky" and "sweetest sunshine" straying far from the poet and cruelly refusing to answer letters (L102). A few days later another unhappy letter tries to explain what Sue means in the color system. Sue sketches her pictures for her, and it is "their sweet colorings," not this dim reality, that the poet longs for. When her friend is gone, she cannot feel peaceful; she needs "more vail" between her and the staring world (L107).

The engagement formed between Sue and Austin a few days later necessarily and permanently altered the relationship between the two young women, and Emily Dickinson somewhat unhappily adjusted to the change. Writing to her brother shortly afterward, she describes Sue reading a letter from him and looking up now and then at the "blue, blue home beyond" (L118). These are certainly Emily's words, whether Sue's or not. She writes less often to her brother, explaining that she is afraid of sounding "rather bluer" than he would like (L123). Shortly afterward things still "look blue," and she is not even sure Austin wants to hear from her (L128).

Next summer produced a violent rupture between the two young women. Apparently forgetting that Sue is to be her sister-in-law, the poet tells her their friendship is ended. She adds bitterly that she will "simply murmur *gone*" while her boat goes down and the billow dies "into the boundless blue" (L173). Of course she cannot remain in this absurd posture, and the passage of a few weeks finds her begging for letters and describing a fair day, "very still and blue," and a crimson sunset (L176).

Blue is absent from her 1858 poems but reappears in a rough draft letter to an unknown "Dear Master" (L187). Her friend is ill. He has not written for so long that she thought him dead and seems surprised to learn that he is not. "Each Sabbath on the Sea" (life's troubled main) has her counting the Sabbaths till they "meet on shore" (the life beyond), and she wonders whether the hills there will be as "blue" as reported by sailors. The letter has a curiously unreal, manufactured sound, as if to a ghost or a figment of her imagination; it is unlike anything she ever wrote to anyone else. Her expectation that they will meet again only in death suggests that he is already dead, if he ever existed at all outside her fantasy. The blue hills where they are to meet belong to the region beyond the ocean of life. Blue is a death color here.

The other worldly blue reappears in an 1859 poem (78). Here the "blue havens," a reminiscence of Psalm 107:29–30, lead by the hand the "wandering Sails" that have been gathered in from the storms. An 1860 poem has the outward look of death, but the exile of this poem, "haunted by native lands" and "blue, beloved air," may be secretly dreaming of a quite earthly paradise (167); for the characteristic mood of these 1859–60 "blue" poems is ecstatic happiness, or as one poem puts it, they have an "Azure...Transcending extasy" (122). A letter of about August 1859 to her friend Elizabeth Holland makes this association of happiness with a warm and vibrant blue: "My only sketch, profile of Heaven, is a large, blue sky, bluer and larger than the biggest I have in June" (L185). Indian summer is a wonderful "blue and gold mistake" (130). "Breadths of blue" and "withes of supple blue" appear in another 1859 poem that light-heartedly rephrases the great questions of Job (128). Those "Sapphire Fellows," the skies, are constantly spilling their secret to the hills, who overflow to the orchards (191). An 1861 poem (247), offering to exchange "Straits of Blue" and other valuables for one hour of her beloved's face, is less desperate than other 1861 poems, but of course it may have been written in the happy years 1859–60 and copied into 1861 handwriting.

By 1862 the mood has changed. The blue fuzz of the fly that comes between her dying eye and the lighted window is not ecstatic. Its stumbling uncertainty, which projects the stumbling, failing mind, is the eeriest element in the poem, unless it be the cold blue that portends death (465). Less successful but still interesting is a drowning poem in which the billows toss her up like a ball and make "Blue faces" in her face (598). An 1863 poem remembers icicles prickling "blue and cool" on her soul the day she foresaw the loss of her happiness (768). In still another 1863 poem, love, hope, or happiness is a little brig sunk in a storm. The poet adds that the "Ocean's Heart," that is, the lover's heart, is "too smooth—too Blue" to break for this little boat (723). An 1864 poem describes the heart as measuring in "Blue Monotony" like the sea until it is overtaken by the hurricane of suffering (928).

It is obvious that these blues are unpleasant; they are cold, forbidding, quite unlike the ecstatic *molten* blues of 1859–60. Other blues of the 1862–65 period are not so readily assigned. An 1865 poem observes that nature is prodigal of "Blue" (1045), that is, the blue of skies, seas, flowers, or distant hills. On the other hand, an early 1863 poem, which declares that "Blue is Blue" throughout the world, is not talking about nature's blue at all. Although not precisely an invitation to suicide, the poem seems to urge the other person ("Seek—Friend") to risk flight into the next world for the blue that is unavailable in this (703).

A curious poem of 1862 assigns the color blue to the brain, not in the commonplace sense of melancholy but rather in the sense of the infinity, hence the omnipotence, that is symbolically associated with the blueness of sky and sea. The brain, says the poet, is wider than the sky, deeper than the sea, "just the weight of God" (632). If brain and sea are held "Blue to Blue," the brain will absorb the sea just as a sponge absorbs a bucket of water. The poet is saying, as she has repeatedly said elsewhere in different ways, that her brain has the quality of the infinite. The psychologist calls it omnipotence of thought or magical thinking. It is strictly an infantile or primitive way of feeling about oneself, although by no means absent from the unconscious of the civilized adult. Undoubtedly the curious power of Emily Dickinson's work derives in part from its success-ful embodiment of infantile fantasy.

In an early 1863 poem the moon's blue dimities refer to the blue sky, the moon itself appears to be identified with a beloved lost friend, and the blue may also symbolize an unattainability like that of the sky (737). This is clearly the meaning in an 1862 poem, where the moon has "vaulted" so far above the poet that the latter cannot follow the moon's "superior Road" or its "advantage—Blue" (629). Another 1862 poem begins in the recollec-tion of a childish fear that the blue sky might fall on her, but in the last stanza it is precisely the distance, the unattainability, of this blue that worries her. She *wants* "Heaven" to "tumble—Blue" on her (600). To races that have never seen the light, runs another 1862 poem, can you repre-sent "Blaze" in "Cochineal," "Noon" in "Mazarin" (581)? The poet is questioning the adequacy of all symbols, to be sure, but she is seldom merely didactic. When she generalizes—a habit that grew upon her two years later—she generalizes on her own recent experience. Noon is a fre-quent symbol of love, as are blazes and red of all descriptions. To those who have never known love, can even the intensest blue properly sym-bolize it?

The remaining blues of 1862–63 are clearly associated with the lost beloved. In an 1863 poem, the poet remembers painfully a time when the "Heaven below" obscured the one above with a "ruddier Blue" (756). Her first editor changed the phrase to "ruddier hue," missing entirely the symbolism of the paradisal blue of happiness suffused with the warmth of life's blood. In another 1863 poem, the lovers are united by a noon blue that unwinds from east to west until it covers them both like a warm blue blanket (710). An 1862 poem combines the symbols of paradisal blue and a warm, alluring Italy; the lost beloved, or perhaps the remembered happiness of their love, becomes the longed-for "Blue Peninsula" (405). Obviously these blues have been warmed to the temperature of the molten blues of 1859–60.

Only one poem mentioning the word *blue* can be dated with any cer-tainty between 1865 and summer 1877. Written about 1872, it tells of her liking for March, always a favorite month, and rather oddly ascribes to March a "British Sky" in which "Blue Birds" are exercising (1213). The explanation may be that March was the birth month of Kate Turner, who was in England in 1872 and again in 1873. But 1877, the year of Kate's visit to Amherst, is the *annus mirabilis* for bluebirds as well as the last year in which the poet originated many blue poems. In August 1877 she sent to Higginson a poem describing a bluebird as first to come in March, last to adhere at summer's end, and a model of "Integrity" (1395). The same latter also carried an exuberant description of Nature in her "Opal Apron" (var., "Bluest Apron") mixing fresh air (1397). About the same time she must have worked at the draft of another bluebird poem, which she finished some years later. In its 1877 form it begins by asking who would care about a bluebird's tune when all that it sung for had been "undone" (1530). About the same time she copied off the last lines of the 1872 bluebird poem on a scrap of paper where she also confided that she no longer "Yearns...for that Peninsula" (the full text of this 1877 "Peninsula" poem (1425), describing the sweeping away of her soul by an "inundation," is preserved on other paper). The following March, it would seem, she rewrote the whole 1872 bluebird poem in fair copy, as if intended for some friend. About the same time she rewrote an early 1862 poem concerning two butterflies and introduced the word "Peninsula" into her confused draft (533). Such a thickening of peninsulas and bluebirds, unique in her poetry, makes 1877 (and the two or three months immediately following) an interesting though puzzling year. It is also, proportionately, the richest color year in her poetry, with an average of 0.057 color words per line, reflecting perhaps some strong but transient excitement. In the last of her 1877 blue poems, the "parched Corolla" of the gentian is dried azure, the beatification of Nature's juices (1424). Later than other flowers, it comes to assist "an aged Year" and is a symbol of "Fidelity," in which, incidentally, it resembles the bluebird. This "dried azure" would seem to be the final reduction of her molten blue. The following year the color words fell to an average of 0.015 per line and the rich palette of 1877 was reduced to a ghostly "pallid" and a "snow."

4

Yellow is Emily Dickinson's workaday word, used seventeen times simply to describe the sunlight. It is not surrounded by an aura of value like gold or golden, does not share with amber the sense of something delicate, precious, shining, and is not attended by any of the sacrificial quality that seemingly attached to gilt or gilded. (Topaz, which occurs twice, and saffron, daffodil, and gamboge, once each, are exotics of no great importance.) Yellow can be humorously used, as in the sunset's yellow play (496), the yellow boys and girls climbing the purple stile of evening (318), the daffodil's yellow bonnet (134) or yellow gown (348), the yellow knee on which the poet as awkward little bird falls adoringly (941). Other uses of the word yellow, suggesting that it is sometimes too bright, too painfully stimulating, recall the fact that the poet spent many months in Boston during 1864 and 1865 for treatment of her eyes. The affliction was apparently neurotic, but it may have left her oversensitive to bright light. On the other hand, it would seem that she anticipated her eye trouble some years before it happened.

In an anguished poem written about spring 1861, the poet describes the loss of love as "Blindness" (236). A year later she recalls the happy time before she got her "eye put out" (327). In another 1862 poem she is looking into the "face" of a cannon, whose "Yellow eye" glares death into her eye (590). About this time occurs one of her early references to lightning: it plays, sings, "alarms us"—and has "Yellow feet" (630). The following year the poet herself becomes a "Loaded Gun" and lays "Yellow Eye" and "emphatic Thumb" on her "Master's" foes (754). About 1864, the year of her first eye treatment, comes a graveyard poem that adjures the sun not to "interrupt this Ground" with any "yellow noise" (829); synesthesia converts intrusive light to intrusive sound. Of the same period is a poem describing how the lightning "showed a Yellow Head" and a "livid Toe" (824). A revision makes the lightning more cruelly terrifying: "Yellow Head" becomes "Yellow Beak" and "Toe" becomes "Claw." About 1870 the lightning is described as a "yellow Fork," the "awful Cutlery" of the sky (1173). A few months later the sun takes down his "Yellow Whip" and drives the fog away (1190). Finally, an undated poem places the "yellow lightning" in a context of volcanic cloud and mangled limbs (1694). No other shade and indeed no other hue has precisely these connotations of fear, violence, and cruelty.

Gilt or *gilded* appears to be associated with pain or with the effort to conceal pain. The earliest instance is an 1861 poem about a "clock" that has stopped, its "Gilded pointers" indicating a "cool—concernless No" to anyone who importunes it (287). An 1862 poem describes a lip "gilded" with a smile to hide its pain (353). Another 1862 poem, which affirms that heaven has a hell to "signalize" itself, says every sign in front of heaven is "Gilt with Sacrifice" (459). The "Gilded Hands" of another clock seem tormented with anticipation of a joy that proves short-lived (635). The last of these poems, written apparently in 1863, describes the torture of a balloon, a "Gilded Creature" that tries desperately to fly but rips apart on a tree and falls into the ocean (700).

The yellows of all shades are too brilliant to be suitable graveyard colors, the yellow sun being specifically asked to stay away. The honorific *gold* or *golden* can be and is applied to the world beyond the grave, but rarely and with no great conviction. On her return from Baltimore, Susan Gilbert is to shun the golden wings of angels and people beckoning from the clouds. Looking toward the "golden gateway beneath the western trees" (the direction from which Sue will actually come to the Dickinson house on Pleasant Street), the poet seems to make some half-conscious association between the golden West and the next world (L96). A few months later the association is explicitly made. Once more looking toward the West, the poet calls it the "golden West" and speaks of the "silent Eternity for ever folded there," which will presently open its arms and gather Sue and her in (L103). Writing in January 1856 to Mrs. Holland, she imagines herself a rather unusual mill wheel translated to the new stream of heaven where her "belts and bands" will appropriately be of gold (L182).

In the poetry, two rather perfunctory uses of *golden* suggest the next world. The "more golden light" of an 1854 poem sent to Susan Gilbert appears to be the light of heaven (5). The "golden floor" of another poem is that of the heavenly city (117). Finally, the "Yellower Climes" toward which the birds precede the poet may allude to the next world where alone she has any hope of being with her lover (250).

Amber and gold or golden, the shades most in esteem for their preciousness, are those applied to love, the beloved, or some particularly admired friend. The lost "guinea golden" of an 1858 poem (23) may be Sue or, less probably, some other girl friend who is being urged to answer letters; the poem looks early and is recorded in packet 82, where some of the vanished 1850–56 poems may have been preserved. An 1862 poem, describing the haze of pain through which a former delight is now seen, says it makes the latter pictorial like the amber haze surrounding a mountain, which, when approached, flits and becomes—"the Skies" (572). The shifting of the amber to the skies may be an involved way of alluding to the possibility of regaining the lost delight in heaven. In a poem already mentioned, where "Blue is Blue" and "Amber—Amber," it would seem that amber also symbolizes the love that must be sought in the world beyond (703).

Although gold or amber is associated with the sun-lover, it is equally the color of the moon as beloved. Just as the moon controls the sea with "Amber Hands," so does the lover's "Amber Hand" control the poet (429). Another 1862 poem explicitly identifies the lover with the moon, which continues the "Golden Same" throughout its period of waning until it is cut away by "slashing Clouds" (504). Still another 1862 poem, mentioned earlier, has the moon sliding away, "independent Amber," like a guillotined head or a "Stemless Flower" (629). A poem of early 1863 appears to identify the moon with some particular person. Only a "Chin of Gold" a few nights ago, the moon now turns a "perfect Face" on the world below. If the "Lips of Amber" should ever part, what a smile the moon would bestow upon the poet, who longs for the privilege of being even the "remotest Star" taking its way past the moon's "Palace Door" (737).

The lamp of an 1861 poem "burns golden" even when its oil is gone, signifying the continuance of her love after the other's love has been withdrawn (233). A curious poem sent to Samuel Bowles in late 1861 is more obscure. The subject is love, and the "Eagle's Golden Breakfast" that *"dazzles"* her is suggestively erotic on the oral level so common in her work. If Bowles, who was pretty well informed, had been urging her to take her women friends less seriously, this is her answer. The poet is neither an eagle nor attracted to eagles (a conscious male symbol in her poetry); she is explicitly a "robin," whose little mouth is better suited to cherries or crumbs. She is so far from desiring the "Eagle's Golden Breakfast" that in a revised version she says it "strangles" small-mouthed creatures like her (690). A few weeks later she sent Bowles the curious poem mentioned in chapter 3 describing some unconsummated love relationship. She says she has *not* had the swoon that ensues when "Garnet" cleaves to "Garnet" and "Gold—to Gold" (1072). Superficially there is not much resemblance between a "Golden Breakfast" and the orgasmic swoon of united garnet reds and golds; in the reconciling universe of symbols they may nevertheless be the same. According to one brave theory, however, this powerful sexual imagery of golden flesh and garnet blood expresses a maidenly yearning for a double-ring ceremony![3]

Another 1862 poem recalls the period of happiness when she dealt words of "Gold" to everyone; now the "Wilderness" has rolled back along her "Golden lines" (430). Poem 452 in the same year laments her failure to dive for the pearl she thought too precious for a "Vest of Amber." But in a poem of the same period she is fearlessly diving for her jewel and hopeful that her next dive may be the "golden touch" that obtains it (427). Saturated with Shakespeare as she was, it is possible that she recalled these lines from *The Two Gentlemen of Verona*:

> For Orpheus' lute was strung with poets' sinews,
> Whose golden touch could soften steel and stones.[4]

Her poetry is precisely what she would use in any attempt to win back an estranged friend. That a person is intended would seem to explain the tender, caressing references to the jewel, which is addressed as "you." In another 1862 poem she is waiting for death, when her lover will take her home in an "Equipage of Amber" (603). A disillusioned poem of 1864 sums up her history as "Finding...loss...Expedition for / The 'Golden Fleece'...no Discovery...no Crew...no Golden Fleece," and poet-Jason doubtless sham, too (870).

A poem of 1866, taking a mournful farewell of a "Retreating" person, states that a "Perished Sun" is doubly more endearing than all the "Golden presence" (1083). It is reminiscent of the earlier poem linking some important person with the sun, especially with the setting sun. Although the other person is surely alive, the tone is elegiac and final, as for the apotheosis of the golden beloved. There are no later poems linking any shade of yellow with any cherished person.

5

Purple, amethyst, Tyrian, violet, lilac, and *iodine* are freely interchangeable throughout Emily Dickinson's poetry, perhaps because the color word, without ever losing a sense of deep rich color, is far more important as symbol than as epithet. This also appears true with respect to the poets who influenced her. Milton's Love not only lights his constant lamp, he waves his "purple wings";[5] and Keats's Psyche and Cupid sleep in each other's arms on a couch of "budded Tyrian." [6] Though not rich in color words, Shakespeare makes occasional telling use of *purple*. The "purple pride" on the loved friend's soft cheek has been "grossly dyed" in "my love's veins" (Sonnet 99). Emerson calls love's illusions "bandages of purple light." [7] Elizabeth Browning used most of her purples descriptively, but she gave amethyst a prominence that caught the eye of her disciple. It occupies the most important position in *Aurora Leigh,* being the absolute last word, uttered with meaningful emphasis. Moreover, in the thirty-eighth of the *Sonnets from the Portuguese* Mrs. Browning compared her lover's first gallant hand-kiss to a "ring of amethyst," adding that the eventual kiss on the lips "was folded down / In perfect, purple state."

For *iodine* as a color word Emily had no poetic predecessor or successor, but having discovered it as a usable word from her scientific vocabulary, she was reminded by her dictionary that "its vapor is a beautiful violet" and that the name originated in the Greek word for violet (she read etymologies). Under the definition of *purple,* she found that it was a much-admired color worn by Roman emperors and hence signified imperial government. In poetry it might be "red or livid; dyed with blood." Purple of *Mollusca,* she read, is "secreted by certain shell-fish ... and is supposed to be the substance of the famous Tyrian dye." That Emily Dickinson avidly collected color words, studied definitions, and tried out new specimens is fairly obvious. She knew something about the theory of colors too. From Denison Olmsted's *Compendium of Natural History,* another textbook used at Mount Holyoke, she would have learned about optical properties and the nature of the prism. In a love poem she writes that the love of the other is a "Prism" (prismatic color?) "Excelling Violet" (611).

To these associations of love, happiness, dignity, imperial state, she added that of death, perhaps because it was to her the most important of all state occasions. She may also have known that the pall thrown over coffin or tomb in ceremonious funerals might be purple velvet instead of black. An early poem describing the funeral ceremony says that this is a "purple," a "Crown," that no one can evade (98). In another poem, the "Modest Clay," the erstwhile "Democrat," now lies in a state "Full royal" and "purple" (171). A poem in late handwriting describes death as a brook that must be leaped to secure the "Flower Hesperian" or "Purple Flower" (1558), recalling Shakespeare's "little western flower ... purple with love's wound." [8] According to these poems, death levels upward, and the humblest, most impotent denizen of earth (herself perhaps) may achieve dignity in death—and possibly the satisfaction of desire in the world beyond.

As a color word for flowers, *purple* is infrequently used. The clover blossom is a "Purple Democrat"—an intended oxymoron (380)—and the lilacs sway with "purple load" (342). The most important instance is the

"Purple Creature," the gentian of an 1862 poem, which, after the humiliating failure of its summer-long effort to be a rose, is brought to "Tyrian" perfection by the frost (442). The gentian of this poem is a personal symbol, referring either to her belated love affair or to the dramatic efflorescence of her talent under the sharp stimulus of personal tragedy.

In two poems purple signified blood—the "purple brook" in the breast (122) and the "purple" in her vein, every drop of which she would give in order to live over one particularly happy hour (663). The "purple Host" of poem 67 doubtless has blood as one of its connotations, for it gives and sustains wounds on the field of battle; but it is also triumphant and victorious, attaining the supreme value that purple appears to symbolize in a number of poems. In one such poem she offers to buy an hour of her lover's face with "Purple" from "Peru," itself another symbol of supreme value because of the wealth wrung from it by the conquistadores (247). The "purple line" of another poem (137), around which the butterflies of "St. Domingo" are cruising, may be nothing more than the deep violet of a summer day; on the other hand, this may be one of many instances where metaphor appears to hesitate on the border of symbol. Elsewhere the butterfly is a symbol of the beloved, and "St. Domingo" is one of several place-names symbolizing the South of erotic happiness and freedom. In brief, "Butterflies" may be butterflies here, the "purple line" the noonday summer sky, and "St. Domingo" only a playful way of suggesting summer warmth, yet Emily Dickinson could not write this poem without being aware of the possibilities of symbolism. This "purple line" is very close in feeling to Pizarro's "purple territories" and to the "amber line" or "golden lines" which explicitly signify former happiness (73).

Purple is a favorite sunrise and sunset color and is associated with hills, the four cardinal points, sun, noon, autumn, spring, and peculiarly with the month of March. Most of these poems give the reader an uneasy feeling that he is reading about something more, or other, than sunset, sunrise, or the season of the year. This ambiguity is the subject of one poem, which states that purple is "fashionable twice"—at this season of the year and in that inner season when the soul knows itself an emperor (980). Since love is the supreme value in poem after poem, to be an emperor is to be loved; or, in slightly different words, she would "rather be loved than to be called a king in earth, or a lord in Heaven" (L185). When she writes that on the "Purple Programme" of the East every dawn is the first one, she is describing the lover's sense of miraculous uniqueness, an interpretation already made in the opening stanza (839). In another poem she deliberately spells out her metaphors: the beloved's absence is night, the beloved's presence is dawn, and this presence, in another metaphor, is the "purple on the hight" that is called morning (1739). In short, as the poems witness, the beloved is frequently represented by purple, hill, and morning.

Because the beloved's departure ushers in the night, the beloved is just as often, indeed more often, represented by the setting sun and *its* purple. In an 1861 poem, the poet, now an "Eastern Exile," tries vainly to climb the "purple Moat" that once led her over the "Amber line" into the sun-drenched West of love (262). In a poem discussed in the "blue" section, the "East" keeps her "purple Troth" with the "Hill," and at night North signals to the separated lovers by blazing in iodine—displaying violet auroral light (710). Sun, amber, and purple are once more united in an 1863 poem. Purple is "the Color of a Queen," with "Amber" "Sun at setting" (776).

About March 1859 she sent an earlier poem across the lawn to her sister-in-law. It may be concerned with flowers, or with Sue herself, or it may be a comment on, or a tribute to, some new woman friend whose recent departure resembles the evening stealing "Purple and Cochineal" after the day (60). In a love poem of the same period, the Daisy (always a personal symbol of the poet) steals after the sun toward the "parting West," the "Amethyst" (106). The following year the color is scantier and has little personal reference, but in troubled 1861 the price of "purples" rises as high as death (234). She strives to climb the purple moat and would give Peruvian purple for an hour of her beloved's face; but the unattainable "Heaven" (her own quotation marks) merely decoys her with its "teazing Purples" (239). If not in this life, however, there can still be hope in the next, and she thinks of herself as dropping her life into a "purple well" so plummetless that it will not return before eternity (271). Less extravagantly, she says she has lost a gem and now has only an "Amethyst remembrance" (245).

After 1861 the purples are less frequently, or less obviously, concerned with a real person and a real situation. There is of course the 1862 poem offering the purple in her vein for one remembered hour of love (663), which is so intense in feeling and so heavily italicized as to read like a misplaced member of an 1861 group in packet 37; but this is a puzzling exception to the general rule that the later poems appear less urgent, less immediate and painful. Purple shares in the general dimming of her palette after 1865.

6

Although the reds of the 1850–56 letters are less important than the yellows or even the greens and blues, Emily Dickinson was already using *crimson, red, rose, ruddy, scarlet,* and *pink.* In 1858 she added *carmine*; in 1859, *cochineal, vermilion,* and *damask*; in 1860, *ruby*; in 1861, *rouge*; in 1862, *garnet, coral,* and *blood.* The other additions are a doubtful *hyacinth* in 1864 and a possible *cardinal red* in 1882. The importance of red is due to its association with vitality, with blood, with the heart and other vital organs. It is not necessarily of special importance to a woman, for Elizabeth Browning uses rather less red than her husband or Emerson or Tennyson; and the reds in Shakespeare's nondramatic poems average twenty percent, or very little less than Emily Dickinson's.

Not surprisingly, red is well-nigh absent from the graveyard. The earliest poem that in any way associates the two makes a strong point of the fact that no "ruddy fires" appear on the hearth of this curious "Inn," the grave (115). But after the poet becomes anxious for the early demise of the person with whom she wishes to spend eternity, the grave turns ruddy. She says she can see the other person better in the dark and through the lapse of years and best of all in the grave. Its "little Panels" are "ruddy with the Light" (the lamp of love) she has been holding high all these years (611).

The symbolic red usually indicates a quality or a state rather than a person, but there is some evidence that cochineal points toward a particular individual (60). The poet chooses for her "Knitting" a "Cochineal" that "resembles Thee" and a "Dusker" border that represents her dimmer self (748). But in poem 334 she identifies herself with a "Ruby" flower, and elsewhere she may be the collective "Flowers" that waste their "Scarlet Freight" in lonely isolation (404).

Red is Emily Dickinson's color. Outwardly she may wear the white of martyred renunciation, but inwardly she is red, scarlet, carmine, vermilion, whether in ecstatic happiness or in the violence of loss and suffering— until after 1865, when the vitality drains away and the white so gains upon the red that the latter pales to pink. The earliest of the reds occurs in a poem written about summer 1859. If this is "fading" or "sleep" (her own quotation marks), then she wants immediately to "fade" or sleep. If it is "dying" (her own quotation marks and a possible indication that she remembered the 1847 Webster definition for die, "To languish with pleasure or tenderness"), then she wants to be buried "in such a shroud of red" (120). The occasion is a happy one, however else it may be interpreted. In an 1860 poem, the "Rose" capers on the cheeks of two unidentified lovers (208). In an 1862 poem about her lost happiness, she remembers that she once "told it—Red" in the color of her cheek (430). Very early in this year she tends her flowers in memory of her "Bright Absentee" and muses sadly that she "had as lief" they bore no more "Crimson" (339). Another 1862 poem, which appears to recall a declaration of love, tells of the "Carmine" tingling to her fingertips (470).

In early 1863 she spells out her symbol in terms of opposites. The "Zeroes" of her unloved life taught her that there must be a "Phosphorus," and the "White" of deprivation and asceticism convinced her that "Red— must be" (689). Later in the same year she remembers the "ruddier Blue" of that one-time "Heaven below" (756). Rejected by "Morning" and condemned to "Midnight," she asks in poem 425 whether she cannot at least look toward the "Red" East.

By 1864 the "Crumb" that once satisfied the little robin is the "crumb of Blood" that momentarily "eased" her tiger-self (872). Another poem gives a more detailed account of her love experience. At some time in the past there bloomed a "Single Noon" (a frequent symbol for love's zenith) with a flower "distinct and Red." As in many another poem, she believes she did not properly value it at the time. Too late she learns that this was the one and only flower intended for her (978). The flower with which the beloved is identified is commonly the rose, and in the rose poems the red color may be presumed.

Red is life, vitality, erotic ecstasy, in Emily Dickinson's models no less than in her own work. Undoubtedly she knew a line of Emerson's essay "Culture" that salutes "Love, red love, with tears and joy," [9] and she must have been equally well acquainted with that curious passage in which Milton's Raphael, extolling a kind of sexual activity among the angels, blushes "Celestial rosie red, Love's proper hue." [10] But red is also the color of suffering, and this meaning attaches to it early, perhaps initially to describe the pain of temporary separations. A poem that appears to belong to spring 1860 says wounded deer leap highest and cheeks are reddest where they sting (165). This is no more than an anticipation of real pain. The difference is apparent in a poem written a year later, perhaps about April 1861. Here no attempt has been made to polish metaphors or achieve a neat finish, and more than half the words are underlined. In an anguish of abasement, the poet describes herself as her lover's little spaniel whose life is leaking "red" (236). Of the several spaniels that she found in her reading about this time, one that she undoubtedly has in mind here is Helena's. To the stony-hearted beloved, Helena cries:

I am your spaniel; ...
The more you beat me, I will fawn on you.
Use me but as your spaniel—spurn me, strike me,
Neglect me, lose me; only give me leave
(Unworthy as I am) to follow you.[11]

A poem written later in 1861 suggests that if one could only foresee the end of pain, if the depth of the bleeding and the "drops of vital scarlet" were limited, then it would be bearable (269). Another 1861 poem says she will keep singing. Like the robins, though more slowly, she too will journey southward with her "Rhymes" and her "Redbreast"—a play upon the robin's common name and the emotional wound she has suffered (250). A poem written in late 1861 and sent with autumn leaves to Kate Turner in Emily's brother's house makes unique use of the word *rouge*. There is no explanation other than that the recipient had a fair command of French and liked to display it. The poem says that the red of the leaves cannot mean "Summer" (her own quotation marks and hence a symbol), for Summer—with the slight dash that often suggests a catch of the breath—"got through." It is too early for "Spring" (her own quotation marks and hence another symbol), and besides she must first cross "that long town of White." Nor can it be "dying"; it is "too Rouge," and the *Dead* shall go in White." Since the leaves point neither to the vanished summer of love nor to the resurrection of love after the long white town of the grave (and they are "too Rouge" for the intermediate stage of dying), their redness would seem to symbolize not love but suffering (221). It is a queer, puzzling poem; but in October 1861, according to a hint given T. W. Higginson next spring and by the evidence of other letters and poems, Emily Dickinson was almost out of her mind with fear and suffering.

In an 1862 poem she says she had chosen the "Scarlet way" of suffering and renunciation (527). A poem in the same packet, however, calls her renunciation the "White Election" (528). By this white election and by the "Sign in the Scarlet prison" (her suffering self), she hopes to reclaim her lost happiness. Still another 1862 poem suggests that the symbolic white is the incandescence of the passionate red. In this white blaze the "impatient Ores" are refined until they become the "Designated Light" itself and quit the human forge (365). Oddly enough, she called this poem "Cupid's Sermon" in a letter to Higginson (L675). It may therefore express the apotheosis of love rather than suffering and owe its origin to a line from Margaret Fuller's "Notice of George Sand"; "She knows passion, as has been hinted, at a *white* heat, when all the lower particles are remoulded by its power." [12]

As early as spring 1860 Emily Dickinson began to associate her inner turmoil with a volcano. Happiness is a delectable vineyard that she holds on uncertain lease in the shadow of some danger symbolized by a volcano overwhelming a Pompeii (175). By early 1861, according to one of the so-called Master letters (L233), the cataclysm has occurred. As her tension increased, so did the violence of her metaphors. A confused poem of 1862 says the ordinary person lives a peat life of steady, subdued warmths; hers has the heat and violence of "Popocatapel" or "Etna's Scarlets" (422). In another 1862 poem the "peat" lives become "natures" this side of "Naples" and denizens of the cold "North." These passionless innocents "cannot detect," let alone understand, her "Solemn—Torrid—Symbol," the "still—Volcano" of suffering that has opened the "hissing Corals" of its lips and destroyed her "Cities" (601). About 1869 she wrote, or more probably rewrote, a poem making the only other use of the "Garnet," the "Naples," and the "Etna" of these 1862 poems. A one-stanza poem, it is probably a redaction of a longer poem contemporaneous with the earlier volcano poems. Naples, she says, fears a basking and purring "Etna" even more than one that "Shows her Garnet Tooth" (1146). Although the poem has no manifest personal application, it would be a mistake not to suspect one. An undated poem about a volcano (in a transcript made by Sue Dickinson) resembles these earlier ones and probably belongs with them. Her volcano, she observes, is now overgrown with grass and looks a "meditative spot," but the fire is rocking "red" below (1677).

The last poem in what might be called her red period is one of the saddest. She has sung birdlike from her heart, dipped her beak in it to help out her song, offered up her death as her only wealth. If the tune drips too much or seems too "Red," she begs her erstwhile lover to forgive the "Cochineal," accept the "Vermilion," suspend "Liturgies" and "Chorals" while she repeats that lover's "Hallowed name" (1059). This poem was written about 1865.

The most curious aspect of her color system after 1865 is the dulling and fading of her palette. Prior to that time she employed an unusually high proportion of vivid colors—saturated reds, sky blues, rich golds, imperial purples. The browns, though treated mostly as warm, comfortable colors, are few in number; and the achromatic whites, grays, and blacks, which make up forty to fifty percent of the color words employed by other poets, amount to little more than twenty percent of Emily Dickinson's. There is a disturbing impression of intense, restless color in a period of raging creativity and of powerful emotional tension. Little wonder that the image of an erupting volcano or of a blazing fire recurs and recurs.

By 1865 the fire is virtually extinguished. "Ashes" now indicate the "Fire" that was, and the poet begs respect for this "Grayest Pile" in memory of what it symbolizes (1063). No reds appear in the 1866 poems, and no colors at all in the 1867–68 poems. During 1869–70 there are a few "red" poems, some or all of which may have originated in the earlier period. The Naples-Etna-Garnet poem (1146), it was suggested, belongs to the period around 1862, and a "rose" and "vermilion" poem in 1870 handwriting recalls the love affair with a surprising immediacy and in the vocabulary of the early 1860s (1171). It is a curious fact, however, that a worksheet draft originating perhaps late in 1868 describes a temporary reheating of the fire, suggesting that she has recently seen the disturbing friend of the earlier period. Such a blowing upon the "smouldering embers" (1132) might initiate new poetry on the old theme or incite her to review and tinker with the older poetry. But even if these particular "red" poems originated in 1869–70, they modify only slightly the impression of diminished vitality, almost of bloodlessness, that distressed Higginson in late 1873.

Higginson was unpleasantly struck by her pallor and by the white garments that she now wore habitually. His friend Helen Hunt Jackson made a similar visit in late 1876 and had a similar reaction. An apologetic letter shows that she berated the poet for living out of the sunlight and told her she looked ill ("so white and mothlike").[13] If Mrs. Jackson or Higginson had had any real acquaintance with her poetry, they would doubtless have found symptomatic the curious bleaching of her once vital red. Whether a conscious and deliberate act or not, the symbolic white appears to have invaded the red and lightened it to pink. In the early letters, for example, the color word *pink* occurs just once—in contrast to seventeen reds, crimsons, and the like. The letters of 1858–66 employ four pinks (all of them names or descriptions of particular flowers) as against seventeen assorted reds; and the poems of that period exhibit a mere three pinks as opposed to the overwhelming vividness of ninety-four reds, scarlets, crimsons, cochineals, carmines, vermilions, and the like. But in the 1870s the reds begin to fade into pinks, and the various browns multiply. In some poems of the midseventies, as her variants show, she can be seen hesitating between a pink and a red, as if no longer sure of her preference. Perhaps conscious of declining vitality, she begs her heart to put up its "Hoary work" and take a "Rosy Chair" (1310). (Rose or rosy, incidentally, is treated as a fairly deep color—in one poem as an autumn color.) In the letters of 1869–86 there are now a dozen pinks to fourteen of the more vivid red shades, and in the poems of the same period the proportion is ten pinks to sixteen assorted reds.

It is not alone the employment of the word *pink*; the context in which it occurs becomes oddly symbolic. Shame is a "shawl of Pink" and even the "tint divine" (1412). The general flesh becomes "that Pink stranger" (1527), and, in an 1881 poem apparently recalling some more or less decorous struggle with an admirer, their particular flesh becomes the "Pink Redoubt" (1529). One wonders whether an undated dream poem describing a pink worm, lank and warm, that turns into a terrifying snake "ringed with power" might not have been written at this prevailingly pink date (1670). The dripping of February eaves, she writes, "makes our thinking Pink" (L450). Hearts are now pink (letters 654, 845), Cupid drives a "Pink Coupe" (L723), and in the final weeks of her life she writes that the idea of her stirring about is rather like the arbutus, "a pink and russet hope" (L1034). The words are curiously descriptive of the impression made by her colors during the last decade or so of her life.

Although creativity and color alike seem diminished to a uniformly low ebb after 1865, a more careful inspection discovers occasional puzzling ripples. A temporary increase in color around 1869–70, it was suggested, may be due to the reappearance of the person who caused the original disturbance. There is another such increase in the middle seventies, apparently tied to a fire poem of about 1877, which describes the reappearance of the "Witch" and the uncovering of supposedly dead embers by the hand that once "fondled them" (1383). But after reaching its absolute peak in 1877, the color incidence once more tumbles abruptly. There is a peculiar flatness and lack of color in the poetry written during Judge Lord's courtship of the next several years. After his death, surprisingly, the old brilliant colors, the old symbols, made a last flickering appearance in letters and poems. And then she too died, having locked up her life in transparent image and symbol.

I judge from my Geography [1705]
This Travel may the poorest take [1263]
Unto the Dead / There's no Geography [489]
We will talk over what we have learned in our geographies [L34]

"I do not cross my Father's ground to any House or town" (L330). So wrote Emily Dickinson to her friend T. W. Higginson, who had invited her to drop in at a meeting of the Boston Woman's Club to hear his lecture on the Greek goddesses. The absurdity of his invitation may have provoked the grandeur of her reply, but it is true that the last twenty years of her life were bounded thus narrowly. In earlier years she may have hoped to see a little more of the world she was reading about. As a girl of nineteen, she excitedly proposed to some friend that they "talk over" what they had learned in their geographies; and an 1874 poem, speaking of "Lands" she had expected to visit someday, appears to recall a dream long dead (1293). Whether or not her father forbade her to travel, as she once declared to Higginson—and she was capable of inventing a stern father to gloss over her own refusals (L319)—there were stubborn facts not to be evaded. Like virtually all women of her time, she was dependent and penniless; and she turned eagerly to books as the "Travel" that even the poorest—herself, for instance—might take without "oppress of Toll" (1263).

To her friend Elizabeth Holland she wrote hyperbolically of the snow on the neighboring hills, "I saw the sunrise on the Alps since I saw you. Travel why to Nature, when she dwells with us?" (L321). No physical boundaries stayed her mind, which overleaped them to roam at large through a world charted for her by her reading. There is nothing technical or scientific about her geography. She made a close study of Milton's poetry, and must have been struck by the effective geographical imagery, but she was no more tempted to use his learned names than to write sonorous blank verse. Maps and geographical facts were of interest to her not for themselves but as she could use them symbolically to identify and order the more subtle elements of the mind's world. For this purpose the simplest language suffices.

A map drawn to incorporate her geographical names would differ hardly at all from the maps in the geography readers she must have studied as a child. Those of "Peter Parley" (Samuel G. Goodrich) may serve as an example.[1] A youthful nonsense poem in which she exclaims, "Hurrah for Peter Parley!" (3), has several lines suggesting humorous recollections of his books on geography, biography, history, and science, a series begun in 1827 for the instruction of young children and so popular during the next thirty years that those decades have been called the Peter Parley epoch. A fine April day might even be described as a kind of Peter Parley heaven that prepared children for the sublimer weather of the next life (65).

Peter Parley dealt in the larger elements of geography, and customarily so did Emily Dickinson. The vast majority of her geographical names are those that appear in the maps and text of Peter Parley's geography, and in one fashion or another she used a very large percentage of those names he thought young children should know, including Appenine (misspelled in his fashion), Azof, Buenos Ayres, Cashmere, Caspian, Chimborazo, Dnieper, Don, Himaleh, Kamchatka, Potosi, Sicily, Teneriffe, Timbuctoo, Tripoli, Tunis, and Van Diemen's Land. In a letter of 29 January 1850 exotic place names like "Alps," "Switzerland," and "Asia Minor" appear for the first time; a few months later come such words as "Alp," "Ande," and "Olympus," and a bit later, "Hindoostan," "Appenine," "Canaan," "Australia," and "Chinese Tartary" (letters 31, 34, 37, 107, 110). It is an indication, together with the excitement of letters of this period, the increasingly rhythmical prose, and the studied introduction of color words, that she had begun to write poetry and to build that vocabulary of symbols so warmly recommended by Emerson in "The Poet." Geographical terms and place-names would form a significant part of her vocabulary, and she found them everywhere. She read incessantly in the Victorian writers, to a lesser extent in the romantics and such late neoclassicists as Cowper and James Thomson, and was saturated in the Bible and Shakespeare and Milton. The better journalistic writing of her day, that of the *Atlantic* and *Harper's,* for example, afforded another source of language, and she might draw upon the travel books of a John Stephens and an Elisha Kent Kane or the work of popular historians like William H. Prescott.

There is no reason to suppose that she ever deliberately set herself to construct a geographic symbolism neatly parceled out according to continents. Geographic stereotypes were all about her, and she picked them as needed and elaborated them extravagantly. Furthermore, they are symbol clusters, in which all the differently named oceans mean the same thing, and all the warm countries—Italy, Africa, Brazil, for example—are the same heart's country, and all the mountain ranges and individual peaks are one and the same (except her volcanoes, which are a different kind of mountain and have their own unique function). Still there are certain vague but distinguishable differences. Her Latin American imagery, which appears to be the most carefully and consciously elaborated, owes its characteristic features to tales of early Spanish exploration, and Asia, except for the Bible lands, is the domain of exotic luxury. The continents even have their characteristic color associations, purple for South America and the Caribbean, sky blue and scarlet for Europe, unspecified "tint Cashmere" for Asia (110), and for Africa the gaudiest hues drawn from circus posters and vague notions of savage taste. Of these several color associations, the purple of Latin America is the most readily explained.

2

The analysis of her color words has shown that purple is a favorite sunset color, and from an association with sunset to an association with the western or sunset land is an easy step for an inveterate symbolist. Peru is purple—no doubt alliteratively, but also because it is, above all others, her western land. The literal-minded objection that Peru lies east of most of the United States, like a similar objection to Etna overawing Naples (1146), is scarcely in point, since Peru and Etna and Naples alike are states of mind, needing only the slenderest footholds in fact to establish their validity as symbols. Again, Peru is purple because it is her royal color, evoking the classic tradition of royal purple and signifying power—the power of emperors, queens, great conquistadores, great wealth. And of course Peru is wealth. The tale of a golden hoard wrenched from the Incas by the bold conquistadores was the property of every imaginative schoolboy, so that "Ik Marvel" could remember as his greatest triumph acting the part of one of Pizarro's chieftains in the school exhibition;[2] and fabled Peru recurs and recurs in the works that Emily Dickinson read. Among the family books was Prescott's *Conquest of Peru,* from which she derived information she was not likely to find in other sources.[3] To this rich and complex symbol Sir Thomas Browne's "I have not Peru in my desires" may have contributed, all the more probably since "Peru" was what Emily did have in her desires.[4] On the other hand, it would appear that "Peru" was sometimes in her gift. In a poem beginning "What would I give to see his face" (247), she offers—besides such items as bags of doubloons from bees, spicy stocks, shares in primrose banks—this final, climactic wealth, "And Purple—from Peru—."

A poem beginning "Who never lost, are unprepared" (73) declares that only the thirsting can really taste the flagons and cooling tamarind; only the weary foot is fitted to explore "The purple territories / on Pizarro's shore." As for the purple Peru hinted at in these linked symbols, it would appear to be that quite earthly heaven for which she sighed elsewhere, "but not / The Heaven—God bestow—" (636).

In a poem beginning "I envy Seas, whereon He rides—," the Peru of incalculable wealth reappears in a metonymy. The lover has gone, and the poet envies the spokes of his chariot wheels, the fly on his pane, the happy leaves at his window. They enjoy a privilege "The Ear Rings of Pizarro / Could not obtain for me—" (498). A vivid passage in Prescott's *Conquest of Peru* describes the sons of the Inca nobles kneeling before their sovereign to have their ears skewered with gold bodkins, which were left in place until the holes were large enough to receive the enormous wheel-shaped ornaments denoting their rank.[5] To secure a brilliant image, she has made the earrings stand for all the enormous wealth torn from the Incas and has hung this wealth pirate-fashion from the ears of the great conquistador.

The notion that Peru was to be identified with biblical Ophir receives scornful attention from Prescott, but an idea need not be true to make a satisfying poetic metaphor.[6] In a series of couplets written in the late seventies, Emily Dickinson once more played with her symbolic Peru. The first couplet begins "Brother of Ingots—Ah Peru—." The second, which suggests a possible recollection of Prescott, begins "Sister of Ophir—Ah Peru," and is addressed to her sister-in-law. A third, written two years later as an elegiac note on the death of a townsman, drops the now inappropriate Peru but keeps the biblical Ophir as a suitably reverent tribute to the worthy dead: "Brother of Ophir, Bright Adieu" (1366).

Years earlier, as was shown in the discussion of her jewel imagery, the poet made a far more elaborate association of her sister-in-law with the fabulous Peru. According to this 1862 letter-poem (L258), she had thought herself a "Millionaire," in the little wealths that girls boast, until her new friend arrived—apparently somewhat in the manner of continental drift, for Sue is represented as *drifting* her "dominions," which are "broad as 'Buenos Ayre'" and a "Different—Peru," out of some black unknown into the poet's ken, whereupon Emily's riches showed as bare poverty compared to sharing "Life's Estate" with the adored Sue.

Not only "Peru" and "Buenos Ayre" but indeed all South America, the Caribbean, Mexico, and Central America are embedded in this matrix of symbols signifying incalculable wealth or unattainable desire. To her sources should be added the family copy of John L. Stephens's *Incidents of Travel in Central America, Chiapas, and Yucatan*, from which she plausibly derived the line "Fresh as a Cargo from Batize" (1148). The name appears to be an editorial misreading of "Balize" (present-day Belize, The Republic of Honduras), for Stephens has much to say about

Belize and its important mahogany exports.[7] In addition, his long descriptions of cochineal plantations, earthquakes, and volcanoes reinforced similar accounts in other books the poet read. Surely it was this lively interest that led her father to give her and Austin the two-volume *Exploration of the Valley of the Amazon* by William Lewis Herndon and Lardner Gibbon. It is the report of an official navy expedition and of little interest except to the enthusiast. Herndon's volume has numerous engravings and interminable discussions of the "Cordillera." The rather more lively Lieutenant Gibbon talked of "the pampas of Buenos Ayre and Brazil," of "Potosi" and its wealth, and of *diving* for diamonds in the rivers of Brazil.[8]

The finest Brazilian diamond, the great Star of the South, was discovered in 1852 at the outset of Emily Dickinson's poetic career, and Brazil would remain the principal source of diamonds from 1740 until some years after the first African discoveries in 1867. Throughout Emily's poetic career Brazil would be as reasonable a symbol of inestimable wealth as Golconda at an earlier period or Kimberley at a later. In a poem already described (621), in which God figures as "the Mighty Merchant," she names the symbolic "Brazil" as her heart's desire and offers "Being" as the purchase price. Of about the same date as this despairing appeal to an indifferent God is a poem that implies a proud self-sufficiency—and misplaces the diamond. A prosperity of inner resources, she says, is as safe as a "Diamond" in distant "Bolivian Ground" (395).

Bolivia was rich enough without diamonds, for the silver mines of Potosi were the most fabulous bonanza the world had yet seen. For a century or more the *villa real* of Charles V was the largest city in both Americas, and its wealth and luxury brought its name into common use as a symbol of incomparable riches. Even Edward Dickinson writes to Samuel Bowles in late 1868 that he would rather have borne the latter's name "on that night in Ludlow St. jail ... than to have owned the mines of Potosi." [9]

Certain poems suggest that Brazil may be imagined in color, perhaps the red of brazilwood, as described in Emily's copy of Silliman's *Chemistry* and her dictionary, or even a royal purple, like so much of her Latin America, for it is demonstrably associated with her "Queen." According to one poem, the late summer drops "bright scraps of Tint" and leaves "Brazilian Threads" on shoulders (574). "A Moth the hue of this," begins poem 841, "Haunts Candles in Brazil," suggesting that Brazil may be visualized in the hue of some tropical moth or butterfly. The possibility increases with a poem in which a brief ecstatic experience is likened to a "Spice" or a "Rose" that could have been plucked but was not, to "Stars" that were close last night but are "Foreigners" this morning, and to a "Butterfly" seen on "Brazilian Pampas" at the noon high point of life or love, after which the "License" to see the butterfly closes (541).

The interrelatedness of her poetry is strongly indicated by another butterfly poem (397), which does not name a South American country but does repeat three symbols associated with South America. "When Diamonds are a Legend, / And Diadems—a Tale," it begins, reminding us of the diamonds for which she was diving and which she proposed to make into a diadem in poem 427. The next lines suggest that she is now self-sufficient and makes "Brooch" and "Earrings" for herself, the latter being at least reminiscent of the "Ear Rings of Pizarro" (498). In a return to self-deprecation she implies that she is no longer important to anyone, but she can remember a "Summer Day" when her art, presumably her poems, enjoyed "Patrons"—a "Queen," a "Butterfly." According to poem 776, the "Queen" of her poetry has the royal color purple. Lines 388–89 of Byron's *The Giaour* are clearly a source of Emily Dickinson's poem about the schoolboy hopelessly following a purple queen-butterfly: "As rising on its purple wings / The insect queen of Eastern spring." [10] It is altogether possible that Emily Dickinson transferred Byron's purple-winged butterfly queen from "Kashmeer" to a no less exotic Brazil. Her "Brazilian Threads," her "Moth" that haunts Brazilian candles, and the very human butterfly she was licensed to see once only at noon on "Brazilian Pampas" may one and all be the color of her queen in poem 776 and of her Peru in poems 73 and 247.

The "Butterflies from St. Domingo" have already been noticed "Cruising round the purple line" (137). This is a quite early poem, and the butterflies seem to have no special symbolic importance, though the "purple line" is her equator of the heart, her code sign of the emotional tropics. It is of no significance that the actual West Indian island is still many degrees north of the real line. This poet was quite capable of running the equatorial heart line between East and West, as in the poem about the "Eastern Exiles" who strayed across the "Amber line" and have been trying ever since to climb back into Eden (262). In a tone of reproach ("That Distance was between Us"), she writes elsewhere that it is the "Will," not the "Equator," that separates the lovers (863).

Her West Indies images are consistently playful rather than intense; they are metaphors for the delights of summer weather, blooming flowers, and poetic success, plus a store of pleasant flatteries to be dispensed to friends. Rum and a tropical climate are their substance. Responding to some kind words about her poems, the poet tells Higginson, "I tasted Rum before—Domingo comes but once—" (L265). To her sister-in-law she writes flatteringly, "What depths of Domingo in that torrid Spirit!" (L855). A poem sent with jewelweed says she could bring the recipient "Odors from St. Domingo— / Colors—from Vera Cruz— / Berries of the Bahamas," but this flower alone seemed dower enough for a "Bobadilo" (697). The last-named has been plausibly identified with Columbus's enemy Bobadilla who seized the admiral's gold, plate, jewels, and other valuables plus an enormous treasure in gold wrested from the islanders.[11] Dower indeed! Admittedly, neither this nor any poem of the West Indian group deserves to rank high as poetry. It is occasional verse employing clever little tricks of style.

Mexican place-names have only a small role in her geographical game. Besides the colors associated with "Vera Cruz" of poem 697, the "Popo-catapel" of poem 422 is a symbol for the heat of vitality or, more exactly, of passion. The "inference of Mexico" of another poem, which describes a storm in terms of "Barricade," "martial Trees," "Armies," "Massacre," and the like, surely owes something to Prescott's account of the Spanish conquest, the barricades, the running fights through Tenochtitlán, and the frightful *noche trista* in which Spaniards and Aztecs alike were massacred (1471).[12] A bare reference to a "Mrs Morene of Mexico" in one of the poet's last letters completes the list (L1034). It is possible, however, that Mexico enters into her poetry more importantly as the associated jewel word *emerald* and color word *cochineal*.

Cochineal, a natural dyestuff used in producing scarlet, crimson, and other tints, and in preparing lake and carmine, was clearly well known to Emily Dickinson. Her use of the word *lake* in its special color sense (451) suggests that she may have looked into the uses of cochineal. She certainly knew that the insect from which the dyestuff is made is native to Mexico and Central America, for her books told her that. John Stephens makes several allusions to cochineal and devotes some space to accounts of the growing of the insects and the preparation of the dye.[13] In his *Conquest of Mexico*, Prescott makes an interesting comment on native dyestuffs: "Among them was the rich cochineal, the modern rival of the famed Tyrian purple." [14]

The emerald is as conspicuous in Prescott's *Mexico* as is the cochineal, and perhaps more so. Speaking of amethysts and emeralds, Prescott says: "They [the Mexicans] fashioned these last, which were found very large, into many curious and fantastic forms." He describes the Indians' golden eagle standard as "richly ornamented with emeralds and silver-work." The cloak and sandals of Montezuma, we are told elsewhere, were sprinkled with pearls, emeralds, and jade. When Montezuma prepares to expostulate with the Aztecs besieging Cortes, he dons a costume decked out with "emeralds of uncommon size." And Cortes gave his young bride "five emeralds, of wonderful size and brilliancy," carved into flowers, fishes, and other remarkable forms. These instances suffice to show that emerald as well as cochineal is firmly associated with the "Mexico" image.[15] But so also is the hummingbird. Prescott repeats, somewhat skeptically, the Indian Deluge story, in which, not the dove, but the "little humming-bird, *huitzitzilin,* was then sent forth, and returned with a twig in its mouth." Or he writes "of that miniature miracle of nature, the humming-bird which delights to revel among the honeysuckle bowers of Mexico." Of

Mexican featherwork, he says that "the fine down of the humming-bird, which revelled in swarms among the honeysuckle bowers, supplied them with soft aerial tints." [16] Most astonishing is the possibility that the terrible Huitzilopochtli, the hummingbird god, has made his own slight and perhaps unconscious contribution to the poet's symbolic hummingbird. Poem 1463 in appearance is a reworking of the hummingbird poem (500) dating back to the winter of 1861–62, but the transformation is so complete that only a careful study reveals the connection between the two. A striking difference is that except for the suggestion inherent in "Ripest Rose" the early poem is barren of color, whereas the later version is, in her own words, a "Resonance of Emerald—/ A Rush of Cochineal—."

Huitzilopochtli, war god and sun god of the Aztecs, whose "fantastic image was loaded with costly ornaments," whose "temples were the most stately and august of the public edifices," whose "altars reeked with the blood of human hecatombs in every city of the empire," this "sanguinary monster," as Prescott calls him, does seem incredibly remote from the tiny hummingbird that ravished a rose in an Amherst garden or, more exactly, in a "Garden in the Brain" (500). According to myth, Huitzilopochtli was once a human being. During temple attendance one day a devout woman "saw a ball of bright-colored feathers floating in the air" and, putting it in her bosom, subsequently brought forth the dread war god, who came into the world, "like Minerva, all-armed—with a spear in the right hand, a shield in the left, and his head surmounted by a crest of green plumes." His name means "hummingbird" and "left," because his image has "the feathers of this bird on its left foot." Besides the rich emerald of his plumes and the cochineal of his bloody sacrifices, Huitzilopochtli has in common with Emily Dickinson's hummingbird that power she so much desired and for which she once wrote she would sacrifice the "kingdom" and the "glory" (L330).[17] She is of course the all-conquering hummingbird, just as she is by turns, though less ardently, the consenting flower. This alteration of roles, expressed more commonly in the bee-flower symbolism, is explicit in her work from the very first poem preserved. All elements of her final hummingbird poem had been in her mind as far back as the early 1860s. As observed in the jewel chapter, the June 1860 *Atlantic* essay, "The Humming-Bird," is the indubitable source of this poem in mood and metaphor. In the late 1870s, perhaps during the excitement of Kate Turner's last visit, Emily apparently took a renewed interest in this poem (as in the "two butterflies" poem), revised it, and destroyed all earlier copies and worksheet drafts.

The Emily Dickinson here described is not the passive, sentimental little figure of popular (and biographical) fancy but rather the woman whose intensity overwhelmed and exhausted the visiting Higginson (L342b); the poet who describes herself as dancing "like a Bomb, abroad" (512), who talks of holding her mysterious secret like a "Bomb" to her breast (443), whose powerful kinesthetic imagery may well be the most effective aspect of her work; the woman, moreover, who retired into seclusion to keep from being torn apart by the violence of energies for which society afforded no outlet to the women of her time. The miniaturizing of her images has deceived careless readers. They are as compact as hand grenades.

The remainder of her geographic imagery does not differ markedly in theme or even in properties. The Latin American imagery is doubtless the most distinctive and original as it appears also to be the most deliberately cultivated. The reliance on Prescott's histories, which still furnish themes to American writers, may account for the impression of greater unity. Apart from Prescott's appeal, Emily Dickinson may have been drawn to her Latin American images by a kind of hemispheric patriotism. Emerson urged his countrymen to forsake the "courtly muses of Europe" and employ homely names like Massachusetts, Connecticut River, and Boston Bay; but except for a very occasional "Amherst" or "New England" Emily Dickinson could make no use of local names. Apparently the word must be somewhat exotic, somewhat removed, before she could raise it to a symbol, but if she thought of herself as particularly American when she used her Latin American names, she would have shared a common and amiable illusion of her countrymen.

3

Compared with her Latin American imagery, the African looks at first like a humorous and motley collection made at haphazard. In 1851 she wrote to Austin Dickinson that their father was as uneasy without him as a trout in Sahara (L45). To a neighbor she sent a gift described as "this little Vat of Numidian Wine" (L994). "The Weather is like Africa," she wrote to Mrs. Holland in July 1880, adding that her own "Numidian Heart" was "neither slow nor chill" in its response to this friend; and from his "Numidian Haunts" her friend Samuel Bowles brought a "vivid Face" and "besetting Accents" (letters 650, 438). When her neighbor and future editor, Mabel Loomis Todd, sent her a yellow jug painted with red trumpet-vine blossom, her playful acknowledgment suggested that the young woman had given her an Africa of barbaric color (L978). To young Theodore Holland, thanking him for a sketch, she said she approved "the Paint" and took it to be "a study of the Soudan" (L921). She was writing in the summer of General Gordon's expedition to Khartoum, and her swift association with Africa implied that young Theodore's sketch was gaudy. Like the incessant Domingo of her Latin American imagery, these Niles, Sudans, and Numidians seem mere tricks of style—bows fastened to gift boxes. They have no serious intent, even though they spring from her symbolic South, and the "Numidian" heat has a plausible source in the fire of passion bursting from the "Numidian veins" of Byron's Haidee.[18]

The African imagery of the poetry appears equally tentative and superficial, as if it had not put down roots in her symbolism. The butterfly has a "Numidian Gown," a purely decorative metaphor, because of its gaudy colors and its association with the poet's tropics of summer (1387). The Sahara appears twice as a fairly conventional metaphor for the droughtiness suffered by a rejected lover (1291, 1664); and a rather late and tired version of the sunset poems of her early period tries for color with a "Red Sea" and a "purple Pharaoh" (1642). Revising a bee-flower poem, she seems to have thought, at least for a time, that the words "I know the family in Tripoli" were an eligible substitute for the delightful "A Rose is an Estate / In Sicily" (994). According to another such poem, a little bee fills earth and sky with his "gay apostasy"; then, with a scratch of the poet's palette knife, no autumn's chill "Appals that Tripoli"—and neither pair of lines seems at all inevitable (1526). Her roses from "Zenzibar," "Dawn in Timbuctoo," and "mail from Tunis" (247, 981, 1463) are picturesque metaphors for distance and speed—dabs of paint rather than integral parts of the structure, though her Tunis has compacted within it a fairly rich borrowing from Shakespeare's *Tempest*.[19] The "Teneriffe" of poem 666 is Alpine rather than African, and her Helena is only another Chillon (letters 242, 233). Somewhat more African is an extended metaphor employing the Libyan desert. She has kept toiling at her "Garden of a Rock" and after repeated disappointment has made this "Soil of Flint" yield fruit: "Seed of Palm, by Lybian Sun / Fructified in Sand" (681). The proud and bitter stoicism of this poem may owe something to a line in Elizabeth Browning's *Aurora Leigh* ("The palm stands upright in a realm of sand"), and the Libyan desert that replaces Mrs. Browning's nameless sand may be a borrowing from Milton's "Libyan Air adust" or Shakespeare's barren "banks of Libya." [20] But in general she could do little with a continent which, aside from Egypt, had not been much cultivated or enriched by English writers and seemed more dependent on popular stereotypes.

"When the sun goes down," wrote Peter Parley, "all Africa dances." [21] Geography books, minstrel shows, and circuses—these are the memories that inform the poet's "African Exuberance" (1516), and of these memories the circus appears to be the most lively. The New England village of her childhood afforded no higher excitement, no richer feast of the exotic and marvelous, than some traveling circus or menagerie. In childhood she had certainly been taken to one or more of these, for she knew the routines. Joking about a tree that was said to shiver, she proposed to make it a little coat, or rather several coats, "and put them on as the circus men stand on each other's shoulders" (L372). Once she wrote half jokingly, half seriously, from the recollection of wide-eyed, wondering childhood:

"Friday I tasted life. It was a vast morsel. A circus passed the house—still I feel the red in my mind though the drums are out" (L318). When a bad foot kept her awake one night, she found compensation in her vigil: "the birds insisted on sitting up, so it became an occasion instead of a misfortune. There was a circus, too, and I watched it away at half-past three that morning. They said 'hoy, hoy' to their horses" (L390). Next year, "We are to have another 'Circus,' and again the Procession from Algiers will pass the Chamber-Window" (L412). In June 1877, "There is a circus here, and Farmers' Commencement, and Boys and Girls from Tripoli" (L506), and a year before her death, in the note thanking Mrs. Todd for the gaily painted jug, she linked the words "Circus" and "Ethiopian Face" (L978). "Circus" meant color, gaiety, life, "African Exuberance." Her response was part of that irrepressible playfulness that made her long for playmates beyond the grave (1549).

In the fall of 1861 she wrote "I've known a Heaven, like a Tent—" (243), in which her lost happiness figures as a circus that has plucked up its stakes and disappeared, all its marvels and men and feats and dazzling ring dissolved as utterly now

> As Bird's far Navigation
> Discloses just a Hue—
> A plash of Oars, a Gaiety—
> Then swallowed up, of View.

The circus, with its colorful extravagance, its exotic strangers, its "Boys and Girls from Tripoli," seems an effective metaphor for the exciting years 1859–60, when friends collected around her, poetry was writing itself after years of dryness, and life seemed beginning again; but the shift in metaphor from tent to vanishing bird suggests a narrower focus. Consciously she may be using the tent and circus feats to recall a glorious experience that has now ended, but at a deeper level the tent, like the bird, appears to represent the person who created the experience. For example, seventeen-year-old Maggie Kelley is dying and her bed is to be moved so that she "can see the tents" of the expected circus. "Folding her own like the Arabs gives her no apprehension," writes the apprehensive poet wonderingly (L372). In Sue Dickinson's 1860 copy of Charles A. Dana's popular anthology, *The Household Book of Poetry*, she could refresh her memory of a passage from Thomas Moore's *Lalla Rookh* affirming that "tents with love" are better than "thrones without." [22] More powerfully erotic, after her own favored device of bees and flowers, are the following lines from James Russell Lowell's "To the Dandelion":

> Not in mid June the golden-cuirassed bee
> Feels a more summer-like warm ravishment
> In the white lily's breezy tent,
> His fragrant Sybaris, than I [23]

Still closer to her theme of happiness and loss is a passage from Lowell's "She Came and Went": "The tent is struck, the vision stays;—/ I only know she came and went." [24]

In an excited letter of 11 January 1850, the exuberant new poet assured her young Uncle Joel that Amherst was "alive with fun this winter" —sleigh rides, parties, beaux for the taking:" "Have you found *Susannah* yet? 'Roses will fade—time flies on—Lady of beauty,'" a hymn so familiar to Joel that she need not repeat it (L29). The quotation has not been identified, but clearly it urges youth to pluck the rosebud while it may. "Susannah" is an allusion to a new song by Stephen Foster that had become immensely popular over the past year as the theme song of the Forty-Niners. In Foster's original, the singer goes to New Orleans looking for his girl, and if he fails to find her,

> Dis darkie'll surely die,
> And when I'm dead and buried,
> Susannah, don't you cry,
> Oh! Susannah Oh! don't you cry for me
> I've come from Alabama wid my banjo on my knee.

There is a probable reminiscence of this Foster song in an otherwise mournful poem of 1862: "No Black bird bates his Banjo— / For passing Calvary" (620). Odder still, this early reference to Foster's poem may mark the first sign of the poet's Ethiopian identity.

It may have begun in half-playful deprecation. Certainly she was no Ethiopian in looks, for her hair was auburn, the color of her eyes hazel, and her skin notably pale. With such a fair complexion, she appeared to freckle easily and to be somewhat concerned about it. She was, in fact, a very plain, overintellectual, overwitty girl, not very well liked by ordinary folk, and the deprecatory references to her spottedness, like the equally deprecatory "old-fashioned" she sometimes applied to herself, were an indirect bid for sympathetic acceptance of the "freckled Maiden" of poem 275 (also 1094, 1737, and letters 235 and 242), "spotted" (492, 964), "sunburnt" (163), "tawny" (492), "tanned" (L235). Because of her freckles or spots she is a "Leopard" (209, 492), and being unable to change her spots and hence her skin, she is an Ethiopian as well.[25] Again, since all her symbols are wonderfully overdetermined, her spottedness presumes the beloved's spotlessness: "Thou art all fair, my love; there is no spot in thee." [26] And since she apparently knew the Song of Solomon by heart, another possible identification is with the "black" woman beloved by Solomon, herself commonly identified with the queen of Sheba, who was believed to be an Ethiopian: "Look not upon me, because I am black, because the sun hath looked upon me; my mother's children were angry with me; they made me the keeper of the vineyards; but mine own vineyard have I not kept." [27] In letter 222 the poet speaks of "Vineyards" she longs to reach, and in poem 175 her "palpitating Vineyard" is destroyed. The most plausible source of these symbolic vineyards is the Song of Solomon.[28]

Emily Dickinson may also have been an Ethiopian because she read Shakespeare, who commonly uses the word "Ethiope" to deprecate. Among the several poems and plays where the term disparages some woman, it is probable that she was most influenced by *A Midsummer Night's Dream,* and not alone by Lysander's scornful words to his erstwhile love, the brunette Hermia: "away, you Ethiope! . . . out, tawny Tartar, out!" Later in the same scene he abuses her for her short stature: "You bead, you acorn," words reminiscent of a poem in which the poet defends herself against the taunt of being an "Acorn" and of having an "Acorn's Breast" (296).[29]

Milton's "*Ethiop* Line by *Nilus* head" is the equator, in the region "by some suppos'd True Paradise."[30] Emily Dickinson's Ethiopia is dark or spotted, tropical, and perfervid, and no farther removed than Amherst. It could be summer weather, "Ethiopian Days" (1644); but this is a very late poem, when her poetry had been stripped of symbolism and virtually of significance. In her major period, as in poem 422, it was the "Ethiop within," the tropical heart that could be extinguished only by "an Ampler Zero— / A Frost more needle keen" than sufficed to obliterate ordinary folk. In an earlier stanza, she wrote of "Requiring in the Quench" (not the water one would expect but) a "Power of Renowned Cold"; yet implicit in the word "Quench" is her recollection of the flood waters that drown her in poem 537 and, more significantly, these lines from the Song of Solomon: "Many waters cannot quench love, neither can the floods drown it."[31]

Ethiopia could be in or close to Asia, that is, an Asia equally of the emotions. The unhappy "Pard" that has left her "Asia," lured by the promises of a "Civilization" that now spurns her, admits to her spotted gown, her tawny customs, but pleads that these were her nature and hence already known to her "keeper." Why reject her now? At least she was never treated like this by the desert wilderness from which she has been lured (with a possible reminiscence of the Song of Solomon: "Who is this that cometh up from the wilderness, leaning upon her beloved?").[32] Her native deserts approved her "Satin," as did "Ethiop—her Gold" (492). Here the poet apparently adopts the common identification of Ethiopia with Ophir, and since she had just signified her presence in that country, she is once more Ethiopian as well as leopard. Her "Memories of Palm," painfully recalled in this poem, seem to be another allusion to the Song of Solomon: "This thy stature is like to a palm tree, and thy breasts to clusters of grapes. I said, I will go up to the palm tree, I will take hold of the boughs thereof: now also thy breasts shall be as clusters of the vine."[33] The palm tree may well be the tall beloved, whose stature permits a taunt at the poet's acorn breast. All these symbols are somehow involved in the central idea of love as tropical heat, vitality itself, an idea to be found again in her symbolic Italy and its volcanoes.

The poet's Ethiopian heart had found its Susannah—for years to come and in some sense for life. Susan Gilbert was the rose and the lily of the poet's symbolism, as indeed her name entitled her to be. In the Dickinson library were at least four books, perhaps more, which gave the translation of the Hebrew name Susannah as "lily" (two of them, as "rose" also), and it is unthinkable that one of these young women did not make the discovery and pass it on to the other as an item of at least sentimental interest.[34] Girls had then, and perhaps still have, an unquenchable interest in their given names as the only names they are likely to retain. There was also among Victorians a regular cult of flower significance, which may be dimly reflected in Emily Fowler Ford's account of the girls in their set giving each other flower names and calling Lavinia Dickinson the pond lily, whereupon her sister Emily "answered so quickly, 'And I am the Cow Lily,' referring to the orange lights in her hair and eyes." [35] Since the poet herself could be a lily, and since her friend Kate Turner was also both rose and lily during 1859–60, the symbolism could not have been exclusive; still, Susan's name itself must have given her a large claim.

"I am the rose of Sharon, and the lily of the valleys. As the lily among thorns, so is my love among the daughters," reads the Song of Solomon. Writing to Sue from Cambridge, about 1864, the poet concludes a letter of passionate affirmation with these words: "Take the Key to the Lily, now, and I will lock the Rose—" (L288). It is a clear allusion to the Song of Solomon and perhaps to the double significance of Sue's name, but what else it may have meant only the poet and doubtless Sue herself would ever know. In September 1864, still at Cambridge, she wrote again to Sue: "Did you save the seed to the pond Lily?" And she ended her letter on a note of strong dependence: "Should I turn in my long night I should murmur 'Sue'" (L294). Six months later, to her cousin Louise Norcross, she described in all innocence an erotic dream that had given her much happiness: "I dreamed last night I heard bees fight for pond-lily stamens" (L304).

In another letter the poet spoke of sending her friend Mrs. William A. Stearns some pond lilies, adding: "I shall bring you a handful of lotus next, but do not tell the Nile. He is a jealous brook" (L612). Here the linking of pond lilies with lotus and the Nile with jealousy hints at an underlying, perhaps half-conscious association with Mark Antony's "serpent of old Nile," Cleopatra herself. Indeed it may have been wholly conscious, for she read in Higginson's "Water Lilies": "Rock softly on the waters, fair lilies! Your Eastern kindred have rocked on the stormier bosom of Cleopatra." [36] To Higginson himself she once made the startling remark: "'Field Lilies' are Cleopatra's 'Posies'" (L405). This identification of Christ's lilies of the field with Cleopatra's lilies has at least one of its associative links in their splendor, for the poet observed to Maria Whitney: "I never pass one without being chagrined for Solomon, and so in love with 'the lily' anew, that were I sure no one saw me, I might make those advances of which in after life I should repent" (L824). The Higginson letter that elicited her comment was the one urging her to cultivate the "ruddy hues," the yellow and scarlet of the field lilies. These were precisely the colors she discovered in Mrs. Todd's painted jŭg, which made her think of "Circus" and "Ethiopian Face" and then of Cleopatra, for her note to Mrs. Todd concluded: " 'You knew, Oh Egypt!' said the entangled Anthony—" (L978).

There are no marks in the copy of *Antony and Cleopatra* most probably used by the poet. A pink string bookmark indicates the beginning of Antony's monument speech ("I am dying, Egypt, dying"), and a piece of cloth inserted in act 5, scene 2, marks the beginning of Cleopatra's "Show me, my women, like a queen." They sound like passages in which the poet would have delighted, but of course it is not possible to know who placed the markers there. In her quotations she appears always to take the role of "entangled Antony," and her Cleopatra seems to be her sister-in-law, Sue Dickinson. Perhaps Sue's dark coloring as well as a certain arrogance and opulence of personality, mentioned by those who knew her, favored the identification, but some oral symbolism appears to be involved also. There is much playing upon food and drink in Shakespeare's *Antony and Cleopatra*. Pompey talks of "your fine Egyptian cookery" and, to make the jibe clear, alludes to the rumor "that Julius Caesar / Grew fat with feasting there." Enobarbus says of Antony, "He will to his Egyptian dish again." The most famous instance, part of Enobarbus's description of Cleopatra's first meeting with Antony, recurs in a note from Emily Dickinson to her sister-in-law: "Susan's Calls are like Antony's Supper—'And pays his Heart for what his Eyes eat, only—' " (L854).[37] When she sent the same quotation to her nephew two years later, she added, in instant self-consciousness, "Excuse the bearded Pronoun" (L1026).

At a much earlier date the poet sent to Sue Dickinson the bare quotation, "Egypt—thou knew'st" (L430), which was intended to evoke for Sue all the following lines:

Egypt, thou knew'st too well,
My heart was to thy rudder tied by the strings,
And thou shouldest tow me after. O'er my spirit
Thy full supremacy thou knew'st, and that
Thy beck might from the bidding of the gods
Command me.[38]

The consistency of this poet's symbolism, from the earliest period of her poetry, suggests the possibility that the line "Loved One, thou knowest!" in a letter of April 1852 to Susan Gilbert was also intended to call up these lines (L88).

The lilies that rocked on Cleopatra's stormy bosom may have affected the symbolism in still another way. The passage quoted earlier from Higginson's "Water Lilies" is followed by these lines: "The Egyptian Lotus was, moreover, the emblem of the sacred Nile ... and the god Nilus still binds a wreath of water-lilies around the throne of Memnon." Given Emily's remarkable powers of association, it would be unsafe to say that this passage has no link with her "'Memnon' of the Desert" (261), although at first glance the poem seems to be a missed opportunity rather than a rewarding instance of her African symbolism. In her Webster's dictionary she would have read no more than this: "The name of a celebrated Egyptian statue, supposed to have the property of emitting a harp-like sound at sunrise"; and that is the material with which she appeared to content herself. "Put up my lute!" she begins. The one person, the "sole ear," that she has ever wanted to charm, now "laps" her "Music," that is, her poetry, as "Passive—as Granite," and she might as well sob as create poems. In the second stanza she turns to the Memnon statue and begs to be taught the particular "strain" that "vanquished Him— When He—surrendered to the Sunrise—." So instructed, she might be able to awaken "them," which is simply the beloved person, the "sole ear," of the first stanza. Clearly the strain to which Memnon vibrates is love's music, and the "Sunrise" to which he yields, as so often in this poetry, is love's sunrise or dawn. In the past the "sole ear" has vibrated like a Memnon too, and this resemblance suggests other reasons for associating the two. In a number of sources the poet would have read about the Ethiopian prince slain by Achilles and of his vocal statue, which, as her Bulfinch's *Age of Fable* and her own wide reading would have assured her, was "a favorite subject of allusion with the poets." [39] The classical dictionaries of Lempriere and Anthon, both conveniently at hand, not only made the handsome black prince an appealingly tragic figure but also linked him with Susa or Susiana, city of lilies. Memnon was the lily prince, just as Higginson had suggested, and this association may explain why the lily-beloved rather than Emily is the Ethiopian of this poem. [40]

The death chill that invades so much of her poetry is not altogether absent even in hottest Africa. Although the Memnon-like person, the "sole ear" that she ever wanted to charm, is obviously alive but indifferent to her, death images abound. The other person is "Passive—as Granite," a stone image; the poet might as well sob (for her dead love) as attempt to sing. Even the language of passion—"vanquished," "surrendered to the Sunrise"—has a chilling sound. An 1864 poem associates Egypt with mortality in the line, "Though Pyramids decay" (946). A somewhat earlier poem, "We dream—it is good we are dreaming—" (531), makes death itself Egyptian. The "livid Surprise" of waking from this illusion called life cools us to "Shafts of Granite"—petrifies us into our own tombstones, carved with name and date and "perhaps a phrase in Egyptian," the very name suggesting not only deadness but also the strangeness, the ineluctable foreignness, of death.

Her only African river, the Nile, is the "jealous brook" of Cleopatra, who functions at least playfully, as the love goddess of this symbolism (L612). More significantly, the Nile is death, an identification explicitly made in a letter of early May 1866 to Mrs. Holland. The latter had paid a visit to Amherst, and the poet, whose devotion to Mrs. Holland must be described as intense, was still reverberating from the effects. In retrospect she felt she had not sufficiently enjoyed her visitor: "The supper of the heart is when the guest has gone." Extravagant allusion to a recent circus gave her some outlet for these uncomfortable emotions, and then, as often happened in letter and poem, intense love converted to intense fear. Recalling a neighbor who had died recently, she continued: "I thought since of the power of death, not upon affection, but its mortal signal. It is to us the Nile" (L318). As she observed to Higginson a few days later, translating his word "Immortality" into the fear most potent in her mind, "That is the Flood subject" (L319).

Careering circuses daubed with red and yellow paint, dark minstrels thrumming banjos and dancing soft-shoe, as it were, in everlasting pursuit of the elusive Susannah, rose of Sharon and lily of the valley, leopard and Ethiopian Sheba, Cleopatra and entangled Antony, granite Memnon and flooding Nile—her African imagery is a kaleidoscope of color and shape incessantly changing and yet remarkably the same. There are but two themes, two aspects of the Nile, and all her art is devoted to securing the illusion of variety and change. That she uses her life as material has been abundantly indicated, but it is imperative to realize that this is only the beginning of understanding. Of her own Circus Animals, Emily Dickinson would have said no less certainly than Yeats,

Heart-mysteries there, and yet when all is said
It was the dream itself enchanted me.[41]

4

The Asiatic imagery is drawn in general from three broad areas (with much overlapping and a few outriders): the Bible land, India and the Indies, and an intermediate region consisting of Arabia, Turkey, Persia, and the Caspian Sea. Chinese Tartary, "Kamchatka," and Japan receive solitary mentions in three widely separated letters (110, 685, 976); and a few words like Asia, Asiatic, Orient, or Oriental allude to a remote, mysterious region of fabulous wealth and luxury. In the short but symbol-rich note acknowledging Mrs. Todd's jar, Emily thanked the young woman for showing her not only an Africa of barbaric color but also an Asia of exotic wealth brought home and naturalized in Amherst: "The Orient is in the West" (L978).

In her letters she commonly uses as mere ornament the imagery that may be quite seriously intended in her poems. Repetitively she assures engaged couples that they have found the passage to India that Columbus was seeking, or she thanks Sue Dickinson for the gift of a George Eliot book that is likewise a passage to India, or Mrs. James S. Cooper for flowers that are an "Indies" in the hand, or Mrs. Thomas P. Field for flow-ers that prove her ownership of the gates to India" (letters 575, 900, 456, 543, 552). Her conservatory is her "Spice Isles," and her sister-in-law has just called and left a "Cashmere print"—perhaps another flower or simply the grace of her visit (L315). These are mere ribbon knots and posies of rhetoric, no more and no less sincere than that kind of writing usually is.

Much the same may be said of her middle eastern imagery, which is based largely on recollections of the *Arabian Nights*. In early letters she speaks of her brother's enjoyment of the *Arabian Nights* (letters 19, 22), and no doubt she enjoyed the book too. A pretended fairyland, a world of genies and magical transformations, surrounds Sue Dickinson, whose "Arabian Nights" unsettle the poet's heart for life's arithmetic (L335). Among her repetitive orientals are her cherished sweet sultans, which are sent across the lawn as "Turks" to Sue's East or, surviving a frost, become sultans and viziers (letters 345, 655, 746). The "little Smyrna" in a dish sent by a friend, Mrs. Edward Tuckerman, appears to be something to eat, perhaps figs; and the poet sends Mrs. Henry Hills "Persian Hues," said to be red lilies (letters 795, 848).[42] In extravagant mood, the poet's flowers become all "Asia" (L650).

The biblical place-names in the letters are not especially rich in associa-tions. "Ophir" implies the golden worth of Mrs. Holland, Higginson's writ-ings, Sue Dickinson, and a deceased fellow townsman (letters 395, 593, 985, 677). Zion and Jerusalem are the New Jerusalem of Revelation (let-ters 46, 189, 727, 1042), and the frequent Edens are a this-world paradise. Her brother's engagement to Susan Gilbert is his arrival in "Canaan" (L110). Her sister's garden is a "Bethesda" in which Vinnie heals a bruised spirit (L521). A photograph of her young niece Martha impresses her, hyperbolically, like the vision of John on Patmos, and her cousins' move to Cambridge is a move to Ephesus with Paul for neighbor (letters 787, 962). Neither these nor any of the Asian names of her correspondence have more than a superficial connection with the symbolism of her poetry.

Only one of her correspondents, Elizabeth Holland, called forth Asiatic symbols approaching the depth and resonance of the poems written in

1859–65. A letter of early January 1881 to Mrs. Holland is rich in symbols. The phrase "Sister Golconda," to be sure, begins on a note as insincere as any of the thank-you notes sent to prying neighbors who tried to bribe their way into her presence; but it is in fact a playful tribute to a genuinely loved friend who has received a Christmas gift of diamond earrings. Further on in the letter, the poet tells of a runaway little boy who, when asked his destination, replied, "Vermont or Asia." Meditating on this "pathetic Crusoe," and perhaps thinking of Dr. Holland's ill health, of her failing mother, even of her own death, she adds that many will go farther than Asia. The intense cold of these early January days reminds her of that coldest part of Asia, and she observes that the rose in her "Puritan Garden" has been dimmed by veils of "Kamtchatka." Perhaps she means only that she is having trouble heating her small conservatory, and yet the insistence on *Puritan* garden hints at a chafing against constraint. And though she speaks of a recent eclipse of the sun as a "stimulus," the tone seems desperately ironic. According to the local paper, a fourteen-year-old boy did run away from Amherst at this time, but he is not likely to have said, "Vermont or Asia." The naive geography is the invention of the poet, who credited it years earlier to her sister. "Vinnie," she once wrote to Mrs. Holland, "thinks Vermont is in Asia" (L473). The would-be runaway is herself stirred to new longing for a symbolic Asia (L685).

The Asian imagery of the poems begins quite early in 1859 with what might be called the poet's Byronic or Thomas Moore vocabulary. Such words as "Cashmere," "Circassian," and "Turk"—and one might also note "turbaned" and "cimitar"—appear sporadically through 1864 (the "Circassian" of poem 970 is the last), then vanish entirely. The favorite is "Cashmere," which she owed to Moore's romance about the Princess Lalla Rookh who falls in love with her young minstrel en route to a royal marriage in Cashmere, only to make the happy discovery that the minstrel is her fiancé in disguise. There is much emphasis on the rose gardens of Cashmere, and the separate tales and the connecting narrative are lushly romantic.[43] In the Dickinson copy of *Lalla Rookh,* three passages dealing with the pleasures, pangs, and disillusionments of love are marked in what seems to be the poet's usual fashion.

The section of *Lalla Rookh* entitled "The Fire-Worshippers," which contains the second and third of her marked passages, may have been the poet's favorite. In a somewhat confused poem she compared her own idolatrous passion with that of a "Persian" girl who turns away, baffled, from her "shrine," to lift up a "Crucifixal sign" toward her adored "imperial Sun" (506). This seems to recall the emir's daughter Hinda and her love for the Persian fire worshiper Hafed; the words "shrine" and "Persian" and references to the worship of sun and fire are frequent in this section of *Lalla Rookh.*[44] At the close the doomed lover immolates himself in the sacred fire of his holiest shrine, Hinda watching from a distance. In her poem Emily Dickinson appears to be both the Persian burning in the sacred fire and the apalled onlooker at her own immolation.

Other poems may draw upon the lines in which Hinda invokes the "glorious stranger!...So loved, so lost," agonizes over the "wrong" or "crime" of her love, fears that she is "Forgetting faith—home—father—all" and is even worshiping her earthly idol above God himself:

> For, oh, so wildly do I love him
> Thy Paradise itself were dim
> And joyless, if not shared with him![45]

The glorious "Stranger" is a recurrent figure in the poetry of Emily Dickinson—the atom of clay she preferred to all others but can acknowledge only after death (664), the "Countenance" from a neighboring horizon that vanished with tragic swiftness (752), the angelic "Stranger" whom she wrestled and overcame and from whom she sought a blessing (59). Closest to Moore's lines is a poem in which she writes that, for the sake of a "paltry One," for the novel companionship of a "Stranger," she has forgotten "Wealth," "Station," "Home," everything, and has dropped the "timid Pebble" of herself in the other's bold sea (966). In poem 640 there is no hope of happiness; their love is indeed a crime, like Hinda's, and the poet expects to be punished, chiefly by separation from her love. This earthly idol has "saturated Sight" until the poet has no eyes left for such "sordid excellence / As Paradise." The lover's face would "put out Jesus'," and the latter's "Grace" would look "plain and foreign" unless the beloved "Shone closer" to her. Both poems would seem to illustrate her skill in reworking and heightening another writer's themes.

One final Asian place-name, which may have come from "The Fire-Worshippers," is her symbolic Caspian. It is her generic sea, just as the Sahara is her generic desert. In poem 1291 the sands suffice the "Desert" until it discovers the "Caspian Fact" that "Water" exists, whereupon "Sahara" ceases. A second stanza, however, implies that all satisfaction is relative and temporary, that today's "Enough" is a mere halting place on the endless road of desire. Another Caspian poem views the dilemma from a somewhat different point of view; her present "drought is destitute," but she has the memory of the "dew"; the Caspian has realms of sand as well as sea and without its "sterile" perquisite" could not be a Caspian (1754). A poem too unfinished to make its meaning clear has the line "A Caspian were crowded," implying that its nature is to be uncrowded, solitary (1107). In "Many a phrase has the English language," she recalls the words "I love you," spoken in happier times; even now she seems to hear the phrase, or perhaps the murmur of the loved voice, like "Caspian Choirs" (276). A quite early poem identifies the beloved as "My Caspian" and the poet as "least" river obedient to her sea (212).

Apparently the name was more usable than those of her other seas,

Baltic, Mediterranean, Red, and Azof, which all together appear only six times in her poems. Euphony, geographic remoteness, even the fact that the Caspian is landlocked and does not open into another sea or ocean, may have helped to make it poetically viable, but initially she would have been drawn to it by the romantic attractiveness of *Lalla Rookh*. For example, Moore speaks of a drowned Persian hero who "sleeps in the Caspian," of "hills of crystal on their Caspian shore," of "fountains of blue flame / That burn in the Caspian," of "the Caspian's Iron Gates" and the "broad Caspian's reedy brink." Still more suggestive, a peri describes the drowned heroine of "The Fire-Worshippers" as purer than any pearl in its shell and proposes to "seek where the sands of the Caspian are sparkling / And gather their gold to strew over thy bed." [46]

A number of Asian place-names or related words, mostly late in the poetry as in the letters, are suggestions of wealth, color, and exoticism—her several "Orientals" (813, 1048, 1526), her "Indies in the Ground," which in the same poem is described as another "Potosi" (1117), her "East India" (202), her "Golconda" (299), her "Indiaman" (791). The golden oriole has the "splendor of a Burmah" (1466), and "Love" with a mere penny outvies "India" (1477). Elsewhere "African Exuberance" is succeeded by an "Asiatic rest" that appears to echo Tennyson's cycle of Cathay (1516).[47] An earlier poem belonging to the years of loss and suffering describes her as once more separated from the beloved by a "Desert" and compares the sand grains blocking her horizon to the uncountable water drops of "Asiatic Rains" (550). The "spicy isles" and "Isles of Spice" (368, 580) are now manifest sex symbols, but they call for no special notice. These metaphors are so commonplace and their sources so nearly legion that inquiry into their origin would be as impossible as it is unprofitable.

The two most important examples of her symbolic India were discussed in chapter 3. The first was the letter-poem to Sue Dickinson, "Your—Riches—taught me—poverty!" (L258), which asserts that the privilege of being constantly close to Sue without "stint" or "blame" would be an "India" of incredible wealth. The second, mentioned in passing, is an 1862 poem that begins "It would never be Common—more—I said" (430) and recalls a happy time when she seemed to fly rather than walk, when she felt her joy "publish" itself in eye and cheek, when she dealt out words of "Gold" and dowered the world. Suddenly her riches disappeared, a "Goblin" drank her "Dew," and the "Wilderness" rolled back along her "Golden lines." Once more she sees her old sackcloth hanging on the nail, but what has become of her "moment of Brocade," her "drop—of India?" This last appears to be the "Dew" that the "Goblin" drank and to be related to all the nectars and dews and assorted liquors that represent ecstasy in her poetry, but it also incorporates all the vague riches of the India symbol, including the pearl of the letter-poem to Sue. In the poetry of Emily Dickinson dewdrops are quite likely to be pearls.

Whether the place-names Cashmere and India represent the passion of love or the person of the beloved, the latter is always part of their meaning. The "Asia" of poem 492, however, more nearly represents the poet herself and appears to have affinities with that East of poetic wealth to which she invited Kate Turner in the spring of 1859: "Dare you dwell in the *East* where we dwell? Are you afraid of the Sun?" (L203). In the "Asia" poem the beloved woman is called "Civilization"—quite literally in the sense of being elegantly dressed, sophisticated, and worldly—who is at first attracted to, then spurns, the unsophisticated, primitive beauty of the poet's "East." Between this poem and Master letters 233 and 248 there is an obvious kinship. The beloved has elegant "Tailor made" clothes (L233), not the poor handiwork of the village dressmaker, successor to the poet's mother, whose own pathetic "apologies made up from dry goods" were so mortifying a recollection of Emily Dickinson's youth.[48] The poet fears that her "Backwoodsman" ways may have offended the beloved, teased that finer nature, and she begs to be taught "patrician things" (L248).

Although the biblical place-names in her poems might seem to be so involved in religious myth as to have little geographic reality, they are in fact about as real, or as unreal, as any of the other place-names. "Calvary" is explicitly contrasted with "Cashmere" (725), and in poem 506 the poet compares herself not only to the Persian girl of the fire-worshiper sect but also to the biblical Rebecca who turns "ravished" toward (a not-yet-existent) "Jerusalem."[49] Neither is a religious poem, except as it serves that religion of erotic passion so conspicuous in the 1859–65 poems. An 1862 poem affirms that happiness in this world would have disqualified her for the next. Struggling through the "Reefs" of "Old Gethsemane," she begs a "Savior" who appears to be as much the human lover as the biblical Jesus to "Crucify" her (313). To the lost beloved she demonstrates her love by exhibiting her "Calvary" (549). Desperately hoping she may have "it" (the lover) when "it" is dead, she imagines a time when the two of them will have waded through this "Deep" of suffering and can smile back on "Old Times—in Calvary" (577).

The place-name Bethlehem is handled with equal freedom, meaning Christ himself, wherever he may appear, or the poet or her lover as Christ. For example, a statement made at the Last Supper is said to be uttered in "Bethlehem" (85). In poem 236 the "*Faint* Star of Bethlehem / *Gone down!*" is both the person of the western lover and the destruction of hope. In a very late love poem, which may be simply a late revision, "Bethlehem" becomes the heavenly Jerusalem where the lovers will be united (1237), and in a later poem, titled "Christ's Birthday," "Bethlehem" figures as birthplace and Calvary at once (1487). In a final poem, which lists "Bethlehem" among the "Subjects" of Bible myth, the place-name represents the entire New Testament.

5

Naturally enough, Europe supplied metaphors drawn from fine manufactures. For example, the human body is compared with expensive porcelain made at Sèvres (640); the flashing "Cutlery" of the squirrel's teeth eclipses the finest implements manufactured at Birmingham or Manchester (1374); a carpet of pine needles is like the carpets loomed at Brussels and Kidderminster (602). Even so exhausted a metaphor as "turned to stone" acquires a new if somewhat precious appearance in the words "wrought Carrara in me" (1046). A poem that describes the dead body as the snowy pendulum of a stopped clock states that "Geneva's farthest skill" could not start this pendulum again (287); and of course the clockmaking skill of the Swiss was common knowledge. Finally, with whatever depth of conscious or unconscious irony, she could not fail to associate "Geneva's farthest skill" with her meddling sister-in-law, who grew up in Geneva, New York, made frequent return visits, and married Austin Dickinson there in July 1856.

Europe is also the realm of art, of high fashion and social rank. According to a poem of late 1861, the admired friend has a "Bonnet like a Duke" and an "Orleans in the Eye" but puts her manner aside for "humbler company" like the poet. Since the friend is also "Half Child—Half Heroine," she is apparently a Maid of Orléans as well as a duke (283). In the more bitter mood of poem 468, the court of "St. James" figures as the symbol of artificiality and social pretense as opposed to ugly, unfashionable truths of suffering and death (468). On the other hand, the poet might dream of waking up a "Bourbon" and bestir herself to overcome little rusticities, so that she would not be caught in "Arragon" with her old gown on and the surprised air of a rustic unexpectedly summoned to "Exeter" (373).

Another poem of this group describes a rose in terms of fashionable dressmaking. Introduced as one of the "Velvet people from Vevay," the flower seems to owe its habitat to the combined charms of alliteration, the velvety texture of petals, and the popularity of a Swiss watering place. In the next stanza we are told that "Paris" (a famous center of dressmaking then as now) "Could not lay the fold" (presumably, gather the petals into folds) of stem and leaf, nor could "Venice...show a cheek / Of a tint so lustrous meek" (138). These lines about a lustrous Venice and a green Paris seem to be a condensation of a passage from Elizabeth Browning's *Aurora Leigh*:

Of fair fantastic Paris who wears boughs
Like plumes . . .
The city swims in verdure, beautiful
As Venice on the waters, the sea-swan.[50]

According to the last stanza of the "Vevay" poem, the poet would rather dwell like her little rose than be "Duke of Exeter"—perhaps another reminiscence of the rustic beauty and the eccentric nobleman.

A second "Vevay" poem so perplexed her first editors that they refused to publish it. In paraphrase, the "Flower" is asked not to blame the "Bee" that keeps turning up at her door but to instruct the "Footman from Vevay" to deny the lady to future callers (206). Since the rose-lady herself is "from Vevay," and since the bee, who is writing the poem, assuredly would not beg to be rejected, the most plausible explanation is that the mischievous bee is now installed as footman and proposes to exclude all later arrivals. The idea of being a footman, curiously enough, did once occur to the youthful Emily. "If I loved a girl to disstraction [*sic*]," she wrote to her brother in July 1851, "I think it would take some coaxing before I would act as footman to her crazy friends—yet love is *pretty solemn*" (L49).

The European imagery affords no Golconda or Domingo or Indies for inexpensive flattery in letters and notes. She wrote to friends in Europe and mentioned the European travels of other friends. Sharing the nineteenth-century adulation of Raphael's Sistine Madonna and of Shakespeare, she observed to Higginson that his seeing "Stratford on Avon—and the Dresden Madonna, must be almost Peace" (L553). A hint of warmer weather is a "Sicilian symptom" (L690), but January cold is "Norwegian Weather" (L764), and elsewhere November is the "Norway of the Year" (L311). According to a poem mentioned in chapter 4, which makes only this seasonal point, the winter solstice is the "Sun's objective" and the year's "Finland" (1696). A remark that the present savage March air would dismay any bird, even "Gibraltar's Feathers" (L808), is a rather eccentric treatment of her customary symbol for firmness and impregnable strength; other references to Gibraltar are more conventional (350, 1502; letters 319, 377, 722). In the new spring the Dickinson hens are "touched with the things of Bourbon" and assume airs that make "republicans" like the poet feel out of place (L339). Pretending to have a report of furnishings that are all marble, "even to the flies," she asks her cousins whether they "dwell in Carrara" (L264).

Among the romantic poets, she once named Keats as her master (L261), but his influence is not especially marked. Her real model seemed to be Byron, as he was also that of Charlotte Brontë, Elizabeth Browning, indeed every Victorian woman who felt herself disadvantaged; and on his side Byron came at least halfway toward his preponderantly feminine audience by urging them to treat him "as a favorite and somewhat forward sister." [51] In poetry and life-style, Emily Dickinson strove to be as Byronic as her sex, total obscurity, and penniless isolation permitted her to be. She was a Byron imprisoned at Chillon. Implicit in the poems complaining of her captivity, the name itself appears in letters to correspondents as varied as the unnamed beloved, her friend Samuel Bowles, her sister Lavinia, and T. W. Higginson (letters 233, 249, 293, 1042). In a note to Sue Dickinson, written in the last few weeks of her life, she describes her illness, or perhaps life itself, as "This long, short penance" and quotes, with slight changes, the concluding words of "The Prisoner of Chillon": "'Even I regain my freedom with a Sigh'" (L1029).

Her borrowings from her father's four-volume set of Byron's works, supplemented by Sue's more inclusive 1854 text, are minute and incessant and deserve more thorough study than can be given here. To Byron she owed much of her interest in the Greek struggle with Persia, a struggle to which his last months and early death provided a striking new illustration, Byron's life being at least as influential as his poetry. She read "The Isles of Greece, the Isles of Greece! / Where burning Sappho loved and sung" and remembered that "The mountains look on Marathon / And Marathon looks on the sea." Lines to the "extinguished Spartans . . . In their proud charnel of Thermopylae" imposed their romantic coloring on the Doric gravity of the epitaph recorded in her school books: "O stranger! tell it at Lacedaemon, that we died here in obedience to her laws." These are the bits of Greek history that kindled her imagination, for these alone appear in her work.

The application is sometimes curious. Barred from happiness by "Decalogues," according to poem 485, she thought of herself as dying in obedience to moral law: not a physical death, she observed pointedly—"The merest Greek could that"—but the living death she saw as her destined and total experience (1013). Once she escaped from egoistic suffering long enough to lament the Civil War, then in its second year, in a poem that calls the dead soldier "This Spartan" and imagines such another memorial "Stone" to honor him (444). With this exception, the martial poems are uniformly concerned with herself as little soldier, with her private wars, her special martyrdom. After the "merest Greek" of 1865, however, the theme of the brave little soldier, victorious in defeat, remained more or less dormant for some twelve years.

About mid-June 1877 she sent Higginson a poem indicating renewed interest in Spartan heroism. First the reader is told to lay his "Laurel" on the one who "triumphed and remained unknown" or, in a revised version, was "Too intrinsic for Renown"; then the laurel is directed to fell its "futile Tree" or "veil" its "deathless Tree," since there can be no victor, or, in the revised version, the victor is "Him you chasten" (1393). The poem has been interpreted as a tribute to her father, dead these three years, but it is more plausibly read as Emily's tribute to herself. Higginson's meandering "Decoration," on which her brief poem is an avowed comment, explicitly rejects the heroic male as subject and turns instead to a low grave without roses or wreath. No higher, warmer heart ever dared battle-storm, he says, no prouder eye ever gleamed in the forefront of battle, no firmer foot ever trod on the field of dead hope:

> Youth and beauty, dauntless will,
> Dreams that life could ne'er fulfill,
> Here lie buried; here in peace
> Wrongs and woes have found release.

And the last stanza finds this champion of woman's rights "kneeling where a woman lies" (any woman) and strewing "lilies on the grave" of the braver sex. No wonder Emily admired it. She had been saying the same thing, notably in "Success is counted sweetest" (67), for almost twenty years. Even the beloved lilies echo through the poem, both in the last lines and in the Vergilian epigraph: "Manibus date lilia plenis." But since she could not envision her father as a specimen of martyred Victorian womanhood, she apparently used his name to mask a more immediate agitation. In mid-June 1877 she had something other than his anniversary to trouble her. A friend from whom she had long been estranged, the former Kate Turner, now widowed a second time, was visiting her brother's house and wanted to see her.

The reverberations of this visit (for she did consent to see her old friend) can be traced through a number of poems, but it is in the letters that her Greeks revisit the light. On the death of Mrs. Higginson in September she wrote to the widower that the dead woman "reminded me of Thermopylae" (L519). The significance of Thermopylae is that the men die by their own choice—in obedience to law—and Mary Higginson could not be said to choose the manner of her death. There are, however, points of resemblance between her long years of hopeless invalidism and the prolonged dying of Emily Dickinson "in obedience to law." That September she also wrote to Jonathan L. Jenkins and his wife that they should have taken her for their "Marathon" instead of going to a new pastorate to achieve triumphs (L520).

A long interval passed before Greek comparisons recurred to her. Most interesting and perplexing is a short poem written about 1882 and surviving in an unfinished draft. From some unidentified source had come a terse, cryptic message, and the recipient prepared to obey without "murmur" and, oddly, without "endearment." But she interrupts to ask whether she is to obey "a Lure—a Longing?" Presumably these are lures after the flesh, for in an apostrophe to "Nature" they are vigorously rejected, and the message delivered is one of heroic self-denial: "To Law—said sweet Thermopylae / I give my dying Kiss—" (1554). A brief note to Mrs. Todd in mid-1884 identifies the yearly death of Nature with that of Leonidas and his Spartans: "We die, said the deathless Thermopylae, in obedience to

Law" (L906). Beneath the playful surface is the grim reminder that the law of the universe is death.

6

Her named rivers are few, but they carry a heavy freight —no less than love and death. The Rhine is her river of love par excellence (123, 230, 383, 583), although it is rather confusingly supplanted by the Danube in a late letter to Sue Dickinson implying that the current of their love persists in spite of barriers: "Beneath the Alps the Danube runs" (L1025). To Emily Dickinson, as to the midnineteenth-century imagination in general, the Rhine connoted the wine of romance. In an early *Atlantic*, she probably read that passage from *The Autocrat of the Breakfast Table* which speaks of

The Rhine's breastmilk, gushing cold and bright,
Pale as the moon, and maddening in her light.[52]

To Oliver Wendell Holmes this Liebfraumilch was hock, and hock was rum, as was burgundy, as was champagne, as were all liquors, whether "distilled from molasses" or "the noble juices of the vineyard"—in a word, the all-purpose "Domingo" of the young woman's poetry.

Many persons "cross the Rhine" in the poet's "cup" and "Sip old Frankfort air" from her "brown Cigar" (123). This poem, preserved in the handwriting of 1859, seems to allude to the romantic cigar of Ik Marvel and may recall lines sent years earlier to Susan Gilbert (in letter 56, 9 October 1851, the poet imagines that she and Sue are walking together and having a charming "Reverie" after the fashion of "that lonely Bachelor, smoking his cigar"). Her symbol draws upon Marvel's "Third Reverie: A Cigar Three Times Lighted," in which the whole business of lighting up, smoking, and relighting a cigar is made parallel to the stages of a love affair.[53] Other aspects of her symbolism are less clear. Why *cross* the Rhine, even in a poetic "cup," unless one is leaving the undesirable side in order to enter some Promised Land on the other shore? She may not have troubled herself about the exact geography, but if Frankfurt is in some sense the land of Canaan, then it becomes necessary to cross the Jordan-Rhine.

An exuberant poem beginning "I taste a liquor never brewed" declares that "Frankfort Berries" (var., "Vats upon the Rhine) could never yield an alcohol like this homegrown bliss that is intoxicating her. She is drunk on air, drunk on dew, reeling from the "Molten Blue" inns of summer days (214). Apparently she is enjoying that "atmosphere of intellect and sentiment" that Holmes found "so much more stimulating than alcohol that, if I thought fit to take wine, it would be to keep me sober." But again, why Frankfurt? The fame of Rhenish wines plus the romance long attached to the river might account for the Rhine symbol, but the symbolic Frankfurt cannot be derived from a history of banking houses, industry, and bustling commerce. In the early fifties, however, she read Margaret Fuller's translation of Bettina von Arnim's *Günderode* (Sue Dickinson's copy) and in the late fifties Sue's copy of *Goethe's Correspondence with a Child,* of which the most striking pages, written at Goethe's request, give a short but anguished account of Bettina's ill-starred attachment to the poet Karoline von Günderode. Both young women lived in Frankfurt am Main and often visited or traveled along the Rhine, and it was on a bank of this river that the young poet carried out her repeated threat to kill herself. In later years Sue Dickinson would compare her romantic friendship with Emily to that of Bettina and Günderode.[54]

Poem 230, with its hock, burgundy, and Rhenish wine, its vat and its vine, may be a direct recall of the passage from Holmes's *Autocrat*. It appears close to the earlier "I taste a liquor never brewed" and may have been composed at almost the same time. In more stoic vein an 1862 poem beginning "Exhiliration—is within—" (383) describes the "Ample Rhine" as an inner resource, like her Bolivian diamond and similar compensations of this period—assertions of proud self-sufficiency contradicted by poems of anguish in the same packet. The last Rhine poem is among the unhappy examples. This "Bare Rhine" that we are ordered to measure—"Naked of Flask—Naked of Cask"—is heart's blood (583).

"Much Billow hath the Sea—/ One Baltic—They," declares a poem that insists on the indivisible self of lover and beloved (587). And her unnamed or variously named seas are themselves one sea, even though this symbol may appear to have much billow. Poem 1029, describing the barriers between the lovers, takes its images from two continents ("Who's Baltic—/ Who's Cordillera?"), as if South American ranges fringed the Scandinavian peninsula. Another poem, "We see—Comparatively" (534), mixing its continents in similar fashion, says "Our Cordillera" of yesterday is today's "furrow," "Our Appenine" a mere "Knoll"; and the "Morning" of poem 300 dawns indifferently on "Teneriffe" or the variant "Appenine." Confusions and identities like these are common in her geographical images; yet they take some of their color from the books Emily Dickinson read or from the general notions she acquired at school or in church or in daily living.

The word "Chimborazo" may be taken as an example. She would not have picked it at random from a textbook list or a gazetteer, since there would have been no reason for choosing this word in preference to others equally foreign to her. But in Emily Dickinson's day the light had by no means faded from the peak which, shortly before her birth, still "had a fame," says Victor von Hagen, "as of some celestial legend as the highest, the greatest mountain in the world."[55] Its fame was linked to that of

Alexander von Humboldt, himself of towering significance, whose ascent to the 19,400-foot level of Chimborazo marked for years the highest point attained by man. His climbs on the peak of Tenerife and Popocatepetl and his explorations around the Caspian were equally celebrated. If she did not read his works directly, she read the works of those who did and was so far impressed as to take Chimborazo for her symbol of unattainable height (453).[56] Mrs. Browning, whose poetry she was reading in the late fifties, describes her heroine Aurora Leigh as learning "by how many feet / Mount Chimborazo outsoars Himmaleh." Apprised of her error, Mrs. Browning altered the line to read, in her collected *Poems,* "Mount Chimborazo out-soars Teneriffe."[57] In his essay "The Poet," Emerson remarks disapprovingly of some writer, apparently Tennyson: "He does not stand out of our low limitations, like a Chimborazo under the line, running up from a torrid base through all the climates of the globe."[58] And in the poem "To a Child" Longfellow stresses the massiveness of "huge Chimborazo's base."[59] These instances from the work of three writers whom Emily admired could be multiplied many times. Chimborazo was the nonpareil, the Everest of earlier days, and was used in the same way to signify the superlative.

Tenerife affords another example of her manner of handling symbols. Although her editors duly note that the peak of Tenerife is the highest of a chain of volcanic mountains in the Canary Islands but of no great absolute height, it held precisely the same significance for Emily Dickinson as did Chimborazo, the Alps, the "Himmaleh," or "Cordillera." She seems not to have remembered that it is volcanic, as she read in Irving's *Life of Columbus,* for she does not identify Tenerife with her volcanoes and in fact describes this tropical mountain, with its light winter coat of snow, its lava, pumice, and luxuriant vegetation, as a snow-girt Alp clad in "Mail of ices" with "Thigh of Granite—and thew—of Steel—" (666).[60] It sounds suspiciously like Ruskin's vivid picture of the Matterhorn in his *Stones of Venice,* but it could be any Alpine giant, for example, one of the Alps of *Childe Harold's Pilgrimage,* "whose vast walls / Have pinnacled in clouds their snowy scalps, / And throned Eternity in icy halls / Of cold sublimity."[61] It is not the actual Tenerife that interests this poet but rather the Tenerife of Mrs. Browning and others, and most especially of that magnificent Satan who "dilated stood, / Like Teneriffe ... unremov'd";[62] for though this mountain is spoken of as "receding" or "retreating," the burden of her poem is that Tenerife is not yielding an inch, and she is "kneeling still" at its feet (666).

Each of the four "Himmalehs" has a different function in the poetry. One represents the almost impossible load under which men grow strong (252), whereas another, expressly compared with Gibraltar, stands for the infinite, the everlasting (350). In poem 862 the "Himmaleh" seems to be simply a remote place chosen to complete a contrast: light glows as impartially on "Squirrel in Himmaleh" as on the poet in Amherst. The "Himmaleh" of poem 481, like the Alps of an earlier poem (124), is the tall lover stooping to the humble daisy (an invariable self-symbol). The admired Alpine "Bonnets" which "touch the firmament" are simply snowy tents of "Himmaleh." Of course, she did not invent this symbolism, however congenial she found it; "snowy breasts" and "icy breasts" were the stock in trade of the male poets she read. When she speaks of the beloved's "Height" as involving "Alpine / Requirements" and "Services of Snow," she is merely making a complicated virtue out of the rejection the male poet would berate and bemoan (914). In a poem written about June 1877, "Unworthy of her breast," she takes an awed pride in falling below the other woman's "exacting" standards (1414).

Another Alps poem seems intended to contrast forbidding mountains with an inviting Italy. "Our lives are Swiss . . . still . . . Cool," till the afternoon the Alps "neglect their Curtains," that is, draw back the curtains and unveil *"Italy."* Yet "we," or rather the poet, can never attain to Italy because the "solemn [warning?] Alps," the "siren Alps," stand "like a guard between" (80). Presumably the word *siren* meant to Emily Dickinson what it meant to her dictionary: "bewitching, fascinating, pertaining to a siren," and it has got into this poem against her conscious intention. The word ceases to be a puzzle the moment we see that the bare-breasted Alps themselves are the alluring and dangerous Italy.

7

Whether covertly or openly acknowledged, sensuality was the quality most often attributed to Italy. All literate Americans knew that Italy was delicious and decadent, just as they knew, for ready contrast, that Switzerland was politically inspiring and scenically sublime, but boasted no higher aesthetic glory than clockmaking. Knowing themselves to be free and crude, Americans of Emily's day readily identified with Switzerland and yearned in unregenerate moments for the alluring South —as did the Germans and the English, and no doubt the Scandinavians, from as far back as the Renaissance or even the Middle Ages. And no doubt there were moods in which Emily Dickinson shared the forthright chauvinism of Emerson's "Prudence" and believed that a bad climate made northerners somehow better than southerners. The three or four pages Ruskin devoted to this gratifying contrast in his *Stones of Venice,* with frequent brief returns to it, were decidedly picturesque. More subtly influential would be Byron's reference to the Italian language as "that soft bastard Latin, / Which melts like kisses from a female mouth / And sounds as if it should be writ on satin." [63] His caressing contempt reappears in her unfavorable contrast of "satin Races" with the northern hemlock that thrives on cold (525). But if the hemlock is admired as a veritable Emerson, there come moods in whi.h Emerson's disciple votes for Italy or boasts her own "Satin" (492).

"Thou art my tropics and mine Italy; / To look at thee unlocks a warmer clime," declares Lowell's "To the Dandelion," a poem Emily Dickinson appears to recall admiringly in a letter of May 1852 (L91) and perhaps more distantly in an 1871 poem about "Lands with Locks" (1195).[64] Robert Browning's "By the Fire-Side," a poem she often quotes or pillages, apostrophizes his adopted home:

> O woman-country, wooed not wed,
> Loved all the more by earth's male lands[65]

In Mrs. Browning's versified novel, the lover calls his cousin Aurora "My Italy of women"; and Emily Dickinson shared her countryman's infatuation with the woman poet who, as she knew, ennobled that blue peninsula with her presence.[66] In an 1862 elegy commemorating Mrs. Browning, the younger poet fairly elbows the bereaved husband aside and with peculiar fervor imagines how "Ourself a Bridegroom— / Put Her down— in Italy" (312).

The sensuous qualities attributed to Italy were warmth and color, notably a brilliant blue, the very qualities that distinguish Emily's paradisal noon. The lushly erotic chapter 23 of *Jane Eyre* opens with a midsummer as splendid "as if a band of Italian days had come from the South," and in *The Marble Faun* Hawthorne agrees that there is a weather found nowhere "save in Paradise and in Italy." [67] The hint of sensuality in Brontë's Italy, less marked in Hawthorne's, becomes explicit with Browning, although he might with more acuity have called this woman-country his *mother* land ("wooed not wed"). There is commonly a strong suggestion of the forbidden, even the incestuous, in this sensual paradise. Elizabeth Browning describes it openly and without anxiety as the never-forgotten Eden of infancy. The hills of Italy toward which Aurora Leigh is hastening are identified with her dead mother. They are "sleeping mothers" who "feel the sucking babe and smile," and by extension they become the entire peninsula—"the white walls, the blue hills, my Italy." [68] And Italy *is* blue. Every northern visitor discovers anew, and reports with astonishment, that Italy is blue. Its hills are blue, its skies deep indigo, and its surrounding seas so dark as to seem well-nigh purple. Emily Dickinson's earliest reference to Italy associates it with its color, and her very last with its sensual warmth. Writing to her cousin John Graves in April 1856, she observes that skies "fairer far than Italy, in blue eye look down" on her, and twenty-six years later she tells Judge Lord that the "Air is soft as Italy," but she spurns a lover's touch that is not his (letters 184, 750).

One of the earliest influences shaping her attitude toward Italy and preparing it to serve as symbol was Ik Marvel's *Reveries of a Bachelor,* which seems to have carried young people by storm in the early 1850s and to have evoked a reciprocal hostility from their elders. Perhaps Marvel's attitude toward the Switzerland-Italy contrast occasioned some adult disapproval. No man could be quite steady and American who expected his readers to enjoy Italy's "soft warm air, its ruins, its pictures and temples, better than those cold valleys of Switzerland." The central episode of the book is a sentimental stay in Rome followed by a trip through the Apennines. Admiringly, Marvel observes the "thin, lazy mists" on the Apennines and notes how "the mist lifted, and the sun brightened," apparently giving rise to Emily Dickinson's comparison between "laces" that "just reveal the surge" of a bosom and "Mists" that reveal the "Appenine" (210). In a vision Marvel sees Walter de Montréal's brother "crowd over the Campagna, and put up his white tents, and hang out his showy banners" on the slopes of the Apennines.[69] By a trick of memory, the white tents transform the showy banners into snowy ones (more exactly, the two images merge into one), and Emily Dickinson writes of the "Himmaleh" stooping compassionately to the "Daisy" at her feet, "Where Tent by Tent—Her Universe / Hung out its Flags of Snow—" (481).

The symbolic "Italy" is rarely named in her work, but it often appears by implication. About May 1860 she wrote a guarded but emotional letter to Kate Turner, begging her friend to return to Amherst. She closed her letter by recalling a winter visit some months earlier: "Its but a little past—dear—and yet how far from here it seems—fled with the snow! So through the snow go many loving feet parted by 'Alps' how brief from Vineyards and the Sun!" (L222). Here the eroticism is centered in the "Vineyards," and the Alps appear as simple barriers, their siren quality suppressed but latent in the symbol. The best comment on this letter is a poem written apparently at about the same time and describing some temporary anguish, perhaps the pain of separation. She has never seen "Volcanoes," she says, but has heard that these "phlegmatic mountains" can suddenly erupt and swallow whole villages. Now suppose a similar "Volcanic" stillness in a human face trying to keep features smooth over a "Titanic" pain, and picture the "smouldering anguish" breaking out at last to overwhelm the "palpitating Vineyard" (175). But the poem may be less desperate than it looks. Emily could suffer grievously over trifles (in late April 1860 she wept bitterly over her sister Lavinia's going to Boston for a few weeks!), and the last puzzling stanza may be more playful than self-pitying. She wants a "loving Antiquary" to come restore the buried vineyard—"Oh! our condor Kate! Come from your crags again!" (L222)—and if not, then "To the Hills return!" Both letter and poem seem further tied by slight suggestions of a rereading of Poe's work. The rather dreadful volcanic-titanic rhyme is a probable borrowing from "Ulalume," Kate's condor may come out of Poe's "Romance," and when the poet writes to her friend, "Distinctly sweet your face stands in its phantom niche," she may have

"To Helen" in mind. On the other hand, a story in the May *Atlantic,* with its partial quotation, would remind her afresh of Mrs. Browning's lines:

And, in my Tuscan home I'll find a niche,
And set thee there, my saint . . .
And burn the lights of love before thy face
And ever at thy sweet look cross myself

The volcano poem has connections with a letter of more serious character, indeed of tragic nature, written in the summer of 1861 to an unnamed person who appears to be the former "loving Antiquary." The poet admits her difference from other people, but "God made me," she urges painfully. "I did'nt be—myself." God built the heart in her too, which has outgrown her, like a little mother with a big child, so that she has got tired holding him. This last curious sentence suggests that she may have been writing at a time late in Sue Dickinson's pregnancy or after the child was born 19 June 1861. Further down she writes: "Vesuvius dont talk—Etna dont [Thy] one of them—said a syllable—a thousand years ago, and Pompeii heard it, and hid forever—She could'nt look the world in the face afterward—I suppose—Bashful Pompeii!" (L233).

Two very probable sources as well as many unknown ones may have gone into the shaping of this important symbol. In the November 1855 *Harper's* appeared a twenty-two page, illustrated article, "A Day at Pompeii," which gave a dramatic account of the eruption and pictured the "many towns and villages that so lovingly nestle amidst the vineyards of sunny Vesuvius . . . undermined by eternal fires." The symbol itself appeared in Thackeray's *The Newcomes,* a work serialized in the 1854–55 *Harper's*: "Which of us that is thirty years old has not had his Pompeii? Deep under ashes lies the Life of Youth . . . the Pleasure and Passion, the darling Joy." And he talks of opening a letter box and rereading old letters which "excavate your heart" and sighs "for the day when the whole city shall be bare and the chambers unroofed—." The buried city of the poet's hopes would also return to haunt her after many years. An undated prose fragment written in the last decade of her life reads: "Pompeii—All its [the] occupations crystallized—Everybody gone away" (PF100). This buried city came to mind again when she described the fire that destroyed much of Amherst's business district in the early hours of 4 July 1879; her paralyzed mother, she notes, had slept throughout the alarm but would never in any event have shopped again "at Mr. Cutler's store, and if it were Pompeii nobody could tell her" (L610).

Italy and the "Vineyards" symbolize either the person of the beloved or the shared experience of love, and if the latter, then the poet too can think of herself as in Italy. Of course she can never be a snow-breasted peak; she kneels at their feet or on occasion tries to climb one. But she can be, and usually is, the volcano, or, as in poem 175, she may describe as volcanic the passionate suffering that threatens to destroy her. Like the snow-breasted Alp, this symbol too is wholly unoriginal. Among the earlier poets, Alexander Pope had his (or, rather, Ovid's) Sappho "consume with more than Aetna's fires," and he said of love, in his youthful *Pastorals,* "Thou wert from Aetna's burning entrails torn." [70] Byron used the "Alp's snow summit" and the "Volcano's eruptive crest" to contrast two types of poetic temperament. At first glance, the advantage might appear to be with the cold Alp rather than with the "scorched mountain, from whose burning breast / A temporary torturing flame is wrung" before its fire is repelled back to the "Hell...in its entrails"; but there is self-indulgence in his portrayal of the volcano. [71] He so often identified himself with this symbol that his friend Moore could only describe him as a volcano that might yet "cool down into...some habitable state." [72] Beginning a description of a woman whose snow concealed the lava within, Byron interrupted himself to jeer at the "tired metaphor" of the "often-used volcano";

Poor thing: How frequently, by me and others,
It hath been stirred up till its smoke quite smothers.

Yet he chose to identify with the volcano once more in lines written at Missolonghi shortly before his death. [73]

Obsessively personified, the volcano acquired lips, tooth, tongue, throat, entrails, heart, breast, and without doubt some unrecognized organs. Lines from "The Fire-Worshippers" compare the quiet moments before disaster to "those verdant spots that bloom / Around the crater's burning lips." [74] Struggling to shake off the crags "piled on his breast," Longfellow's "Enceladus" fills the air above Mount Etna with burning cinders from his "lips." [75] In *The American Scholar* Emerson pictures intelligence as "one central fire, which, flaming now out of the lips of Etna, lightens the capes of Sicily, and now out of the throat of Vesuvius, illuminates the towns and vineyards of Naples." And the "litanies of nations," according to "The Problem," come "Like the Volcano's tongue of flame, / Up from the burning core below." [76] In *Aurora Leigh* Elizabeth Browning suggests that the "burning lava" of song flows from the "paps we all have sucked!" —a confusion of lava with mother's milk found shocking by readers who took calmly the idea of lava expelled by "lips." [77]

To these several poets Emily Dickinson went to school, and especially to Byron, whose volcanic self became a model for her own. She appeared to be impressed by the lines in which Byron jeered at the "nations of the moral North" or declared that

The cold in clime are cold in blood,
Their love can scarce deserve the name;
But mine was like the lava flood
That boils in Aetna's breast of flame. [78]

After the manner of Byron, she perceived a difference between herself and those genteel neighbors passively subdued to the usual occupations of women. Her rebellion would be a silent one, of course, for she never published her poetry: "A still—Volcano—Life—/ That flickered in the night—/ ...A quiet—Earthquake Style" (the oxymorons are violent to the point of absurdity), so subtle that it escapes detection by "natures this side Naples." The cold "North" is blind to the "Solemn—Torrid—Symbol," which (even more grossly personified than in her models) has "lips that never lie," "hissing Corals" that "part—and shut" while "Cities—ooze away" (601). The personal nature of her symbol is equally explicit in the poem, "My Life had stood—a Loaded Gun" (754). When this gun-woman smiles—fires herself—a "cordial light" glows on the "Valley" as if a "Vesuvian face / Had let it's pleasure through"! And the explosive violence erupts again in images of her "Yellow Eye" and "emphatic Thumb."

Less certainly, Etna's "Garnet tooth" is a threatening danger outside herself rather than a self-symbol (1146). On the other hand, two undated poems that appear to belong to these troubled years use the volcano to represent her own explosive suffering.[79] According to poem 1705, volcanoes should be in Sicily or South America; but if she wishes to climb a "Lava step," she knows "Volcanoes nearer here" and can in a moment contemplate a "Crater," a "Vesuvius at Home." The other poem, which appears a direct recall of Moore's lines, begins, "On my volcano grows the Grass." Apparently a quiet spot, a place to attract birds, it would be unpeopled in an instant should she hint at the insecurity of the sod or at the redness of the fire rocking below (1677). One final volcano poem, in 1862 handwriting, says the departure of the beloved effectually ended her own life. Closely akin to the poem about "natures this side Naples," it makes an involved comparison between cold temperaments and an "Ethiop" like herself, between the low "Peat life" of the ordinary citizen and the blazing violence of "Popocatapel" and "Etna's Scarlets" (422).

Whether she writes as martyred poet or martyred lover makes little difference in evaluating these poems. One and all have the same import, and what they reveal is the frustration of a powerful nature expressing in infantile symbols the raging violence of a socially imposed infantilism. Beginning in early 1859, given an agonizing turn in early 1861, her rebellion blazed most hotly through 1862 and 1863 and then rather quickly burned itself out. By 1865 it had pretty well ended, and with it had gone most of her peculiar power, as she herself well knew. Of the bare handful of symbols that managed to cross the gap between her major period and the milder genre poetry of later years, one of the more important, drawn from this Italian complex, is her blue peninsula.

8

For almost forty years, from late 1896 to 1935, the sixteen-line poem, "It might be lonelier" (405), was represented in print by its last four lines only, to which the first editor, Mrs. Todd, gave the misleading title, "Philosophy":

It might be easier
To fail—with Land in Sight—
Than gain—My Blue Peninsula—
To perish—of Delight—

The editor placed this amputated stanza in a section she called "Life," and indeed there is nothing in these four lines to indicate that they come at the end of a painful meditation on lost love. Here is another instance of that persistent fragmentation that has made nonsense of so much of Emily Dickinson's poetry, for the sixteen lines themselves are but a fragment of the total poem.

A related poem, written perhaps a few months later than the "Blue Peninsula," says that a mysterious "They" has come between the lovers and made them as "separate as Sea / And her unsown Peninsula" (474). The imagery is puzzling; either the "Sea" wishes to inundate the "Peninsula" (sow her waters on the land) or the latter wishes to be absorbed into the sea—a geographic disaster on either reading, though it might make erotic sense. According to another 1862 poem, there are as many Calvaries as there are "persons—or Peninsulas" (553). These peninsulas, like the blue one, may be conjectured to represent everything the individual hopes for and strives toward—his life goal, his earthly fulfillment; and since the inevitable destiny of mankind is to be thwarted and deprived, there are as many Calvaries as there are individuals to suffer and life goals to be destroyed. An 1863 poem, "Bereaved of all, I went abroad," says that the life goal, the individual fulfillment, may reappear in another form, a "New Peninsula," only to fail as disastrously as the old one (784).

As often happens with her symbols, the peninsula of these last two poems seems to detach itself from the image of the blue Italy and to drift at large as a vague nimbus of suggestion, perhaps to attach itself to a new image or to dissipate still further until it is at best a code word in the poet's memory. What interpretation, for example, can be given to the "Peninsulas" of poem 661? The poet would like to "ride indefinite" like a meadow bee, flirt with "Buttercups," marry whom she pleases, live now here, now there, run away entirely from the old life without fear of "Police" following her, or even turn boldly and chase the policeman until he jumps "Peninsulas" to escape her. In the remaining lines she is a captive dreaming of a bee's joyful freedom on a raft of air. The stress upon air suggests that the "Peninsulas" are boughs in the blue sky, as appears to be true of the next example. In poem 797 the squirrel with which the poet playfully identifies has a "giddy peninsula," a nest or a favorite bough, toward the top of the pine. The tree itself is described as a "Sea—with a Stem," and the color is implied by the blue jays that "split their route" through the tree to the sky.

Upon the whole, the peninsula would seem to have no one dependable meaning. It is now a bough in the blue sky, now land in the blue sea, and it can be the unattainable earthly paradise and conversely the safe but unexciting land—or bough—one leaves to plunge into the sea of vital experience. As a bough in the blue sky, it may be at least distantly related to a quite early poem, "It did not surprise me" (39), in which the poet complains that some woman friend has stirred her pinions and deserted the faithful nest (Emily) to "Build in gayer boughs." This poem in turn appears to be related to "Misconceptions," a poem from Robert Browning's *Men and Women,* always her favorite among his books. In the first stanza, a "Bird" gives a brief, illusory happiness to a poor spray before choosing a higher and worthier bough, and in the second stanza a "Queen" leans on an ecstatic heart before going to a more suitable mate. Apparently Emily Dickinson remembered Browning's bird, bough, and queen but redistributed the roles in her poem, "Not probable—The barest Chance—" (346). Here a "Bird from journey far" (Emily herself) may "Forget the secret of His wing" and perish with no more than a "Bough" between his "Groping feet" and his "Phantom Queen."

Two late examples of her peninsula, mentioned in chapter 5 as belonging to the crucial years 1877, have ramifications so complex that it is an act of hardihood to try to make sense of them. The associated words are *peninsula, March, bluebird, butterfly.* Sometime during 1877 the poet sent her sister-in-law a poem beginning "March is the Month of Expectation." The work-sheet drafts show an interesting evolution of ideas, most marked in the third line. The first version of this line reappeared in a second draft and then vanished without a trace. She then tried "transports," *"Persons,"* "Treasures," and "aspects" before deciding upon "The Persons of prognostication / Are coming now." To this approaching happiness the next line responds with an effort "to show becoming calmness," then a "becoming firmness," only to find that "silly joy," "awkward Joy," *"pompous"* and, finally, "pompous Joy / Betrays us, as his first Betrothal / Betrays a Boy" (1404). There might be some question as to how frequently the "Boy" is betrothed (she is, as always, identified with the boy), and still more questions as to the choice of March, which is no pleasant month in New England, yet is almost as frequent in her poetry as the prime favorite, June. In his poem, "The Twenty-Seventh of March" (which Emily of course knew), William Cullen Bryant regretfully tells the beloved woman, "thy birthday should rise ... In a June morning." [80] He compliments her on having so well "borne the bleak March day of life" and finds his own delight in the month because it is her birth month. Curiously, Emily Dickinson's first letter to a new friend, written 2 March 1859, reads: "Will you still come? *Then* bright I record you! *Kate* gathered in March!" (L203). Nor was she likely to forget that this friend's birthday fell in March. But the occasion of her poem may be simpler still. Sue Dickinson would know and would tell her sister-in-law that their old friend Kate, now for some two years the widowed Mrs. John Anthon, had recently returned to the United States and planned to visit Amherst—the "Person[s] of prognostication"!

Bluebirds come in March too, which may explain why they so abound in the 1877 manuscripts. On a discarded envelope appear some lines (dated about 1877 by her editor) of the poem, "A Pang is more conspicuous in Spring" (1530). The complete version survives only in a manuscript of about 1881, but earlier work sheets have obviously disappeared. The 1877 fragment reads in part:

When what they sung for is undone
Who cares about a Blue Bird's Tune—

On the other side of the envelope appears a repetition of the first line, together with the curious words, "I dare not write until I hear—." The note of suffering in the poem suggests that the poet herself is the bluebird here. But the other person seems to be remembered in a poem probably written not long after Kate Anthon's visit (delayed, it would seem, until mid-June) and enclosed in a letter of August to Higginson. It begins, "After all Birds have been investigated . . . Nature imparts the little Blue Bird" (1395). In the second stanza we are told that the bluebird is "First at the March." The following line, which gave the poet special difficulty, seems to shape into a vivid recollection. The work-sheet trial lines follow in order:

Her zealous Note Delights it to ascent
Her joyful cry [cordial note] exalts us like a friend
Her gallant note endows us like a friend

and in its final form in the letter to Higginson:

Her panting note exalts us—like a friend—

Since the poem was apparently created in midsummer 1877, it seems to be the friend who excites recollections of March and bluebirds rather than the other way around.

In this same 1877, perhaps about the time of the bluebird poem written for Sue, the peninsula symbol reappeared after a long absence. "The inundation of the Spring," the poet wrote, is a flood in which the soul is "estranged" or perhaps "alarmed" or "submerged." At length "acclimated," it no longer "pines" ("gropes") for "that Peninsula"—or it even "Loses sight / Of aught Peninsular" (1425). Here the peninsula surely stands for the safe bough from which she is swept into the sea of sensation.

On a penciled scrap of the same date appear the words "Yearns no more for that Peninsula," and on the same scrap, as if by a compulsive association, the following version of lines that conclude a much earlier poem, "We like March" (1213):

> With the Blue Birds buccaneering
> On his British sky—

The bluebird is an American species, but Emily could have supposed it was the same as Tennyson's "sea-blue bird of March," actually a king-fisher.[81] In chapter 5 I pointed out that the original of this totemic bird was in England during 1872, the date assigned by the editor to the earlier version of the poem. Kate was abroad seeking medical help for her husband and brother, as her mother wrote to Sue Dickinson, who would have informed Kate's friends in the other house. Emily would not know how serious the husband's illness was, nor would she know precisely where Kate was. She could only write, in another poem of that year, "Somewhere upon the general Earth / Itself exist Today—" (1231).

This bluebird poem interested her once more after Kate's June 1877 visit to Amherst, and she rewrote it in at least two copies, one of which she folded as if to enclose in an envelope. The changes are minor, the most significant being that after Kate's visit the bluebirds are "buccaneering" (as also in the 1877 scrap) rather than tamely "exercising" as in 1872. The poet still likes "March," and "His Shoes are Purple" as before—another color frequently associated with the friend of the March birthday.

About the time the poet wrote her slightly revised bluebird poem, she took up a much older poem, "Two Butterflies went out at Noon" (533) and, after the first two lines, substituted a completely new poem. In its original form, written early in 1862, the two butterflies simply waltzed together and then disappeared. The 1878 work-sheet draft is a far more complicated manuscript, though not at all unreadable. Its tone is elegiac, resigned, at times almost humorous. Half mockingly, the last stanza holds the two of them up as an example, a warning, "To all surviving Butterflies." They had had a wonderful time, reads the second stanza, losing and finding themselves in "eddies of the sun," in "Gambols," "Frenzies," "antics,"

> Till Rapture missed Peninsula
> And Both were wrecked in Noon—

Variants are written above and below and in both margins of the work-sheet draft, but the lines given above are assuredly the poet's first intention. Here the "Peninsula" seems to be the same perch or stable ground the lovers failed to secure, just as in poem 346. It may be no more than coin-

cidence that the other 1877 peninsula poem has a variant "gropes no more /
For that Peninsula"; but there is commonly little coincidence in her close
interweaving of words and motifs, and the notion of *groping* for the beloved occurs in other poems..

These belated peninsula poems have come a long way, it would seem,
from their geographic source, but somewhere in the background an image
of the blue peninsula must be hovering still. After all, it was the living
original who recalled the peninsula and the blue of birds to the poet's mind
in the summer of 1877. "My Italy of women," Mrs. Browning wrote. The
line was marked in Sue Dickinson's copy of *Aurora Leigh,* and perhaps
it was Emily Dickinson who marked it.[82]

SEVEN ❧ THE CARDINAL POINTS

The four points of the compass have had an enduring appeal to the practitioners of magic and poetry alike as a means of codifying experience, of achieving at least the appearance of order in the chaos of sensation. An early poem by William Butler Yeats entitled "He Bids His Beloved Be at Peace" makes summary but illuminating use of a cardinal-points symbolism. Above the shadowy, horse-shaped Pucas of Irish myth, the North is said to unfold "clinging, creeping night" and the East a hidden joy, while the West weeps dew and passes away in sighs and the South pours down "roses of crimson fire"; a further line associates the North with sleep, the East with hope, the West with dreams and fading things, and the South with "endless desire." There is also a suggestion of the four-elements pattern that Yeats developed more fully in later work; the poem makes the traditional association of fire with the South, and of water—weeping and dew—with the West. In a note to another early poem, "The Valley of the Black Pig," Yeats cites John Rhys's *Celtic Heathendom* and Sir James G. Frazer's *Golden Bough* as his sources for myths about death-winter doing battle with life-summer.[1] A still better example of the elaborate patterns into which such symbolisms have evolved is afforded by the "Five Activities" of the Chinese. In this system North is associated with water, black, tortoise, winter; East with wood, blue-green, dragon, spring; South with fire, red, vermilion bird (phoenix), summer; West with metal, white, tiger, autumn; and in the center, earth, yellow, man, all seasons.[2]

The cardinal-points symbolism of Emily Dickinson is a deliberate, self-conscious product of her reading and has much in common with that of Yeats and with the general tradition that attached emotional and mythic significance to the points of the compass. It plays a very important role in her work—more important than students of her poetry have yet recognized, although they have noticed individual elements of this symbolism.[3] In brief, she associates each quarter of the compass with its traditional time of day and season of the year, assigns it a color, or colors, and usually an element, and equips it with a certain range of emotional significance; she has also two symbolic movements of the sun corresponding to her North-South and East-West divisions. On this double axis she has suspended literally hundreds of poems, many of them interlocking with scores of other symbol clusters, and the whole producing a notable economy of allusion and effect within a tightly organized corpus. Indeed, it is not too much to say that by means of these interconnected symbol clusters she has effectually organized her emotions and experience and unified the poetry of her major period, making of it a more respectable body of work than the faulty and too often trivial fragments in which it is customarily presented. As we have seen in earlier chapters, the clue to understanding and evaluation lies in a study of her symbolism.

Her first and perhaps most influential model was Ralph Waldo Emerson. In early 1850 the nineteen-year-old girl mentioned the gift of "Ralph Emerson's Poems—a beautiful copy" from her friend Ben Newton, and toward the close of her life she noticed with sadness the death of the man "whose name my Father's Law Student taught me" (letters 30, 750). From his poetry she turned to his prose, if her friend Newton had not already introduced her to the essays. Nowhere else would she receive stronger encouragement toward the inveterate symbolizing that would distinguish the poetry of her major period. In his essay on *Nature,* Emerson wrote that words are symbols, natural facts are symbols of spiritual facts, and nature herself is the symbol of spirit. Here Emily Dickinson would have found still other suggestions for her cardinal-points schema: "every hour and change corresponds to and authorizes a different state of the mind, from breathless noon to grimmest midnight"; and "is there no intent of an analogy between man's life and the seasons? And do the seasons gain no grandeur or pathos from that analogy?"[4] So habitual did this ordering by hours, seasons, and cardinal points become that in late 1871 she could write to her friend T. W. Higginson: "If I exceed permission, excuse the bleak simplicity that knew no tutor but the North" (L368).

In "The Poet," Emerson asserted that "the fascination resides in the symbol." According to a marked passage, which Emily herself may have bracketed, in the Dickinson copy of the *Essays,* this symbol need not be large and important in itself, the poorest experience being "rich enough for all the purposes of expressing thought. Why covet a knowledge of new facts? Day and night, house and garden, a few books, a few actions, serve us as well as would all trades and all spectacles. We are far from having exhausted the significance of the few symbols we use. We can come to use them yet with a terrible simplicity."[5]

To an aspiring young poet, who would restrict even more narrowly a life already restricted by her sex and her times, it must have been reassuring to know that she possessed everything needful. House and garden she certainly had, together with a few books and a few actions. She had also night and day, sun, moon, stars, seasons, colors, the four cardinal points, and a host of biblical imagery, out of which she constructed her network of symbols. There is nothing very difficult or subtle about her symbol clusters; to anyone accustomed to making the translations required, they read more readily than does ordinary prose discourse. Emerson had recommended "a terrible simplicity," and she followed his advice. She was in fact a naive symbolist who carefully spelled out her symbols, even announcing that such and such *is* a symbol, so that the reader is rarely obliged to guess or interpret. A few require some knowledge of the Bible and of her more specialized reading, but on the whole they illuminate each other and offer no great problems. And she used this symbolism like a second language, or a species of shorthand, into which she translated the sensations, events, hopes, or dreams of her life; but here again she had the authority of Emerson, who had said in "The Poet" that "Dante's praise is, that he dared to write his autobiography in colossal cipher, or into universality." [6]

Emily Dickinson had a highly developed word sense and a superstitious feeling for the magic potency of a name; she can be discovered in the act of choosing gem names or adding to her stock of color words or of "Royal names" (722). "Shall I take thee?" she asks of a "propounded word" (1126). Like Emerson, she read for language, "for lustres," "for a mechanical help to the fancy and the imagination," and she must often have agreed with him that their relationship to a good author was "to find my own, though it were only to melt him down into an epithet or an image for daily use: 'Into paint will I grind thee, my bride!' " [7] These lines from his "Nominalist and Realist" so exactly describe her practice that she may have had them in mind when writing to Higginson that she would "never consciously touch a paint, mixed by another person" (L271); that is, like all poets she sought her pigments—vocabulary and germinal suggestions— in the work of other writers and mixed them to her own specifications.

Another possible debt to Emerson is the marked polarizing of her symbolism, most obvious and frequent in the opposed cardinal points and their related images. In *The American Scholar,* Emerson calls polarity "That great principle of Undulation in nature, that shows itself as the inspiring and expiring of the breath; in desire and satiety; in the ebb and flow of the sun; in day and night; in heat and cold," and the like. Speaking of the "law of polarity" in his essay "Prudence," he illustrates with the usual and dubious contrast between the snowy homeland, hard life, and strong character of northern man and "the fixed smile of the tropics," its easy life, and its too easy people. This favored notion reappears at greater length in his essay "Character," where he exalts the North or the "positive" pole as male, spirit, will, and character, opposing it to the southern or negative pole, which is female, superficial, and without character. Female souls are drawn to the southern or negative pole, concerned as they are with the profit or hurt of an action and unable to "behold a principle until it is lodged in a person"; most damning, they of the southern or female pole "do not wish to be loved." [8] This same opposition polarizes the symbolism of Emily Dickinson, but unlike her male model she is never more than intermittently persuaded of the superiority of the northern or masculine pole.

2

The word *North* or *northern* occurs no more than eighteen or nineteen times in her poetry. Recognizable substitutes are "Arctic" (four) and "Polar" (seven). The diurnal equivalent is night, more specifically midnight; the seasonal is winter, which brings in associations of sleet, snow, frost, glaciers, freezing, icicles, darkness, and blindness. The color is white, partly out of a natural association with snow, frost, and ice but also out of an arbitrary (cultural) identification of chastity or virginity and its associated white with northern cold. The reader may have a sense of black in connection with night and blindness, but the color black proves to be conspicuously rare in the poetry of Emily Dickinson. There are two surprising occurrences of iodine as a northern color, apparently references to violet auroral light (710, 776). Less certainly, the North is associated with the element air.

In one poem, it is true, the poet's home is an island surrounded by the North and oceans (631); and of course sleet, snow, glaciers, and icicles are water, although their symbolic importance appears to reside in their whiteness and coldness. On the other hand, there is a rather piercing breeziness in poems dealing with the northern quarter. Indeed, it is only in this quarter that the reader is made particularly conscious of the air, and several poems make reference to winter air or northern winds. The North has "Vast Prairies of Air" (564), and the compass needle wades "thro' polar Air" (792). There are several references to summer air, however, and it remains likeliest that the poet used the sharp wind as part of the wintry context without elaborating a special relationship between element and compass point.

Myth and magic alike have long associated the North with the powers of cold, darkness, and death. Less potent but influential is the "good" myth, which assigns to the North such desirable characteristics as virtue (including the rather special form of female chastity), hardihood, independence, faithfulness, and so on. Although this countermyth must be as old as northern civilization, perhaps older (the contrast between Teutonic virtue and Roman decadence appears in Tacitus's *Germany*), it became dominant only with northern imperialism in the nineteenth century. Emerson's prepossession and his influence on Emily Dickinson have been noted. She was also acquainted with Ruskin's famous sixth chapter on Gothic architecture in *The Stones of Venice,* which expounds the nineteenth-century "philosophy of the imperfect" and is a notable restatement of the myth of northern superiority. Several of her poems can be dotted along the pages devoted to this notion that precisely for its rudeness and wildness northern architecture—northern man himself—"deserves our profoundest reverence." As Ruskin explains it, the great man will continue working up to his point of failure ("Of human work none but what is bad can be perfect, in its own bad way"); and, secondly, imperfection is the very sign of vitality and of progress and change, the universal law being that "neither architecture nor any other noble work of man can be good unless it be imperfect." [9]

Poem 1067 adopts this philosophy of the imperfect and asserts that only the smaller lives are smoothly spherical and swiftly ripe. The "Hugest of Core," those with "awkward Rind," grow slowly and in proud independence, not clustered, and ripen only "far after Frost." [10] According to poem 332 ("There are two Ripenings"), the "Velvet product" of the first or outer ripening is also "Spheric" and drops early to the ground, whereas the later, "homelier maturing" (apparently that of a nut within its "Bur") is disclosed by "teeth of Frosts" in "far October air." [11] Both poems were composed in 1862, when, according to her letter of 25 April to Higginson, she was most deeply engrossed in Ruskin and might have had under her eyes passages lauding "this out-speaking of the strong spirit of man, who may not bask in dreamy benignity of sunshine," this "magnificence of sturdy power, put forth only the more energetically because the fine finger-touch was chilled away by the frosty wind." [12]

Some lines earlier she would read, "We know that gentians grow on the Alps, and olives on the Appenines," and she would observe the contrast Ruskin established "between the district of the gentian and [that] of the olive." A third maturation poem (442), closely related to the two already described and written about the same time, employs the late-maturing gentian for its symbol. All summer the gentian has vainly striven to imitate the rose, which ripens early and lushly like the "Velvet" fruit of poem 332 or the small spheres of poem 1067; but "Frosts" are the requirement of the gentian (as of the October nut and the Hesperidean fruit), and the flower comes in "Tyrian" (royal) purple only when the "North" invokes her.

One further poem appears to owe something to Ruskin's chapter on Gothic architecture and northern superiority. There is also a resemblance to a passage in his *Modern Painters,* which she may have read, contrasting the warrior strength and domestic justice of northern peoples, "taught them under the green roofs and wild penetralia of the pine," with the "dissoluteness" and "degradation" of southern Europe.[13] The poet's tree is the hemlock, chosen perhaps for euphony, since the Dickinson grounds afforded plentiful specimens of both trees. The hemlock, she says, likes snow, thrives on cold, finds its "best Norwegian Wines" in northern winds. It has need of "Lapland," of "Wilderness . . . Desert . . . the Hoar, the Bald." The hemlock means nothing to the "satin Races," but (with imagery borrowed from Psalm 19:4–5) beneath its "Tabernacles" the hardy children of the Don play and the Dnieper wrestlers run (525).

Apart from the maturation poems, this quarter of the compass offers little that is affirmative or life enriching. In general, the North and its associated symbols represent chastity, asceticism, deprivation, suffering, isolation, and death. On this sliding scale toward death the poet placed herself now here, now there, according to her need. In late December 1861 or early January 1862, she sent to her friend Samuel Bowles the poem, "Title divine is mine," with a little note implying that it described an important relationship with some other person (L250). Apparently upon anxious second thought, she began another letter to him with the words "If you doubted my Snow," followed by a poem intended to assure him that she had resisted sexual temptation and had gone forward on the path of martyrdom, like the compass needle wading painfully toward the North (L251). In a poem written not many weeks earlier, she begged some perhaps imaginary lover to leave her "snow Intact" (275). At about the same time she wrote another martyrdom poem inspired by Revelation 3:5, 7:13–14, and 14:4. Those who have come out of "Tribulation," she says, are "Denoted by the White"; they have overcome a great temptation and wear "nothing commoner than Snow" (325). According to her biblical source, those worthy to wear white have not defiled themselves with sexual intercourse, "for they are virgins" (Revelation 14:4). In late October 1861 she sent to another friend an apparent nature poem with a significant line and a significant underlining, "The *Dead* shall go in white" (221), a complex reminiscence of the white robes of the martyred dead in Revelation and an allusion to these same passages by the heroine of a book Emily Dickinson admired. Defying the restrictions on Victorian womanhood, Elizabeth Browning's Aurora Leigh said she would live as seemed good to her or else take her part "with God's Dead, who afford to walk in white."[14] More somberly, Emily Dickinson limited her experience to the "Austerity" of the hemlock on its "Marge of Snow" and declared that asceticism, indeed agony, was the price of her achievement as a poet. Natures like the hemlock's, like hers, had a Lapland necessity that hedonistic satin races could neither share nor understand. The gentian could not bloom, the Hesperidean fruit could not ripen, until they had suffered the toothlike frost of frustration and denial.

Not surprisingly, it is in the North that this child of the Puritans located God. Intending to pray, she "stepped upon the North" to see her

"Curious Friend" but was so awed by an "Infinitude" of nothing that she worshiped instead of praying (564). Here may be a partial reminiscence of lines from another book she apparently knew well, Job 26:6–7: "Hell is naked before him, and destruction hath no covering. He stretcheth out the north over the empty place, and hangeth the earth upon nothing." Not alone the language of Job but also considerable mythology locates Hell and the demons in the North. According to *Paradise Lost,* which Emily Dickinson studied as a poetic textbook, Satan possesses the "Quarters of the North," intends to erect his throne in the "spacious North," comes "into the limits of the North" to regain his royal seat, appears in arms with his banded powers "in th'Horizon to the North," and, perhaps keeping in character, lights "in the Mount that lies from Eden North" when making his reconnaissance of our ancestral seat. Even in hell he somehow holds to the North, for he burns like a comet that fires the length of Ophiucus in the "Artick Sky." [15] But Emily Dickinson makes only playful reference, in poems 1545 and 1479, to the orthodox devil as a "Brigadier" and a possible friend. God is her Satan.

"By the breath of God frost is given," reads Job 37:10; and the "Approving God" of Emily Dickinson oversees the assassin frost at its work of beheading human flowers (1624). Evil is the inexplicable side of God, and symbolically it belongs to the North. Whether her attitude is awed and worshipful, as in poem 564, or defiant and reproachful, as in many other poems, he is the jealous Jehovah who deprived her of love and will someday deprive her of life. In a poem related to the "white" and "snow" poems above, she describes the triumph of slowly handing back "Temptation's Bribe," not without one eye on the "Heaven" being renounced and the other on the "Rack" of suffering this renunciation entails, yet with the severe satisfaction of being acquitted from the "Naked Bar" of Jehovah's "Countenance" (455). "God is indeed a jealous God," begins one short poem, adding that he cannot tolerate his creatures' preferring each other to him (1719). He is once more a "jealous God" in a poem lamenting the departure or loss of some friend (1260). In a letter to her Norcross cousins, written in the fall of 1861 during a period of intense suffering, she implies that she may soon be dead and adds that heaven may be better, only to correct herself immediately with the bitter observation that a God who begrudged earthly happiness did not inspire trust in heavenly bliss (L234).

Judged by the number of poems, this loss of love and the resultant isolation and suffering far outweighed the meager comfort of asceticism. For every poem that austerely chooses the North, there are dozens that lament its midnight blackness and cold. If only the mistake of her life could be rectified, she wrote, and her soul escape its "Polar Night" (646). This black night or, still oftener, midnight of the spirit is the subject of many painful meditations. A poem written in early 1861 calls the loss of the beloved a

"Sunset," a "Blindness," an "Eclipse at Midnight" (236). An undated poem that appears to stem from the same turbulent period describes her heartbreak as a "night" partly lightened by the belief that the other person shares her Calvary (1736). An 1862 poem recalls the day when her "Night" or, rather, "Midnight" began (400). According to another 1862 poem, her "Midnight" began at "Noon" and her "Eclipse" came without being predicted; that is, she was betrayed at her moment of happiness. Furthermore, it was God's fault; his "Watch" was "wrong" (415). About the same time she wrote bitterly to Higginson that her family, religious except for herself, prayed to an "Eclipse, every morning—whom they call their 'Father'" (L261). Another 1862 poem, suggesting that this love was hopeless from the beginning, says the lovers confronted "Blank," "Wilderness," and "Night" (458). "Midnight," according to another poem, is the maiden state she will leave behind when her future climbs the stairs toward the beloved (461). Imagining this reunion, she dreams of telling the beloved how this "Midnight" of separation felt, how all the "Clocks" in the world stopped, and how the cold pinched her (577). In an 1863 poem she recounts her efforts to smother suffering with busy work, only to find that the "Darkness" braced itself as firmly as if her whole purpose had been to "confirm" the fact of "Midnight" (786). Yesterday she lived in a rose-colored and vermilion world; now the bright "Goods of Day" have been superseded by the "awful Pattern of Midnight" (1171).

Sometimes the fear of losing the beloved is remembered as "Icicles" prickling "Blue and Cool" on her soul (768); or the loss and loneliness are represented as frost upon the garden of the self (195, 631). One such poem describes the action of the frost in terms of a symbolic castration: the "Garden" self has suffered a "Gash," a "crease," a "stain," which it "Cannot correct" or "counteract" (951). In poem 216 and variant stanzas she multiplies her metaphors: death is snow, hoarfrost, eclipse, icicles, "Northern Zones," polar caverns, midnight in marble. Poem 422, which appears to commemorate love's death rather than physical death, speaks of "Renowned Cold," the "Climate of the Grave," an "Ampler Zone," a needle-keen "Frost."

According to an 1862 poem describing the tensely awaited arrival of some important person, she performs her "timid service" of love, then takes up her "little Violin," by which she may mean her poems, and removes "further North," that is, into the region of lovelessness (635). In another poem anticipating some guest, she or perhaps Death gives command to light "my northern room," and the remainder of this grim little poem suggests that the "northern room" is the actual grave (1661). After her death the cruel beloved will remember how "cold" she looked and will hasten to open the door, only to discover that the "little Girl" on the doorstep has a mouth full of ice and can no longer thank her would-be rescuer (874). Or the neglectful beloved will bring a tardy "Heaven" to

the polite "Sufferer" now dressed in "White" (388). Sometimes this sufferer is tormented by the memory of a summer of "Bloom" that makes her
present "November" so hard to bear that she loses her way and perishes
of "cold" (898). Similarly, the dream of a climate warmed by "unsus-
pended Suns" can make her "Winter" more poignant (562). The rather
curious poem 1756 (undated but assuredly written during these disturbed
years) recalls that her "summer paused," making "ripeness" impossible and
sentencing her to perpetual "winter"; but in two frantic closing lines the
poet threatens to come as "Tropic Bride" and melt the beloved's icicle
breast.

These poems of northern cold and darkness always imply their opposites
and sometimes plainly state them. For example, in a happier season the
poet is an "Arctic flower" on the "polar hem," "wandering down the Latitudes" into summer and sun and Eden (180). Again, like "Arctic Creatures" stirred by a "Tropic Hint," there are lives too humble for hoping
that nevertheless receive an unexpected heaven of love (513). In a poem
beginning "The Zeroes—taught us—Phosphorus" (689), where phosphorus
appears to mean both heat and light, the poet explicitly contrasts the symbolic North and South. "When a Boy," she says, she learned to like fire
by "playing Glaciers" and guessed at "Tinder" (heat) by her acquaintance
with its opposite. Eclipses imply that there are suns, and "Paralysis" is her
dumb primer to "Vitality." Finally, according to a most interesting variant,
if there is a "White," then there must surely be a "Red." Northern cold
and southern heat, white paralysis and red vitality, are nowhere more
clearly spelled out than in this little poem.

3

Symbolically the poet inhabits the cold dark North, and
symbolically she longs toward the South of light, warmth, nakedness,
erotic pleasure, and childlike irresponsibility and freedom. The word *South*
or *southern* occurs seventeen times, that is, with about the same frequency
as *North* or *northern,* but the idea of *south* is much more commonly attached to southern regions—Italy, Naples, Sicily, the "blue peninsula" of
Italy, various Caribbean isles and cities, South American countries, Asia,
"spicy isles," Africa, Ethiopia, Tripoli, and so on. The time of day is noon
or "meridian," and the season is summer or midsummer (June is the
month most frequently named in her poetry, although by her own account
August was more significant for her life). These words are freely interchangeable, as her variants show. It is the south or summer or high noon
of sensual freedom, erotic enjoyment, fullness of life. The color is red; the
associated element is fire. So far her symbolism is in substantial agreement
with that of other northern poets, for whom the South also represents

escape into erotic freedom; then comes a rather surprising turn. A real or fancied love relationship ends with violent suddenness, and the South shudders in earthquake and erupts in volcanoes; the color is again red— the red of suffering—and the element is still more fiery.

In July 1859 the poet sent flowers across the lawn to Sue Dickinson's brother, Thomas Dwight Gilbert, with verses about the "south winds" that accompany flowers (86). Birds come back from the "South" (743), and at summer's end nature goes "south" (1324). In an undated poem, the "South" unrolls a purple fan, ushering in a summer rain (1693). Some dozen of the South poems are of this literal and casual order, leaving only five or six in which the usage appears to involve symbolism.

An 1862 poem beginning "I think to Live—may be a Bliss" (646) says that her present loveless condition is metaphorically a polar night, a death. She tries to imagine what it would be like to have "Certainties of Sun" (var., "Noon"), "Midsummer" (var., "Meridian"), a "steadfast South" on her soul, leaving behind its "Polar time" (var., "Polar Night"). The poem concludes by wondering what it would be like to have the whole "mistake" of her life "rectified" by the lover. In short, the words *life, sun, noon, midsummer, meridian, South,* and *love* appear to mean pretty much the same thing and to be freely interchangeable. Their opposites are *death, darkness, night, polar night* or *winter, North, cold,* all of which signify the absence of love and hence are equally interchangeable with each other. It would appear that many a supposed death poem is actually a poem about death in life that ensues upon the loss of some real or imaginary erotic bliss.

A poem beginning "What care the Dead, for Chanticleer" (592) reads at first like a generalized account of physical death. The dead are as indifferent to "Day" and "Summer" as they are to "Winter"; they freeze as readily in a "June Noon" as on a "January Night." No "Solstice" is hot enough to melt the snow before their tomb, and if "One Bird" has a tune that can thrill their "Mortized Ear," it deserves to be cherished by all mankind. For all the good it does these dead, the "South" might as well deposit her "Breeze" of "Cinnamon" in a stone and try warming it with another stone. "Spices" should be given to the living, not to the dead. It becomes clear that the poem is a bitter reproach—very much in the spirit of those poems in which the tardy lover comes back to find the sufferer already in her white shroud or frozen on the steps. Once dead, she will of course be as indifferent to the "Day" or "Summer" or "June Noon" of love as to the "Winter" and "January Night" of cold neglect. The "One Bird," presumably the cruel beloved who no longer sings to the living ear, is reminded that the dead ear will not respond. The June "Solstice" is another metaphor for love's heat, and it may also be an allusion to an impassioned summer parting described in other poems. Finally, there is evidence that Emily Dickinson, like other poet-lovers, penetrated the pious allegory of the chapter headings in her Bible and used the Song of Songs in its obvious erotic sense.[16]

An 1865 four-line poem, which might pass as a brief weather report, becomes suspect in view of this pervasive symbolism. Something appears briefly on her "South," she says, and writes on it a "simple Noon," then, "infinite," disappears (1023). A poem of the preceding year describes the blooming of a brilliant red flower on a "Single Noon." Supposing that it will bloom again "another Noon," she neglects her opportunity and finds too late that her failure to take this one "Flower of the Earth" has meant that "Great Nature's Face" has passed "infinite" by her (978). The red flower would seem to be her important rose symbol, and the neglected confrontation with "Nature's Face" would appear to be erotic.

Like all her symbols, the word *noon* exists in several distinct senses and must be treated with caution. It can mean death, as in the "Degreeless Noon" of the stopped "Clocks" (287) and perhaps in the "Noon" chimed by the "Everlasting Clocks" (297). Again, in describing a zone of "perpetual Noon," with no interrupting "Solstice," a zone where "Consciousness" itself is "Noon," the poet may be imagining life after death viewed as the completion and perfection of earthly life (1056). The "Noons" of an early poem blazing on our "*developed* eyes" suggest the dazzling prospect of immortal life (63), and the "Centuries of Noon" through which the "tired Children" are placidly sleeping reflect the heretical doctrine of soul sleep (112).

On the other hand, there can be a "Noon" of this life viewed as the droughty, desert absence of love. A poem written about midsummer 1860, describing a state of intoxicated happiness, rejoices that there will be no more "Desert Noon" (195), and a poem of the same period speaks of escaping from the "Desert" and the "thirst" (209). According to an 1859 poem, there has been a veritable flood of love in March, but if it is not recruited by "*August*" at the latest, it may well go dry one "burning noon" (136). A poem written later that summer, which brings poet and beloved together on an "August day" (124), suggests that the drought *was* alleviated that August 1859; and though the month is unnamed, an 1862 poem appears to recall the same "Summer's Day" of worshipful love (694). Many years later the poet observed to a friend that "special Months" seemed to give or to take away: "August has brought the most to me—" (L775). Of course the event did not create, though doubtless it strengthened, this ramifying erotic symbolism.

There are poems employing the word *noon* in a literal or near-literal sense, as the "summer's noon" of poem 122, the purely descriptive violet "Noon" of poem 469, the "Noon" of poem 517 in which a "Mote" is suspended, the "Noon" that the robin overflows (828), and several others. In poem 620 the "Noons" into which "Mornings blossom," splitting "Pods of Flame," ornament and take their color from the central bee-rose symbol

and seem to hover on the verge of symbolism. Again, the bee whose experience of "Clovers" and "Noon" the poet longs for (916) and the bee
that hangs in the buttercup "all Noon" (956), though literal in themselves,
are the stuff of which her symbols are made; they are readily convertible.
Again, the butterflies of poem 328 that go swimming off "Banks of Noon,"
treated playfully as small boys leaping and plashing, are neighbors to
thoroughly human "Butterflies"—for example, the two "Butterflies" of the
early 1862 poem and its 1878 revision who go out precisely "at Noon"
and waltz madly together at the symbolic zenith love, then are "wrecked
in Noon" or "hurled from noon" (533).

In a poem beginning " 'Heaven' has different Signs—to me—," she says
explicitly that "Noon" is but a "symbol" of that heaven, although she is
less explicit about the kind of heaven she has in mind (575). In poem 960
"Noon" and "Night" are respectively interchangeable for "Life" and
"Death." Most frequently and consistently "Noon" symbolizes the paradise
of earthly love. Though she will come late to her place in "summer," she
will sing a better tune; and she reminds the love that the "Morning" of
their love is but the "seed of Noon" (250). In poem 415 she writes more
painfully of "Eclipses," "Sunset," and "Midnight" on the "Noon" of their
love. Elsewhere she envies the bells that tell her lover it is now "Noon,
abroad"; she wishes to be his "Noon." Yet such is the barrier between them
that she must forbid bee and flower to come together, lest "Noon," that is,
erotic fulfillment, drop both of them into "Everlasting Night" (498). In
another bee-rose poem, the "Bee"-soul escapes from his dungeon, reaches
his "Rose," and is lost in a delirium of "Noon, and Paradise" (512). An
eight-line poem beginning "To my small Hearth His fire came" contrives
to use a number of her symbols for erotic happiness. It is "sudden light,"
"Sunrise," "Sky," "Summer" without decay, "Noon" without threat of
"Night"—it is "Day" (638). According to a curiously ambivalent poem,
however, her "Noon" to dine comes after years of hunger, and she turns
in discomfort and revulsion from the proffered food of love (579).

In at least two important respects Emily Dickinson appeared to draw
upon Milton for her "Noon" symbol. A passage in *Samson Agonistes,*
in which Samson bewails his blindness ("O dark, dark, dark, amid the
blaze of noon"), appears significant in shaping her laments for her own
"blindness" and the "eclipse" on her life.[17] "Noon" is significant for Milton
—and for Emily Dickinson—in another and more puzzling sense. In
Paradise Regained the devil proposes to tempt Christ with women: "Many
are in each Region passing fair," he says, "As the noon skie; more like to
Goddesses / Than Mortal creatures." [18] The association of "Noon" with
temptation is still more heavily stressed in *Paradise Lost.* It is "at highth
of Noon" that the disguised Satan approaches Uriel in the sphere of the
sun and asks directions to the home of newly created man. Having lighted
on a peak north of Eden, he turns and with distorted face curses "the full-

blazing Sun, / Which now sat high in his meridian tower." The temptation and fall take place the next day at the noon hour, and Milton stresses
the hour. Eve promises again and again "To be return'd by noon amid
the bow'r, / And all things in best order to invite / Noontide repast or
afternoon's repose. / O much deceived, much failing, hapless Eve, / . . .
Thou never from that hour in Paradise / Found'st either sweet repast, or
sound repose." She is listening to the Tempter when "the hour of noon"
draws on and wakes an "eager appetite"; noon is the "evil hour" in which
she succumbs to temptation.[19] That Emily Dickinson remembered the
significant hour and interpreted the temptation as sexual, despite Milton's
disclaimer, is the repeated suggestion of her "noon" and "temptation"
poems. A better melody bubbled from Eden's brooks (reads poem 503),
thus explaining "Eve's great surrender" and "the feet—that would—not
—fly." No doubt Milton connected the noon hour with hubris, as his
disciple does also—in part; yet the hint remains that for Emily Dickinson,
if not for Milton also, the danger, or the evil, sprang in some sense from
the desire to *see*. For such voyeurism the punishment is blindness.

After about 1865, the noon symbol, like most of the other symbols, tends
to disappear. An important exception is a poem in the handwriting of
early 1881. Here she remembers a time when she was transfixed by the
"Missiles" of "Torrid Noons," that is, struck by the lightning bolts of love
(1581). Another copy of the poem appeared two years later, about the time
she saluted the "torrid Spirit" of her sister-in-law, Sue Dickinson (L855),
and the following year she sent her the opening lines with the "torrid
Noons" and their "Missiles," suggesting in a note that the event concerned
Sue or was one the latter would remember (L914).

The symbolic *day* and *summer* have about the same frequency and range
as *noon*. Several instances have already been noted, and of the remainder
only the most significant need be pointed out. These are of course dozens
of poems in which the word *day* appears to be literal, and it may occasionally be personified, as in poem 716, where the "Day" undresses herself.
The attributes of clarity and unbroken light make "Day" an appropriate
symbol for the celestial kingdom (101, 113). It may symbolize reunion in
heaven with the lover (174, 850), or the poet may imagine reunion in a
grave so "ruddy" with light that she can dispense with "Day" (611). In
tragic mood she reproaches the lover for opening the chasm in her life
that now swallows up love's "Sunrise" and "Day" (858). Love has ended
with its dawn and does not lead on to "Day" (450). She has been obliged
to renounce love in this life, to put out her eyes just on "Sunrise," lest the
splendor of this earthly "Day" outvie its "Great Progenitor," the jealous
Jehovah of whom she often takes angry account (745).

Several characteristics—heat, redness, sudden destructive violence after
long quiescence, plus the southern location of those volcanoes Emily
Dickinson selected—all united to form her "Solemn—Torrid—Symbol"

(601) of passionate suffering. Involved in this symbol is her notion of what constitutes real life as opposed to mere existence. Repeatedly she insists that "love is life" (549), that "Life means—Love" (961), that to live with her lover "would be Life" (640). In a poem beginning "More Life—went out —when He went" (422), she specifically contrasts this "finer Phosphor" with "Ordinary Breath," and "Etna's Scarlets" and "Popocatapel" with ignominious "Peat life." There is a snobbish hint that ordinary lives and loves will not stand comparison with her own violent passion.

The volcano does not exhaust the imagery of violence and suffering connected with the erotic South. A very agitated poem of early 1862 reports that there is now "Earthquake in the South—/ And Maelstrom in the Seas," and the poet cries to Jesus for help in her great suffering (502). A riddling poem of the next year finds "Midnight to the North," "Midnight to the South," "Maelstrom—in the Sky—" (721). The fire symbol, associated with the volcano as "smouldering anguish," "Etna's Scarlets," "hissing Corals," and the like, can also stand alone as an agent of destructive violence. It is the "Fire" that the "Cloud" lets through, the "Lightning" that burns her at night, blisters to her dream, and sickens afresh on her sight every morning (362). It can be the fire of martyrdom that alone rewards her constancy (1737). Less violent, it is the remembered blaze of love's "Sun" (826). Or the lovers strike sparks in each other like meeting flints, and after their violent parting they subsist on their "single Spark" (958). The fire of love, once ignited, cannot be put out (530). One poetic tour de force, "Dare you see a Soul *at the White Heat?*" (365), converts the southern fire symbol into a refining and purifying agent and equates it with the "North" of maturation and the "white" of martyrdom and purity. The 1865 "Ashes denote that Fire was" comes at the end of these several years of prodigious symbolizing and correctly notes that the fire has played out. On two later occasions the poet observes that the fire has momentarily blazed up—under the spell of the original "Witch," it would seem—and she has still many lines of verse to write. Out of a total production of some 19,500 lines, about 4,500 survive in the handwriting of 1867-86, but they lack the demonic drive of her earlier work. After 1865 the South of passion is dead.

4

"Dare you dwell in the *East* where we dwell?" writes Emily Dickinson to a new friend in early March 1859. "Are you afraid of the Sun?"

The dawning sun would appear to be one of many risks facing the newcomer in this poetic and symbolic East, for the letter to Kate Turner continues: "All *we* are *strangers*—dear—The world is not acquainted with us, because we are not acquainted with her.... We are hungry, and thirsty, sometimes—We are barefoot—and cold—" (L203). And at this point the reader begins to suspect that the poet is paraphrasing well-known lines from the twenty-fifth chapter of Matthew, the word *barefoot,* as elsewhere in her work, being a euphemism for *naked*: "For I was ahungered, and ye gave me meat: I was thirsty, and ye gave me drink: I was a stranger, and ye took me in: Naked, and ye clothed me.... I was in prison, and ye came unto me."

Here the poet herself is the (plural) stranger, hungry, thirsty, barefoot, and cold, who hopes to be taken in and accepted by the new friend. Elsewhere, and with a different emphasis, the unknown other is the "stranger." A poem written in late 1858 or early 1859 suggests that a "Stranger" may have "pressed a Kingdom" into her "wondering hand" (323); an 1863 poem alludes to a "Countenance" from a "Neighboring Horizon" that is no sooner known than gone (752); and a poem written about 1864 speaks of forsaking everything else for "just a Stranger's...Accompanying" (966). Of more immediate interest, both for its ambiguous "Stranger" and for its involvement with the East symbolism, is a poem written early in 1859, that is, about the date of the letter to Mrs. Turner. The theme is Jacob wrestling with the angel and obtaining a divine blessing (59).

Just "East of Jordan," according to "Evangelists" (but not according to the Bible, which is silent about the compass point), Jacob the "Gymnast" meets an "Angel" with whom he wrestles till dawn touches the "mountain." The angel begs to be allowed to go and breakfast, to which Jacob replies, with an unbiblical addition made more significant by the isolating dash and exclamation mark, " 'I will not let thee go, Except thou bless me' —Stranger!" The poet herself appears to be the "Gymnast" Jacob, as she is elsewhere (letters 720, 1035, 1042). As for the stranger, this angelic visitor has a plausible connection with the one angel whom God let the poet "play" with before sending her back to a dull and boyish game of "Marbles" and with that "small Deity" whom she begged leave to worship on a "bashful Summer's Day" (231, 694). The play upon the words *angel* and *stranger* appears also to recall Hebrews 13:2: "Be not forgetful to entertain strangers, for thereby some have entertained angels unawares." Poem 895, with its belated resolve not to pass an "Angel" henceforth with a mere "glance and a Bow," seems to be another such allusion.

The stressing of the cardinal point is not difficult to understand in the context of this biblical symbolism. Jacob is returning to Canaan (the blessing extorted from the "Angel" may be simply the promise that he will be allowed to cross the Jordan and enter into "Canaan"), and for Emily Dickinson as for Jacob and his descendants the Promised Land is always in the West. This was true as early as her schoolgirl attachment to Susan Gilbert, and it remained true more or less to the end of her life.

In earlier years the orphaned Sue had lived with an aunt in Geneva,

New York, a city to which she often returned and in which she would marry the poet's brother Austin. Geneva is some 230 miles west and slightly north of Amherst and would seem west enough for all the purposes of symbolism. At other times Sue might go as far west as her brother's home in Michigan, and the poet might complain, as she did on one such occasion, that no word came back to her "from that silent West" (L177). But Sue was as clearly identified with the symbolic West in the Amherst home of her married sister as with her aunt in Geneva or her brother in Michigan. Moreover, she remained fixed in the West even when she was literally south or north of Amherst. Her year of teaching in Baltimore seems never to have produced any southern associations. Instead, Emily Dickinson remembers that after her friend returns to Amherst she will come from the West to the Dickinson house; the poet looks often "towards that golden gateway beneath the western trees, and I fancy I see you coming" (L96). A few months later Sue spent several weeks in Manchester, New Hampshire, but to the poet she was still in the West, a West now more than a little tinged with death. Grieved by Sue's failure to write, the poet described herself as going outside, apparently in the direction of the golden gateway, to "stand and watch the West, and remember all of mine—yes, Susie—the golden West, and the great, silent Eternity" that would soon gather the two of them to its breast (L103). Three weeks later, she wrote a somewhat reserved letter to congratulate her brother on his engagement to Sue: "I really had my doubts about your reaching Canaan" (L110). Some eight years later, during a painful estrangement from her sister-in-law, she decided that her brother had not entered Canaan after all: "He married —and went East" (L235). And the East, as Emily Dickinson knew, was not a land flowing with milk and honey but instead was desert wilderness.

It is doubtful that she made an explicit association of any element (or any single distinctive color) with the eastern cardinal point; but plainly she lived east of Eden, east of Jordan, east of Canaan, on top of Mount Nebo, in the Transjordanian wilderness, and the element that is oftenest implied and sometimes expressed takes the form of desert sand. In a waking nightmare, she watches away hours of suffering that are like "Grains" of sand, or she struggles westward through a desert of "steady— drifting—Grains" (471, 550). According to another poem, the "realms of sand" are the price she must pay for her Caspian Sea (1754). Still more stoic of mood, she insists that she has been "Fructified" by this experience of sand (681). In some two dozen poems she pursues this theme of a life condemned to desert wilderness.

The East is arid only as part of her East-West axis; taken alone, it has its separate meanings. Several poems using "East" and "Orient" seem to be straightforward descriptions of nature having little if any relation to the symbolism. A small group invokes the East of oriental wealth and fable, an association which in other poems is suggested by exotic objects or by place-names like India, Golconda, or Cashmere. The "Orient" of poem 323 seems to be a combination of nature's East and the East of fabulous wealth, for the poet acknowledges some rich gift of friendship. The same merging of cardinal point with oriental wealth and beauty appears in a description of the lost beloved as "An Orient's Apparition—/ Remanded of the Morn—"; that is, love's rich dawn perishes with the dawn (788). Death is contrasted with the "Oriental Circuit" of life, the mind of some admired person is compared to priceless "Fabrics of the East," and the dead Helen Hunt Jackson is described as a peddler carrying life's empty pack as gallantly as if it contained the wealth of the East (813, 1446, 1562).

A poem with the line "The Vane a little to the East" describes her inner weather after some grievous loss. It is apparently a tribute to men like Samuel Bowles and her clerical friends Charles Wadsworth, Edward S. Dwight, and Frederic Dan Huntington, whose "Broadcloth Hearts" stood firm when the "Muslin souls" of beloved women failed her (278). Although this particular East may derive from nothing more than the experience of biting east winds, her persistent symbolism suggests unconscious associations with the East of desert chill and death. "To the bright east she flies" is an elegy on her mother's death (1573). The early "Sleep is supposed to be," usually dismissed as a mere joke, has an "East of Eternity" that hints at a stately resurrection (13). Poem 608 explicitly connects the East with resurrection, and poems 461 ("Unto the East, and Victory") and 839 ("Old, indeed, the East") look toward resurrection and reunion with her beloved. Perhaps the Christian emphasis upon the East as the altar end of the church helped establish these associations with death and resurrection. She may also have read an article in the *Atlantic Monthly*, "The Eleusinia" (September 1859), which was rich in such associations.

A few early poems are concerned with the beginning of love. "As Watchers hang upon the East" reflects the strained hopefulness of the lover who watches for the sunrise of love (121). Poem 257, apparently written in 1861 during a period of great emotional disturbance, harks back to a time when the poet "asked the East" if the rainbow of love would endure. "Good Morning—Midnight" begins by describing the blackness that overtook her hopeful morning and then begs permission to look at the red East, the remembered sunrise of love (425).

Again and again "sunrise" or "dawn" or "morning" signifies the beginning of love. "Day" was to have been her life with the beloved, but since love ends almost as soon as it begins, "sunrise" commonly ushers in the death of love and becomes almost a death symbol itself. In a poem sent to her sister-in-law, most probably on Sue's birthday, 19 December 1858, the poet writes that she "spilt the dew—/ But took the morn," choosing a "single star," Sue herself, who is also the "morn" and in some sense the spilled "dew" of their youthful attachment (14). In a poem about the same date, she asks the "Orient" whether it has a "Morn" for her, and it lifts its "purple dikes" and floods her with the "Dawn" (323). In a poem of late 1860, which refers to Sue by the nickname "Dollie," the poet fears that she may open "cheated" eyes on a "grinning morn," the "Sunrise" of love still mockingly in sight but inaccessible (156). A poem sent to Sue about 1862 says the poet revealed such secrets as "Morning's Nest," and then "brake" her life in two for the other (446). Elsewhere she remembered that she "looked at Sunrise—once" (542), that "Cunning Reds of Morning" woke her from her "Egg-life" (728), that the "Sunrise" compelled her awake and she *saw* (480).

In a letter of early 1883, recalling the recent death of her revered friend Charles Wadsworth, she seemed oppressed by a coincidence of dates: " 'The first of April' 'Today, Yesterday, and Forever'—'*Can* Trouble dwell with April Days?' " (L801). In a letter written a few months earlier the poet explicitly emphasized such a coincidence: "It sometimes seems as if special Months gave and took away—August has brought the most to me—April—robbed me most—in incessant instances—" (L775). It is a curious fact that the line quoted from Tennyson's *In Memoriam*—"Can trouble dwell with April days?"—appeared as an epigraph to T. W. Higginson's "April Days" published in the April 1861 *Atlantic Monthly,* which Emily Dickinson would have seen in late March. It is demonstrable that the most acute phase of her mysterious suffering began in early 1861. A poem written in April 1861, or shortly thereafter, begins, "If *He dissolve*—then—there is *nothing—more—*." This loss would be no less than "Eclipse—at Midnight" on a life already dark; it would be the setting of her faint Bethlehem "Star," a *"Blindness"* at *Dawn,"* a *"Sunset—at Easter"* (236). If Easter Sunday, 31 March 1861, was indeed followed on Monday, 1 April, by the death of her last hope, then the tragic irony deepens almost intolerably.

Another poem of this packet begins "The *Sun—just touched* the Morning" and implies that her happiness was brief and her hope of a perpetual springtime soon dashed (232). A poem of this same year speaks with envious sadness of those whose "Sunrise" is followed by "Enamored—Day" (294). An 1862 poem protests that "Sunset on the Dawn Reverses Nature" (415). "Morn—didn't want me," complains another poem, "So—Goodnight —Day!" (425). Renunciation, according to the starkly Calvinistic theology of another poem, involves the "putting out of Eyes" just at "Sunrise" lest love's earthly "Day" outvie God himself (745). The beloved has made a "Chasm" in her life, a "fissure" into which the "Sunrise" has dropped, and she is half-tempted to stitch up this living tomb with a final breath (858). Another poem recalls that her "Morning" started bountifully colored but ended early and sere (913). Still another poem says that "Sunset stopped on Cottages" where "Morning" (var., "Sunrise") had just begun (950).

Since the poet had a hope, or at least a fantasy, that she and her beloved would be together after death, the sunrise (dawn, morning, aurora) or the related springtime may also signify their meeting in heaven. The most explicit account of this celestial reunion states that she will be a "Wife— at Daybreak," asks whether "Sunrise" has a flag for her, says she climbs from "Midnight" to "East, and Victory" and meets her beloved in "Eternity" at the top of the stairs (461). In similar mood, she speaks of passing "Midnight," the "Morning Star," and "Sunrise" en route to "Day" and reunion with the beloved in a heaven where the lamps will be lighted and she will finally be able "to *see*" (174). Following a separation that is like a tragically glorious sunset, she looks forward to a heavenly sunrise, the "infinite Aurora" in the lover's eyes (925).

5

The element associated with the West is water—"that Great Water in the West— / Termed Immortality" (726). Symbolically conceived, the West is ocean or sea, an association so consistent that the direction of any of her symbolic voyages may be assumed to be westward. An 1853 poem beginning "On this wondrous sea" gives the destination as "Eternity" and the direction as the "peaceful west" or, in the 1858 version, the "silent West" (4). The emphatic words "I pilot *thee*" underline the curious fact that the person she is piloting to the next life is Susan Gilbert, then absent on a visit to Manchester, New Hampshire. Perhaps this poem accompanied the rather dismal letter in which the poet describes herself as looking at "the golden West, and the great, silent Eternity, for ever folded there." After Sue married and settled down next door, she did not live at the end of a few yards of grassy path but westward across an ocean. In a poem addressed "Sue," the poet says no day is dark to her if its sun sets in the beloved Sue, and no distance is far if she can see the "Ships" that touch the other's shore (808). Appealing for a renewal of correspondence, of ships that are letters, she writes to Kate Turner: "We dignify our Faith, when we can cross the ocean with it, though most prefer ships" (L209). Since Kate lived in Cooperstown, New York, almost due west of Amherst, this ocean of separation or distance appears to be conceived as western.

The draft of an 1858 letter to some unidentified friend is explicable as a symbolic westward voyage. The other person is supposed to have inquired what her "flowers said," and the poet answers with an unmistakable death symbol—"what the lips in the West, say, when the sun goes down." She is writing on the "Sabbath," which gives her church-and-death associations, for she alludes to the recurrent Sabbaths as days "on the Sea," says she is counting the Sabbaths till they too "meet on shore" in the next life, and wonders whether the hills there will be as blue as "sailors say" (L187). In a poem written the next year the blue hills are replaced by "blue havens." Just as the "Ebbing Day" is flowing to the "West," a poor, torn, tattered heart (her own, presumably) sits down to rest, is discovered by angels, and is carried to God (78).

Striving for colorful effect, the poet might describe a sunset as "Ships of Purple" tossing on "Seas of Daffodil" or as a "Yellow Sea" rushing off into the "Western Mystery" (265, 266). Elsewhere the "West" is pictured as "Whole Gulfs—of Red" on which sail "Fleets—of Red" with "Crews—of solid Blood" (658). "Sundown creeps in, a "steady Tide," and everything is extinguished in this "Sea" (354). Initial sunset images of a "Sapphire Farm" or a herd of "Opal Cattle" give way, as if obsessively, to a "Sea" and "Ships" with crews the size of mountains (628). As late as 1885 this conceit reappears, after long absence, and the poet writes of having a "Navy in the West" (1642). Another late poem, "Of Death I try to think like this," makes explicit the death fear that underlies even her most colorful sunset water images. Here the more usual ocean is replaced by a "Brook that seemed a Sea"—in other words, by Jordan's stream and death's cold flood of frightened childhood memory—which she must somehow leap if she is to clutch the "Flower Hesperian," the "Purple Flower," of immortal life beyond (1558).

Despite the frequent red and yellow sunset shades, purple is incontestably the poet's "Hesperian" color. Purple is blood, of course—the *"purple—in my Vein"* (663); it is also the royal color and hence suited to royalize death (98, 171). In a more personal anguish, she speaks of death and the grave and describes the way of salvation as "Costly," adding, "So are *purples!*" (234). Out of the common ground of these symbols blooms her purple Hesperian flower. But purple is also the beloved's color, and not surprisingly; soon or late, or concurrently, every death symbol in this poetry is converted into an erotic symbol and every erotic symbol into a death symbol. Her purple Hesperian flower appears to recall Shakespeare's "little Western flower...now purple with love's wound." [20] The beloved is royal, costly, death imbued, and so persistently linked with the West as to suggest an actual geographic relationship.

In late September 1858 Sue Dickinson made another of her trips to Geneva, New York, and the poet wrote mournfully of the "chink" her "dear face" made, adding that one would not "mind the sun, dear, if it didn't *set,*" and she then invited Sue to repose on her breast in what appears to be the grave (L194). Some fifteen years later she sent across the lawn a poem that describes the "West" as "a little worn" but the longed-for "Gold" as glowing ever "newer." Unfortunately the other woman's (Sue's?) "infinite disdain" has vanquished them both (1249). Other western and purple poems, mentioned earlier, associate Sue with the mountain

Tenerife and its "Purple of Ages," a "Queen" with purple and the setting sun, and the lovers with the "Eastern Exiles" trying to reenter a western and purple Eden.

6

The letter of early 1859 to Kate Turner, the poems of like date concerning Jacob and the angel, and the long-standing association of Sue with the symbolic West are evidence that at an early date the poet began working out the major elements of her East-West symbolism. It was based in good part on the geography of the Holy Land, where she appeared to be so much at home as never to make a mistake. She would have had to study a map of the Bible lands to discover that Jacob struggled with the angel just "a little East of Jordan"—within sight, as it were, of the Promised Land. She knew that the Israelites did not enter Canaan from the Sinai Peninsula in the South but from the Transjordanian East, where they had been wandering forty years in desolate wilderness. She was aware that Adam and Eve were expelled from the garden through the eastern gate, so that paradise was always westward. Unlike more careless readers, she appeared to know that the Wise Men in the East went westward to seek the Star of Bethlehem. Finally, she knew that the Lord took old Moses up on Mount Nebo and allowed him to look westward across the Jordan to the Promised Land, saying, "I have caused thee to see it with thine eyes, but thou shalt not go thither." That she too was allowed a glimpse of a forbidden paradise, symbolically associated with the West, is the theme of many poems.

Conventionally, the East is the place of birth and beginnings, the West the place of death and endings, and this convention is the dark underside of the poet's Canaan symbol. At times the Jordan River is no more than an earthly obstacle that must be crossed to attain a quite earthly paradise, but ever and again it is the cold, dark river of death beyond which there may or may not lie immortal fulfillment. The several poems about Moses illustrate the ambivalence of her Canaan symbol as well as her cumulative and repetitive way of working. Here the Bible is supplemented by the fourth stanza of the Isaac Watts hymn, "There is a land of pure delight":

Could we but climb where Moses stood,
And view the landscape o'er,
Not Jordan's streams, nor death's cold flood
Should fright us from the shore.

The earliest borrowing occurs in an 1852 nonsense valentine. A stanza about Adam and the forbidden apple is followed by the lines "I climb the 'Hill of Science,' / I 'view the landscape o'er'" (3). When she takes up the subject again in an 1859 poem, "Where bells no more affright the morn," she is not so lighthearted. The rooms to which the "nimble Gentlemen" are obliged to keep and in which the "tired Children" sleep placidly through "Centuries of noon" are simply their graves. In a final stanza paraphrasing Watts, the substitution of "Father's bells" and "Factories" for "Jordan's stream" and "death's cold flood" draws curious attention to Watts's original wording, which obviously haunts her and has already given a death chill to her own poem (112). An 1860 Moses poem makes further use of the Watts hymn but now stresses the bitterness of denial. We are asked to stand with Moses, " 'Canaan' denied," and look across at the "stately landscape" (168). An 1862 poem beginning "It always felt to me a wrong" attacks God as a sadistic bully who gets pleasure out of tantalizing Moses with the sight of a Canaan he will not be allowed to enter—a cruelty worse than murder, the poet insists. Late as it is, her sense of justice bleeds for the "Old Man on Nebo" (597). In 1871 she could still write indignantly that Moses had not been "fairly used" (1201).

The memory of a lost paradise, according to an 1858 poem, is like the bubble of brooks "in deserts" on dying ears or like the flame of "Evening Spires" to dying eyes; that is, she thinks of herself as living in the desert and yearning toward the sunset West (20). In an 1859 poem the "brooks in deserts" once more babble on ears too distant to be helped (121). "I did not reach Thee," begins an undated poem, probably written in 1862 or 1863, then describes her efforts to attain the lost beloved. Every day her "feet slip nearer," across rivers, over hill and desert, and finally over the sea. In the end she has apparently crossed three rivers, a hill, two deserts, and the sea, only to learn that death has taken her lover (1664). A very similar poem, written in 1862, makes the western direction clear. In her mind, she says, she keeps crossing a mountain, more mountains, a sea, more sea, and then encounters a desert. None of these obstacles slows her pace or keeps her "from the West," but in the end she is not sure whether she has arrived or whether she is even alive (550). Although the details vary somewhat, these poems are treatments of the same theme, a dreamlike struggle westward toward the unattainable beloved over mountains and deserts and a sea.

7

The poet's cardinal-points symbolism employs two movements of the sun, the diurnal and the slow movement north and south across the equinoctial line. The diurnal governs the East-West axis of her symbolism and is far more important, as discussion of many poems has already demonstrated. Usually the sun is identified with the passion of love or with a most passionate friendship, running a swift and calamitous course from sunrise to sunset. On occasion, however, the sun is the beloved, and on some of these occasions the sun is clearly Sue Dickinson.

In an early 1859 poem that identifies the poet with the "Daisy" and the beloved with the "Sun," she fancies herself stealing closer to the loved friend, "Enamored of the Parting West," its "peace" and "flight" and "Amethyst" color (106). A poem written some three years later recalls a sexual overture by the lover, which the poet rejected, whereupon the "Sun" withdrew to "Other Wests," that is, to Wests more distant and unattainable than the lover's actual residence (643). In a poem of the same year, which describes love's martyrdom, the lovers suffer a mutual sunset (474). Another poem speaks of the beloved face, apparently sunlike, which will accord the poet her "Rank" in death's "West" (336). Of the swift sunset that overtakes her hopeful sunrise, she says the "treason" is not "His," exonerating the lover of deliberate cruelty; rather, it is "Life's," since everything that means life to her has that day "Gone Westerly" (950). A knotty poem beginning "Said Death to Passion" might yield to a similar interpretation. Death robs passion of "All His East" (the lost sunrise of love), but "He," that is, passion, sovereign like the sun, ends the debate by resituating himself in the "West" (1033).

Poem 307, a copy of which went to Sue Dickinson, appears to describe a summer day, but the final stanza has some curious features. The poet writes, "When Orient—have been outgrown—/ And Occident—become Unknown—." She herself is the East so frequently as to suggest that the Orient outgrown is her outgrown self (or is it once more the lost sunrise?), and the Occident that has "become Unknown" seems to hint at her obsessive attachment. Poem 603 says the lover bade her to be faithful to the "East" until he could return and take her home. Perhaps she thinks of herself as waiting once more for the sunrise, but the home to which the lover will take her is assuredly the West. A related poem describes death as the "Drift of Eastern Gray, / Dissolving into Dawn away." Rather surprisingly, the poet adds, "Before the West begin." Apparently she dies in the East but enters upon the glorious resurrection in the West (721).

If the lover is symbolized as the sun, it would not matter greatly whether he lived in Boston or Baltimore or Montreal. Symbolically he would make his transit from east to west, as love dawned, then failed. Yet there are peculiarities in the poems, as well as an urgency and a poignancy, that suggest the coincidence of an actual residence in the West. For example, a poem beginning "The Sunrise runs for Both" says that the East is keeping her "Purple Troth" with the hill. Noon unwinds her blue until it covers both of them. Night sets lamps wicks apart for each of them, by which presumably stars are meant, although this notion of setting out lamps is curiously reminiscent of an anecdote related by Sue's daughter in *Emily Dickinson Face to Face* (the poet, said Mrs. Bianchi, was in the habit of putting a light in her west window as a good-night signal, to which a light in Sue's east window would send back "a fond response").[21] Finally the midnight clasps them in her dusky arms, one of them lying upon her bosom and the other upon her hem (710). Although the interval need not be great, the image does suggest a greater distance than that between the two Dickinson houses. Of course the poem might have been written while Sue was visiting in New York or Michigan, and indeed the markedly feminine identity of the night on which both are lying (between bosom and hem!) favors such an interpretation.

A poem of stronger feeling, perhaps not written to her sister-in-law, makes a vital point of the direction. At the moment of her greatest hope, the poet recalls that she was standing, in bitter weather, at a "Window facing West." Revising the poem, she offers the variant phrase "In a Chamber facing West" (768), suggesting that her bedroom was important as the setting. But it was weather rather than place that she stressed for the next important day in this painful affair. The day she feared—feared, that is, that the love was ending—is described as swimming in a heat that suggests late June, the time of the summer solstice (322). Another 1861 poem beginning "One Year ago—jots what?" points back to the preceding year for the date of this anguished parting (296).

Although the detail about the extreme heat is convincing and other evidence supports the idea of an important development in the summer of 1860, the solstice of poem 322 does not prove that the parting occurred precisely on 22 June 1860. It is too neat a symbol, and it seems to have occurred to her only when she began to write the poem, apparently some-time in December 1861. Still it does point to the probable season, and it works to intensify the symbolic heat of passion, although its principal func-tion here is to signalize the crisis or turning point of this relationship. There are, in fact, two senses in which this symbolic turning point is to be taken. In one sense, the lovers dedicate themselves to a love everlasting beyond the grave and thus pass a solstice that makes "all things new." More realistically, love's sun reaches its farthest northern point in the poet's New England garden and begins its slow retreat southward, never to return.

In a poem written a few months later, the solstice expresses heat alone: no "Solstice" can thaw the dead from their tombs (592). In an 1864 poem, which clearly implies a solstitial movement, her old-fashioned, steadfast heart "swerved" like the suns, or like birds alternating between zones, just for the "merit of Return" (973). Perhaps she remembered a figure in some astronomy book showing the sinuous curve of the sun in its annual prog-ress from solstice to solstice across the equinoctial line; poetically, it might be described as swerving. In the last of these solstice poems, written about 1865, she imagines a "Zone" beyond death, where there is no interrupting "Solstice" but instead a summer everlasting and a "perpetual Noon" of love (1056).

She was now very near the end. The fury of a symbolism that had caught up literally hundreds of poems in one vast cyclonic movement was wearing itself out. After 1865 she could no longer sustain the mood of massive self-deceit that had hitherto fueled her symbolic storm. In 1866 she wrote almost no new poems—perhaps, indeed, none—and though a good deal of occasional verse would be written in later years, almost none of her characteristic symbols had managed to bridge this Lipalian interval. There seems to be nothing comparable in the history of any other lyric poet, major or minor, early or late. At the very least, the study of this web of symbolism would suggest treating the work of her major period not as a series of tiny, fragmented lyrics but as one total poem. So treated, it would be more readily seen as the unique and, indeed, distinguished achievement it is.

NOTES

Introduction

1. See Willis J. Buckingham, *Emily Dickinson: An Annotated Bibliography* (Bloomington and London: Indiana University Press, 1970) for an extensive list of all writings on Emily Dickinson from 1850 to 1968. Since the publication of his bibliography, Buckingham has continuously updated it in the *Emily Dickinson Bulletin*. Although Klaus Lubbers's *Emily Dickinson: The Critical Revolution* (Ann Arbor: University of Michigan Press, 1968) traces the development of critical appreciation of Emily Dickinson as a poet since her first publication in edited versions, the majority of books and articles that appeared before 1955 were concerned with her life and loves. Buckingham cites ten separate publications that deal with the poet's life as opposed to four that focus on the poetry.
2. Thomas H. Johnson, who must be one of the most devoted of Emily Dickinson scholars (and who justly deserves that description), published a three-volume edition of the poems, including all the variants, publication history, some commentary, and a tentative chronology. This was followed in 1958 by a three-volume edition of her letters. *The Poems of Emily Dickinson, Including Variant Readings Critically Compared with All Known Manuscripts*, ed. Thomas H. Johnson, 3 vols. (Cambridge: Harvard University Press, Belknap Press, 1955); *The Letters of Emily Dickinson*, ed. Thomas H. Johnson and Theodora Ward, 3 vols. (Cambridge: Harvard University Press, Belknap Press, 1958).
3. Richard B. Sewall, *The Life of Emily Dickinson* (New York: Farrar, Straus, and Giroux, 1974); Thomas H. Johnson, *Emily Dickinson: An Interpretive Biography* (Cambridge: Harvard University Press, Belknap Press, 1955); Jay Leyda, *The Years and Hours of Emily Dickinson*, 2 vols. (New Haven: Yale University Press, 1960); George F. Whicher, *This Was a Poet: A Critical Biography of Emily Dickinson* (New York: Charles Scribner's Sons, 1938).
4. Clark Griffith, *The Long Shadow: Emily Dickinson's Tragic Poetry* (Princeton, N.J.: Princeton University Press, 1964); Rebecca Patterson, *The Riddle of Emily Dickinson* (Boston: Houghton Mifflin, 1951); John Cody, *After Great Pain: The Inner Life of Emily Dickinson* (Cambridge: Harvard University Press, Belknap Press, 1971).
5. Albert J. Gelpi, *Emily Dickinson: The Mind of the Poet* (Cambridge: Harvard

University Press, 1965); William R. Sherwood, *Circumference and Circumstance: Stages in the Mind and Art of Emily Dickinson* (New York: Columbia University Press, 1968); Genevieve Taggard, *The Life and Mind of Emily Dickinson* (New York: Alfred A. Knopf, 1930).

6. Compare, for example, Laurence Perrine's evaluation that "This may be the most important volume that has been published about the life of Emily Dickinson. It is at once a work of solid scholarship, an exciting exhibition of literary detective-work, and a major contribution to the biographical understanding of Emily Dickinson's poetry" ("Emily's Beloved Friend," *Southwest Review* 37 [Winter 1952]: 81–83) with Elizabeth Bishop's question, "Why do so many books of literary detective-work, even when they are better authenticated, better written and more useful in their conclusions than Mrs. Patterson's, seem finally just unpleasant?" Bishop concludes her review with the comment: "this infuriating book." "Unseemly Deductions," *New Republic* 127 (18 August 1952): 20.

7. The questions of a psychological approach to Emily Dickinson's poetry were raised as early as 1930 with Josephine Pollitt's study, *Emily Dickinson: The Human Background of Her Poetry* (New York: Harper, 1930), and then by Clement Wood, *Emily Dickinson: The Volcanic Heart* (privately printed, 1945), who theorizes that forbidden passion is sublimated in the poems.

8. Cody, *After Great Pain,* p. 183 et passim.

9. David Porter. This comment was included in an early version of his article, "The Crucial Experience in Emily Dickinson's Poetry." See note 33.

10. Women's subjugation was exacerbated in the Victorian era by the onset of the Industrial Revolution and a corresponding move away from rural family life in the English-speaking world. No wonder that women began to rebel and to form suffragist and suffragette movements. With the ushering in of the new era, the question of insanity became predominantly a female writer's prerogative.

11. Edith Perry Stamm, "Emily Dickinson: Poetry and Punctuation," *Saturday Review* 46 (30 March 1963): 26–27, 74. E. Porter's *The Rhetoric Reader,* 23d ed. (New York, 1836), is cited as the poet's possible source.

12. Brita Lindberg-Seyersted, *The Voice of the Poet: Aspects of Style in the Poetry of Emily Dickinson* (Cambridge: Harvard University Press, 1968).

13. Ibid., p. 196. A fuller treatment of the question can be found in Lindberg-Seyersted's article, "Emily Dickinson's Punctuation," *Studia neophilologica* 37, no. 2 (1965): 327–59.

14. No serious study has been done so far on the effect of seeing the dashes in print, in determining the way most readers experience the poetry. Generations of students, when confronted with Johnson's edition as compared with versions that regularize the punctuation, prefer the former. See David Porter's discussion in *The Art of Emily Dickinson's Early Poetry* (Cambridge: Harvard University Press, 1966), p. 143.

15. Richard Howard, "A Consideration of the Writings of Emily Dickinson," *Prose* 6 (1973): 67–97. He quotes Emily Dickinson's line, "Blessed are they that play, for theirs is the Kingdom of Heaven." In his discussion of the poet at work, Johnson comments on the three versions of poem 228: "These copies were set down over a period of five years, from 1861 to 1866, and one text is apparently as valid as another" (*Poems,* 1: xxxv).

16. "Except in instances where direct evidence in letters can be used to date a poem —and they are relatively few—all assigned dates are tentative and will always remain so" (Johnson, *Poems,* 1: lxii).

17. Johnson, *Letters,* 2: 388.

18. R. W. Franklin, *The Editing of Emily Dickinson: A Reconsideration* (Madison: University of Wisconsin Press, 1967). In an appendix to *The Poetry of Emily Dickinson* (Middletown, Conn.: Wesleyan University Press, 1968), Ruth Miller provides a useful list of all the poems in the order they appear in the fascicles and packets and compares Franklin's emendations with Johnson's original ordering.

19. The thirteen poems and the fascicles and packets in which they appear are as follows. Fascicle 11: poem 690, sent to Samuel Bowles, 1861. Fascicle 14: poem 214, published *Springfield Republican,* 4 May 1861; poem 319, sent to T. W. Higginson, 15 April 1862; poem 321, sent to Higginson, 25 April 1862. Fascicle 16: poem 683, sent to Higginson, April 1863. Fascicle 26: poem 299, sent to Higginson, July 1862. Fascicle 27: poem 326, sent to Higginson, August 1862; poem 334, sent to Eudocia Flynt, 21 July 1862. Fascicle 32: poem 327, sent to Higginson, August 1862. Fascicle 33: poem 823, sent to Susan Dickinson, 1860; poem 830, sent to Gertrude Vanderbilt, summer 1864. Packet 84: poem 1067, sent to Higginson, 17 March 1866; poem 1181, sent to Higginson, October/November 1871.

20. Johnson comments that "the evidence now seems to point" toward the fact that the poems were composed at the time the copies were made but provides no supporting argument for this conclusion, except the rather dubious statement at the end of his introduction, "Creating the Poems," that "the inspiration and the act of generation were one and complete" (*Poems,* 1: xviii, xxxvii).

21. It is somewhat surprising that no one has seriously questioned the feasibility of composing 366 poems in 365 days (1862 was not a leap year), given the poet's household duties, by no means unsubstantial in the nineteenth century.

22. Miller, *Poetry,* pp. 270–77.

23. Ibid., pp. 213–19.

24. Robert Weisbuch, *Emily Dickinson's Poetry* (Chicago: University of Chicago Press, 1975), pp. 13–14, 18–19.

25. See ibid., chap. 4, "Persona as Voice, Persona as Style," pp. 59–77.

26. Porter, *Dickinson's Early Poetry,* p. x.

27. Sirkka Heiskänen-Mäkelä, *In Quest of Truth: Observations on the Development of Emily Dickinson's Poetic Dialectic* (Jyväskylä, Finland: K. J. Gummerus Osakeyhtiön Kirjapainossa, 1970), pp. 186–87.

28. Interest is growing in the United States. See, for example, Richard W. Bailey and Dolores M. Burton, *English Stylistics: A Bibliography* (Cambridge: The M.I.T. Press, 1968), and the journals *Language and Style, Poetics,* and *Poetics and the Theory of Literature.*

29. Donald C. Freeman, "Current Trends in Metrics," in *Current Trends in Stylistics,* ed. Braj B. Kachru and Herbert F. W. Stahlke (Edmonton, Canada: Linguistic Research, 1972), pp. 67–81.

30. Irene Nims, "Tone in the Poetry of Emily Dickinson: A Linguistic Analysis with Pedagogical Reflections" (Ph.D. diss., Indiana University, 1971).

31. Elizabeth Perlmutter, "Hide and Seek: Emily Dickinson's Use of the Existential Sentence," *Language and Style* 10, no. 2 (Spring 1977): 109–19.

32. Archibald Hill, "Figurative Structure and Meaning: Two Poems by Emily Dickinson," *Texas Studies in Literature and Language* 16, no. 1 (Spring 1974): 195–209.

33. David Porter, "The Crucial Experience in Emily Dickinson's Poetry," *Emerson Society Quarterly* 77 (1974): 280–90.

34. Roland Hagenbüchle, "Precision and Indeterminacy in the Poetry of Emily Dickinson," *Emerson Society Quarterly* 74 (1974): 33–56.

35. Buckingham, in his 1970 *Bibliography,* cites nineteen languages into which poems by and articles on Emily Dickinson have been translated. She was being translated into German as early as 1898 and into Italian by 1933 (A.v.E., trans., "Emily Dickinson," *Der Westen* [Chicago], 19 June 1898, sec. 3, p. 1; Giacomo Prampolini, trans., *Circol: Rivista di Poesia* [Genoa] 3, no. 6 [November–December 1933], pp. 10–15).

36. Fresh insights into ways of resolving questions of chronology are provided through an exploration of the poet's choice of words and images, and Patterson makes a persuasive distinction between undated poems that may have been written in the poet's most productive years and those that were written later but return to some of the attitudes and passions of the earlier period. We do not have to accept Patterson's specific if conjectural datings to recognize the possibilities she raises of determining to some extent poetic development through textual analysis.

37. Patterson's analysis of the word imagery that went into decline after 1865 is impressive; whether one agrees with her that this constitutes the whole of Emily Dickinson's symbol making is another matter.

Chapter One

1. *Charlotte Cushman: Her Letters and Memories of Her Life,* ed. Emma Stebbins (Boston, 1878), pp. 12–13.

2. Ibid., pp. 59, 92, 17. Biographer Stebbins records with solemn reverence that Miss Cushman adopted as her motto the well-known passage from Longfellow's *Hyperion*: "Look not mournfully into the past ... Wisely improve the present ... Go forth into the shadowy future, without fear, and with a manly heart." No doubt her manly heart had much to do with her achievement of wealth and independence at a fairly early age.

3. Bettina (Brentano) von Arnim, *Goethe's Correspondence with a Child,* 2 vols. (London, 1837), 1: 6; and *Lebensspiel,* ed. Willi Reich (Zurich, 1953), pp. 113–14.

4. Julia Ward Howe, "George Sand," *Atlantic Monthly* 8 (November 1861): 525, 530–31.

5. Elizabeth Browning, *The Complete Poetical Works,* Cambridge ed. (Boston, 1900), p. 103.

6. Margaret Fuller, *Woman in the Nineteenth Century and Kindred Papers,* ed. Arthur B. Fuller (Boston, 1855), pp. 75, 129. That Emily Dickinson knew this book becomes plausible when her poem 365, "Dare you see a Soul *at the White Heat?*" (which she identified as a love poem in letter 675 to Higginson), is compared with this excerpt from a "Notice of George Sand" (ibid., p. 235): "She knows passion, as has been hinted, at a *white* heat, when all the lower particles are remoulded by its power." On page 342 Margaret Fuller writes: "It is so true that a woman may be in love with a woman, and a man with a man. It is pleasant to be sure of it, because it is undoubtedly the same love that we shall feel when we are angels, when we ascend to the only fit place for the Mignons where 'Sie fragen nicht nach Mann und Weib.' " Although Fuller does not mention Raphael's blushing confession to Adam (*Paradise Lost* 8. 619–29), she undoubtedly remembered it. What Emily Dickinson made of these ideas can be discovered only by a careful consideration of her poems.

7. "Visits to Concord," *Memoirs of Margaret Fuller Ossoli* (Boston, 1852), 1: 229.

8. *Elizabeth Barrett to Miss Mitford,* ed. Betty Miller (New Haven: College and University Press, 1954), pp. 125–26, 235.

9. Alexandre Dumas, quoted in the *Encyclopaedia Britannica* (1949), S. V. "Sand, George."

10. Thomas Moore, *Life, Letters, and Journals of Lord Byron* (London, 1838), pp. 209, 229, 1, 353.

11. Jay Leyda, *The Years and Hours of Emily Dickinson*, 2 vols. (New Haven: Yale University Press, 1960), 2: 480–81.

12. In an 1855 letter from Hawthorne to W. D. Ticknor, quoted by F. O. Matthiessen, *American Renaissance* (New York: Oxford University Press, 1941), p. xi.

13. Lydia Maria Child, *Letters from New York* (1848), p. 106. The name of this pioneer feminist was introduced, apparently by Emily Dickinson herself, at the first of her two meetings with T. W. Higginson. The poet even essayed a little feminist joke, which wholly escaped her visitor. Higginson reported with solemn bafflement that after mentioning her domestic duties she added, " '& people must have puddings' this *very* dreamily, as if they were comets—and so she makes them" (L342*a*). Such a redoubtable feminist should have remembered Sarah Grimké's scornful attack on the male dictum that "She that knoweth how to compound a pudding is more desirable than she who skilfully compounds a poem" (*The Equality of the Sexes and the Condition of Women*, 1838). Grimké must have gotten her pudding and her title from "The Equality of the Sexes" by "Constantia" (Judith Sargent Murray), who demanded (*Massachusetts Magazine*, March–April 1790) whether it was "reasonable that a candidate for immortality, for the joys of heaven, an intelligent being, who is to spend an eternity in contemplating the works of Deity, should at present be so degraded as to be allowed no other ideas, than those which are suggested by the mechanism of a pudding?" Royal Tyler's Van Rough approved the general opinion "that if a woman knew how to make a pudding, and to keep herself out of fire and water, she knew enough for a wife" (*The Contrast*, act 1, scene 2, a play almost certainly known to Emily Dickinson). Of course it all went back to Samuel Johnson, who saw the necessity of asserting that "My old friend, Mrs. Carter, could make a pudding as well as translate Epictetus." Best known to Emily was Charlotte Brontë's famous diatribe against those "more privileged fellow-creatures" who thought women should "confine themselves to making puddings" and the like trivial occupations (*Jane Eyre*), although she could not have read Elizabeth Barrett's attack on the "pudding-making and stocking-darning theory" of women's activities noticed earlier (see above, 8). There was something about making puddings that set a feminist's teeth on edge, and Emily expected Higginson to know it.

14. Mrs. S. C. Hall, "Memories of Mrs. Jane Porter," *Harper's Magazine*, 1 (September 1850): 433.

15. Millicent Todd Bingham, *Ancestors' Brocades* (New York: Harper and Brothers, 1945), p. 166.

16. Josiah G. Holland, *Timothy Titcomb's Letters to Young People* (New York, 1858), p. 86.

17. Josiah G. Holland, *Miss Gilbert's Career* (New York, 1860), pp. 27, 88, 152, et passim.

18. Ralph Waldo Emerson, *The Complete Essays and Other Writings* (New York: Modern Library, 1950), p. 258.

19. Bettina (Brentano) von Arnim, *Die Günderode* (Boston, 1861), p. 277.

20. George S. Merriam, *The Life and Times of Samuel Bowles*, 2 vols. (New York, 1885), 1: 168.

21. Martha Dickinson Bianchi, *The Life and Letters of Emily Dickinson* (Boston: Houghton Mifflin, 1924), pp. 26–27; *Emily Dickinson Face to Face* (Boston: Houghton Mifflin, 1932), p. 11.

22. Martha Dickinson Bianchi, "Selections from the Unpublished Letters of Emily Dickinson to Her Brother's Family," *Atlantic Monthly* 115 (January 1915): 36.

23. Theodora Ward, *The Capsule of the Mind* (Cambridge: Harvard University Press, 1961), pp. 70, 73, 14, 8.
24. Howe, "George Sand," p. 521.
25. This Bible is in the Houghton Library collection, Harvard University, Cambridge, Mass.
26. Thomas Wentworth Higginson, "Ought Women to Learn the Alphabet?" *Atlantic Monthly* 3 (February 1859): 143–44.
27. Elizabeth Browning, *Aurora Leigh*, 2. 334–35; 8. 13–15; 3. 161–64. References to *Aurora Leigh* here and elsewhere are to the Cambridge edition of *The Complete Poetical Works*.
28. Bianchi, *Face to Face*, p. 27.
29. Charles Dickens, *The Old Curiosity Shop*, chaps. 33, 36, 63. See also Leyda, *Years and Hours*, 2: 277.
30. Unpublished letters of Samuel Bowles to Austin and Sue Dickinson, Houghton Library.
31. See Leyda, *Years and Hours*, 2: 13.
32. The *Springfield Daily Republican*, 13 October 1860, p. 3. Bowles acknowledged his authorship in a letter of 15 January 1861 to Maria Whitney (see Merriam, *Samuel Bowles*, 1: 317).
33. See Merriam, *Samuel Bowles*, 2: 48, for a quotation from another work by Margaret Fuller.
34. Bianchi, *Life and Letters*, p. 25.
35. Bettina von Arnim writes: "the strawberries so seduced me.... A week has now passed, but I still languish after them; those which are eaten are forgotten, the unplucked still burn in my recollection. Thus I should for ever burn, if I neglected that which I have a right to enjoy." And she makes fairly explicit that her symbol refers to the enjoyment of love. *Goethe's Correspondence with a Child*, 1: 32.
36. This first editor, Mabel Loomis Todd, conceived of herself as a Dickinson and showed almost a family interest in smoothing over the irregular and the unconventional. Thus, she suppressed virtually all evidence of strong religious doubt in letters or poems and emphasized the earlier, slighter, more immature poetry. One example will show her at work. Poem 501 begins "This World is not Conclusion" and goes on for eleven more lines of such stirring affirmation that Mrs. Todd published them under the title "Immortality" in the *Outlook* (53: 25 January 1896, p. 140) and, untitled, in *Poems by Emily Dickinson*, 3d series, ed. Mabel Loomis Todd (Boston: Roberts Brothers, 1896). Not until 1945 did *Bolts of Melody*, edited by her daughter, Millicent Todd Bingham, publish the additional eight lines, in which "Faith" slips, blushes, grasps at mere twigs of evidence, asks directions of a weathervane, and concludes bitterly that strong hallelujahs and pulpit gestures are "Narcotics," unable to still the "Tooth" of doubt that keeps nibbling at her soul. In the early 1890s Mrs. Todd gave a number of lectures in neighboring towns in which one of her appointed tasks was to combat a fairly widespread rumor of the poet's heterodox opinions. These reassurances were gratefully received. For example, one Arthur Chamberlain thought this "graft of liberal thought" on the gnarly tree of Calvinism had borne "some wonderfully fine olives," and he was satisfied to make no further question of the real Christian reverence of Emily's poems, "now that Mrs. Todd had set it forth with that explicit statement of one who speaks with authority" (Bingham, *Ancestors' Brocades*, p. 196). He did not know, of course, how many olives Mrs. Todd thought wise to conceal. At another such lecture, a Mr. Wingate was pleased to find that ideas which made the poet "an irreverent woman ... were explained

away" (ibid., p. 128). "Explaining away" has been the chief business of Dickinson scholars.

37. See below, p. 49, for Ruskin's erotically tinged "Redemption" in a passage known to Emily Dickinson.

38. The lines "You think a woman ripens as a peach— / In the cheeks, chiefly (which Emily, or more likely Sue, bracketed in the latter's copy of *Aurora Leigh*) seem to have combined here with lines from Emerson's "Culture" (which Emily would have read in the September 1860 *Atlantic,* and perhaps again in Sue's 1861 copy of *The Conduct of Life*): "Heaven sometimes hedges a rare character about with ungainliness and odium, as the burr that protects the fruit" (*Complete Essays,* p. 734). Unluckily, both women were snobs about youth and beauty, although it is a curious fact that in a volume of the De Quincey set which the beautiful Kate Turner bought in Boston on 7 March 1859, six days after spending a night with her friend Emily, she marked this revealing passage: "It is unintelligibly but mesmerically potent, this secret fascination attached to features oftentimes that are absolutely plain" (see my *Riddle of Emily Dickinson* [Boston: Houghton Mifflin, 1951], p. 362). Austin Dickinson thought his sister had retired into strict seclusion out of mortification over her appearance, because she knew "how plain she was" (Bingham, *Ancestors' Brocades,* p. 235). His opinion is typically masculine, but it should not be overlooked that her strongest erotic attachments were to two women reputed beautiful. As for her sensitivity about age, there are bits of evidence throughout the poetry (most notably in poem 1130). Writing to the elderly Judge Lord of her "rustic love" for him, she adds: "Oh, had I found it sooner! Yet Tenderness has not a Date—" (L750). Obviously she is not regretting that they had no earlier opportunity to marry, for she is refusing to marry even now that opportunity is battering at her door. In her unspoken but deeply troubled awareness of the psychological barriers, she is all but confessing her distaste, her sense of the ridiculous, in the lovemaking of this sickly, seventy-year-old man. If it had been earlier, if he had been a handsome *young* man, would she have been able to respond? Such appears to be her unspoken question, and certainly it goes far to explain the contrast between her gushy, overprotesting letters to him and the queer, frozen quality of her poetry in those years.

39. Bianchi, *Face to Face,* p. 167; *Life and Letters,* p. 64.

40. References to Shakespeare's works here and elsewhere are to the 1969 Penguin edition of the *Complete Works,* ed. Alfred Harbage.

Chapter Two

1. Bingham, *Ancestors' Brocades,* p. 310.
2. *The Tempest* 5. 1. 88.
3. Song of Sol. 2:16, 6:3.
4. Elizabeth Browning, *Works,* pp. 207, 139.
5. *Aurora Leigh,* 5. 1270–71.
6. Elsewhere "knee" appears to be an unconscious substitution for the more intimidating "thigh," as in poems 186 and 222 and letter 248 ("the knee that bore her once unto [royal] wordless rest"). Compare letter 233 ("If it had been God's will that I might breathe where you breathed—") and "Her sweet Weight on my Heart a Night" (518) and "few can bear a rose...worn upon the breast... wearing her" (L203) for the deeper content of her memory.
7. In an interesting analysis of this poem, John Cody has pointed out that the "Eider-Duck's / Deep Pillow" "connotes the idea of a nest with its cozy security and maternal nurturing" ("Emily Dickinson's Vesuvian Face," *American Imago*

24 (Fall 1967): 175). More exactly, it connotes the female breast itself, an association the poet found in 'The Custom-House" section of Hawthorne's *Scarlet Letter*: "her bosom has all the softness and snugness of an eider-down pillow." The "Doe" this gun-woman hunts is equally feminine. Since she was acquainted with Tennyson's *The Princess,* she may well have remembered the description of the somewhat mannish Princess Ida as a "lovely lordly creature" and "leader" of "a hundred airy does" (6. 69–72). Prince Cyril's uncouth old father clarifies the metaphor: "Man is the hunter; woman is his game. / The sleek and shining creatures of the chase, / We hunt them for the beauty of their skins" (6. 147–49). In becoming a hunter of the doe, Emily Dickinson usurped a male prerogative. Susan H. Gilbert owned a copy of Tennyson's *The Princess* (Boston: William H. Ticknor & Co., 1848).

8. *Harper's Magazine* 11 (July 1855): 213. It was certainly known to Kate, and, through her, probably to Sue and Emily, that Thackeray's most attractive heroine, Ethel Newcome, was closely modeled on a famous New York beauty, tall, dark Sally Baxter, between whom and her handsome cousin, tall, dark Kate Scott Turner, there was considerable resemblance.

9. John Cody remarks that the symbolic latch of this poem "is more fittingly a female phallus—the clitoris suspended above the vaginal vestibule," and he is "tempted to conclude that the sexual threat that stands between the poet and the tender love she craves is in this instance at least a homosexual one." *After Great Pain: The Inner Life of Emily Dickinson* (Cambridge: Harvard University Press, Belknap Press, 1971), p. 138.

10. "Samson Agonistes," *The Student's Milton,* ed. Frank Allen Patterson (New York: Appleton-Century-Crofts, 1930) lines 80–82, 33.

11. Ibid., lines 100–102, 103–105, 155–56.

12. See Johnson's note to poem 249.

13. Since poem 339 manifestly borrows from Robert Browning's "A Lovers' Quarrel," *Men and Women* (1855), and less certainly from Elizabeth Browning's *Aurora Leigh* 2. 12 (1857), it cannot date back to her passionate attachment to young Susan Gilbert (much less to her young friend Abiah Root, who in letter 69 is saluted as "my absentee") but merely shows how certain ideas and images of her early twenties could persist and be evoked by a like situation in her late twenties. The carefully, if unconsciously, detailed paralleling of sexual activity among these flowers is strong evidence that they are in fact one flower set over against or contrasted with modest "Daisy" Emily, and this collective flower which the daisy *tends* is the real center of her interest rather than a barely mentioned "lord" without attributes. Collectively, however, the flowers stand surrogate for "him," and "he" is completely identified.

14. John Ruskin, *The True and the Beautiful,* ed. Mrs. L. C. Tuthill (New York, 1859), p. 101.

15. Ward, *Capsule of the Mind,* p. 14.

16. Henry Wadsworth Longfellow, *Kavanagh,* ed. Jean Downey (New Haven: College and University Press, 1965), pp. 68, 46. See Dickinson letters 30, 38, 68, 102, 133, 342*b*.

17. A transcript of poem 1767 (Amherst College Microfilm, Bingham Collection, roll 2) shows "timid room" as the original reading, the word "mighty" in Mr. Todd's hand appearing above the poem at the end of a long arrow from the word "timid." In the last line the word "fallow" is replaced by a variant "shadows." The variorum edition follows that 1924 *Collected Poems* in using "mighty" and "shadows," with a note that no autograph copy of the poem is known. Editor Johnson appeared to be ignorant of the Amherst transcript. "Timid" is not a

word Mrs. Todd would have invented or even thought desirable, although plainly it had special significance for the poet.

18. Martha Dickinson Bianchi, introduction to *Further Poems of Emily Dickinson* (Boston, 1929), p. xvii.
19. Patterson, *Riddle of Emily Dickinson,* pp. 252–53, 281, 295, 298, 317, and elsewhere.
20. Ibid., pp. 359, 364–65.
21. See Leyda, *Years and Hours,* 2: 27.
22. Unpublished letter, dated 17 March 1863, from Austin Dickinson to his wife, then visiting Gertrude Vanderbilt in Flatbush, in which he alludes with tender regret to news of Kate's engagement, says he "had always meant to hold on to part of her for myself," and begs Sue to bring Kate back to Amherst, which in fact she did (Houghton Library collection).
23. Patterson, *Riddle of Emily Dickinson,* pp. 242, 245, 249–50.
24. Ibid., pp. 88–89.
25. Merriam, *Samuel Bowles,* 2: 426.
26. E. C. Gaskell, *The Life of Charlotte Brontë* (London, 1858), p. 399. Both Sue and Emily owned copies.
27. Leyda, *Years and Hours,* 1: 185.
28. See Robert Graves and Raphael Patai, *Hebrew Myths: The Book of Genesis* (Garden City, N.Y.: Doubleday, 1964), p. 65.
29. Bianchi, *Life and Letters,* p. 74. Mrs. Bianchi had a genuine anecdote, although, as with others she had received from her mother, she attached it where it would do least harm. The truth, of which she was fully informed by her mother, was at all times a perilous possession with Mrs. Bianchi. Burdened with family secrets, she was constantly tempted to give a hint—if for nothing else, then to square accounts with the biographers of her aunt. There is a fairly well authenticated anecdote that she could not resist sharing the laugh with some of her Amherst cronies. Apparently she told her friend Robert H. Patterson that her publisher had urged her to choose a love story for her aunt and stick to it, adding that she "therefore chose the Philadelphia clergyman" without believing a word of the yarn she then spun (see David Higgins, *Portrait of Emily Dickinson: The Poet and Her Prose* [New Brunswick, N.J.: Rutgers University Press, 1967], p. 258). On another occasion she offered some hints to Conrad Aiken, only to be warned by his expression that some truths were particularly offensive to men (Conrad Aiken, "The Dickinson Scandal," *New Republic,* 2 July 1945, pp. 25–26). Nevertheless, if one knows how to look, there is much genuine evidence among Bianchi's somewhat treacly memoirs.
30. Patterson, *Riddle of Emily Dickinson,* p. 302.

Chapter Three

1. George F. Kunz, *Shakespeare and Precious Stones* (Philadelphia, 1916), p. 44.
2. *Othello* 5. 2. 145–46.
3. *Paradise Lost* 6. 750–72. The edition used is Milton, *Poems,* ed. Frank Allen Patterson (New York, 1934).
4. See Aurelia G. Scott, "Emily Dickinson's 'Three Gems,'" *New England Quarterly* 16 (December 1943): 627–28.
5. Perhaps as a consequence of her excited discovery of *Jane Eyre* about December 1849 (L28), Emily Dickinson alluded to Revelation—but not to the foundation jewels—several times between early January 1850 and late 1853 (letters 29, 37, 57, 62, 142). Charlotte Brontë has St. John Rivers read aloud from Revelation 21

"the vision of the new heaven and the new earth" but stress only the wiping of "all tears from their eyes" and the importance of having one's name "written in the Lamb's book of life" (*Jane Eyre* [Riverside ed.; Boston: Houghton Mifflin, 1859], p. 396). Neither St. John Rivers nor Emily Dickinson was ready to see the poetic possibilities of the foundation stones.

6. Rev. 6, 7:11, 21:27.

7. Henry Wadsworth Longfellow, *The Courtship of Miles Standish* 4. 5–9. For Dickinson's reference to this poem, see her poem 357, letter 665, and prose fragment 93.

8. Ruskin, *The True and the Beautiful,* p. 379. For Taine's extraordinary rhapsody, see his *Notes sur l'Angleterre,* 3d ed. rev. and amended (Paris: Librairie Hachette, 1872), pp. 361–63.

9. *Atlantic Monthly* 1 (May 1858): 880; 2 (October 1858): 578: 3 (June 1859): 780; 4 (July 1859): 37; 5 (May 1860): 563.

10. The dates here followed are those established by Myra Himelhoch in her study of the letters of Emily Dickinson to Samuel and Mary Bowles. No letters to the Bowles family earlier than mid-1859 are known to survive. See her article, "The Dating of Emily Dickinson's Letters to the Bowles Family, 1858-1862," *Emily Dickinson Bulletin* 5, no. 20: 1–28.

11. Years later she would remember the occasion when she had talked with Bowles about his "Gem" chapter (L536). Bowles himself was more inclined to thank Sue Dickinson for his new literary interests. In April 1862, en route to Europe, he wrote to Sue that she had introduced him to the Brownings and that the only books in his seabags were the Bible and *Aurora Leigh.* See Bianchi, *Face to Face,* p. 283.

12. Rev. 3:12, 21:4, 14:3.

13. The manuscript of letter 185 is missing, and the editors, who elsewhere corrected many a wild guess by Mrs. Holland, have kept her improbable date for this letter instead of placing it among the summer 1859 letters to which it is allied in substance and tone. For a conclusion similar to mine, see Leyda, *Years and Hours,* 1: 371.

14. Henry David Thoreau, "Autumnal Tints," *Atlantic Monthly* 10 (October 1862): 395.

15. Bianchi, *Face to Face,* pp. 16–17.

16. She had read Robert Browning's *Men and Women* (1855) before she wrote her own poem. In his "A Lovers' Quarrel" are the lines, "Only, my Love's away! / I'd as lief that the blue were grey." Speaking of her roses, Dickinson writes, "I had as lief they wore / No Crimson—more," adding that, with "Her Lord—away," she will dwell in "Calyx—Gray—."

17. Cf. the following lines from Byron's *Don Juan,* canto 5, stanza 77:
And then he swore; and, sighing, on he slipped
    A pair of trousers of flame-coloured silk,
Next with a virgin zone he was equipped,
    Which girt a slight chemise as white as milk;
A four-volume edition of *The Works of Lord Byron* (New York: E. Duychink & G. Long, 1821) was in the Dickinson library.

18. *Atlantic Monthly* 5 (June 1860): 659–60, 662.

19. James T. Fields, "Diamonds and Pearls," *Atlantic Monthly* (March 1861): 361–71.

20. Ibid., p. 365. Fields apparently confuses the Star of the South with another well-known jewel.

21. Ruskin, *The True and the Beautiful,* pp. 125–26.

22. Matt. 7:6, 13:46; Rev. 21:21.
23. *The Merchant of Venice* 3. 1. 87; *The Tempest* 1. 2. 398; *Macbeth* 5. 8. 56; *Troilus and Cressida* 2. 2. 81–82, and 1. 1. 103, 105; *Othello* 5. 2. 346–48.
24. *In Memoriam* 52. 16.
25. George Frederick Kunz and Charles Hugh Stevenson, *The Book of the Pearl* (New York, 1908), p. 405.
26. The simple village maiden was a miller's daughter named Sarah Hoggins married to a plain "Mr. John Jones," who one day told her to pack up and accompany him to his old family home. When they came in sight of Burleigh House, she asked whose mansion it was. "It is all yours," replied the tenth earl, "and you are the countess of Exeter."
27. This theme is touched on by Kate Flores and Eric W. Carlson, *Explicator*, vol. 9 (May 1951), item 47; and vol. 20 (May 1962), item 72. A more thoroughgoing Freudian interpretation is given by Clark Griffith, *The Long Shadow: Emily Dickinson's Tragic Poetry* (Princeton, N.J.: Princeton University Press, 1964), pp. 19–23.
28. Fields's "Diamonds and Pearls" has a vivid description of the pearl diver's risky life: "Appalling dangers compass him about. Sharks watch for him as he dives, and not infrequently he comes up maimed for life. It is recorded of a pearl-diver, that he died from over-exertion immediately after he reached land, having brought up with him a shell that contained a pearl of great size and beauty" (p. 369).
29. *As You Like It* 5 .4. 64.
30. Fields, "Diamonds and Pearls," p. 371.
31. Thomas Moore, *Lalla Rookh* (New York: Leavitt and Allen Brothers, n.d.), p. 196.
32. Theodora Ward, ed., *Emily Dickinson's Letters to Dr. and Mrs. Josiah Gilbert Holland* (Cambridge: Harvard University Press, 1951), p. 48.
33. Bianchi, *Face to Face*, p. 25.
34. *Don Juan*, canto 13, stanza 39.
35. *Twelfth Night* 2. 5. 17; *Henry VIII* 1. 1. 21–22; *Troilus and Cressida* 1. 7. 103; *The Merchant of Venice* 5. 1. 4–6.
36. With regard to the nonreligious meaning of Emily Dickinson's "Immortality," Theodora Ward makes an interesting comment. Writing to the Hollands, the young Emily fears they may smile at her letters, "but so sure as 'this mortal' essays immortality, a crow from a neighboring farm-yard dissipates the illusion, and I am here again" (L133). Mrs. Ward points out that the poet did not mean life after death, as the puzzled Hollands may well have thought, but an "elation," an "enlargement of spirit" brought by ecstatic moments, a "godlike feeling" of being one of the immortals. See Ward, *Capsule of the Mind*, p. 34. As for the apparent masculine identity of the friend, the poet had long ago used masculine pronouns to refer to Sue (L96).

Chapter Four

1. Emerson, *Complete Essays*, pp. 329, 334, 337.
2. Bianchi, *Face to Face*, p. 158.
3. O. M. Mitchel, *The Planetary and Stellar Worlds* (New York, 1852), pp. 211–12.
4. *American Journal of Science* 78 (November 1859): 445–46. See also 80 (November 1860): 141 for the report of a search made for the supposed intra-Mercurial planet. How soon or how extensively Leverrier's new speculations entered the popular press is not known, but in the *Atlantic Monthly* (6 [July 1860]: 118), a

magazine Emily Dickinson read faithfully, a review of O. M. Mitchel's *Popular Astronomy* takes a favorable notice of Leverrier's search for an intra-Mercurial planet.

5. The famous youthful letter to Susan Gilbert, sometimes cited as proof of the poet's "normal blossoming," is illustrative. After some monitory words to Sue about the wives who would envy their maiden lives, Emily goes on bravely: "you have seen flowers at morning, *satisfied* with the dew, and those same sweet flowers at noon with their heads bowed in anguish before the mighty sun; think you these blossoms will *now* need naught but—*dew?* No, they will cry for sunlight, and pine for the burning noon, tho' it scorches them, scathes them; they have got through with peace—they know that the man of noon, is mightier than the morning and their life is henceforth to him" (L93). It is obvious that she is speaking of sex, but less obvious, partly because of her own innocence, that she is expressing in the only language known to her the unconscious fears aroused by her passion for Sue. One cannot read the 1851–52 letters to Sue teaching in Baltimore and fail to realize that the young writer is both absorbed and frightened by this passion. Anticipating Sue's return in July, she says this month had once "seemed parched, and dry...but *now* Susie, month of all the year the best," and for Sue she will give up the spring and its "dew ... exchange them all for that angry and hot noonday" of her friend's sunlike return (L77). At the very mention of Sue's name the sunshine grows "so warm" and out peep "prisoned leaves," and with Sue's coming Emily's garden will bloom: "how many boundless blossoms among those silent beds!" (L92). As the promised day approaches, the impassioned girl can hardly endure this mingled desire and fear: "the expectation once more to see your face again, makes me feel hot and feverish, and my heart beats so fast—I go to sleep at night, and the first thing I know, I am sitting there wide awake, and clasping my hands tightly," and she almost wishes "the precious day wouldn't come quite so soon, till I could know how to feel, and get my thoughts ready for it. Why, Susie, it seems to me as if my absent Lover was coming home so soon—and my heart must be so busy, making ready for him" (L96). In short, Sue is masculinized—she *is* the "man of noon"—and her face is clearly the sun-disc that causes so much heat and fever in the young poet. A few years later a most interesting situation arises when Sue becomes in turn the sun-woman of the poet's brother. In contrast with his sister's passionately heated outpourings, Austin's letter seems curiously feminine and passive: "You are the light and you the genial warmth that have made the closed bud within me to expand and send up its tender shoots—& you the sweetest influence that is to cherish it to its perfect flower." From the Austin Dickinson letters in the Houghton Library, Harvard University, Cambridge, Mass.; quoted by Cody, *After Great Pain*, p. 202.

6. Cody (ibid., p. 429) has observed that the image of the father "functions...as an eclipse behind which blazes still the unrivaled preoedipal mother." Or, one might add, such mother substitutes as Susan Gilbert.

7. For another text of the poem, see R. W. Franklin, *The Editing of Emily Dickinson: A Reconsideration* (Madison: University of Wisconsin Press, 1967), pp. 40–46. He has proved that poem 1712 belongs in this same packet; thus, it would have been written about the same time and would be concerned with the same feelings.

8. It is possible that her "parallax" has some baffling relation to a sentence in Emerson's "Self-Reliance" (*Complete Essays*, p. 255): "What is the nature and power of that science-baffling star, without parallax, without calculable elements, which

shoots a ray of beauty even into trivial and impure actions, if the least mark of independence appear?" This essay appeared in 1841, three years after announcement of the first successes in determining stellar parallax.

9. An indication of the excitement aroused by the 1861 comet is the number of articles it inspired. See the *New York Times,* 4 July 1861, p. 8, col. 2; 6 July 1861, p. 1, col. 6. Other stories about the comet appeared 1 July 1861, p. 4, col. 4; and 26 July 1861, p. 3, col. 1.

10. A very probable source, in a work she admired, would be these lines from James Thomson's *The Seasons (Summer)*:

> Amid the radiant orbs
> That more than deck, that animate the sky,
> Lo! from the dread immensity of space,
> Returning with accelerated course,
> The rushing comet to the Sun descends.

But the 1861 visitor would be her primary source. Comet 1861 (II) astonished all observers by the suddenness of its apparition and by its extraordinary brilliance, which exceeded that of any other comet within the memory of men then living—not excepting the great "Napoleonic" comet of 1811 or the glorious Donati's of 1858. There was some dispute as to whether the earth actually passed through the tail of this comet. The German astronomer Pape of Altona said that it did not, but G. P. Bond of the Harvard Observatory found his calculations in error and announced that a collision did occur on 30 June ("The Great Comet of 1861," *American Journal of Science,* 2d ser., 32, no. 95 (September 1861): 263–64). For a poet, the discussion itself would have been enough. There would be no more great comets until the "sun-grazer" of 1862.

11. On page 18 of a typed account of her married life called "Annals of the Evergreens" (preserved in the Houghton Library), Sue Dickinson recalled that a dance given by the young Dickinsons in their parents' absence was betrayed by a disarranged rug, adding: "I should have explained, of course, that this best parlor rug was never taken up except at the change of solstice."

12. The fourteen poets selected for comparison were Shakespeare, Milton, Pope, Wordsworth, Byron, Shelley, Keats, Tennyson, the two Brownings, Emerson, Bryant, Poe, and Longfellow. Although Emily Dickinson never mentioned Shelley, a copy of his *Poetical Works* inscribed "Susan H. Gilbert. Geneva. 1854" is preserved among the Dickinson books at the Houghton Library, and it is inconceivable that Emily failed to read it. For all the others, she has left written record of her admiration.

13. Albert J. Gelpi discusses "Circumference" as a metaphor for ecstasy and comments on Emerson's influence on Emily Dickinson (*Emily Dickinson: The Mind of the Poet* [Cambridge: Harvard University Press, 1965] pp. 120–27).

14. Although poem 508 appears to be a marriage poem, she may also be recalling line 72 from Browning's "Abt Vogler," a poem she knew well: "On the earth the broken arcs; in the heaven, a perfect round."

15. Thomas Wentworth Higginson, "The Procession of the Flowers," *Atlantic Monthly* 10 (December 1862): 652.

16. The manuscript "Powder," an obvious slip of the pen, makes nonsense of her metaphor.

17. Benjamin Silliman, *Elements of Chemistry* in the order of the lectures given at Yale College (New Haven: H. Howe, 1830–31), 2: 72, 74, 76.

18. In the rough draft of this poem, she at first wrote "Chemist," then put down the more meaningful variants, "happy— / ransomed / A Lover—."

19. *Nature, The American Scholar, The Divinity School Address, Essays: First and Second Series, Representative Men, English Traits,* and *The Conduct of Life.*

20. Mrs. Browning, who strove to be in the van of progress and the new thought, was capable of writing such lines as the following:

That men of science, osteologists
And surgeons, beat some poets in respect
For nature,—count nought common or unclean,
Spend raptures upon perfect specimens
Of indurated veins, distorted joints,
Or beautiful new cases of curved spine,

While we, we are shocked at nature's falling off, etc. [*Aurora Leigh* 6. 172–78] On the whole, it was safer to admire than to imitate her, although her curious recommendation of science may have had its weight with her admirer, and the words *science, surgeons, specimens,* and *indurated* do reappear in the younger woman's verse. When the two women seem most alike, both are usually Byronizing.

21. Emerson, *Complete Essays,* p. 54.

22. Most significant is that vocabulary which demonstrates her fascination with the methodology of science, for example, such words as *accurate, analysis, analytic, analyze, apparatus, ascertain, axiom, classify, criterion, dilute, dissect, dissolve, equation, exactness, experiment, extrinsic, fact, fallacy, formula, function, gauge, generic, hypothesis, inspect, instability, intrinsic, microscope, microscopic, minutiae, observation, precise, probe, problem, process, proof, quality, quantity, refract, regulate, research, scan, scholar, science, scientist, scrutinize, scrutiny, species, specific, specimen, superficies, synthesis, telescope, telescopic, thesis, untenable.* Over half of these words are rare or nonexistent in her poetic models.

Chapter Five

1. See letter 405*a.*
2. *Endymion* 2. 992. The edition used is the Modern Library *Works of John Keats.*
3. Charles R. Anderson, *Emily Dickinson's Poetry* (New York: Holt, Rinehart and Winston, 1960), p. 182.
4. *The Two Gentlemen of Verona* 3. 2. 77–78.
5. *Paradise Lost* 4. 763–64.
6. "Ode to Psyche," line 14.
7. "To Rhea," line 16, in Ralph Waldo Emerson, *Complete Poems* (Boston, 1904), p. 9.
8. *A Midsummer Night's Dream* 2. 1. 166–67.
9. Emerson, *Complete Essays,* p. 736.
10. *Paradise Lost* 8. 619.
11. *A Midsummer Night's Dream* 2. 1. 203–207.
12. Fuller, *Woman in the Nineteenth Century* (Boston, 1855), p. 235.
13. See letter 476*c.*

Chapter Six

1. Samuel G. Goodrich [Peter Parley], *Peter Parley's Method of Telling about Geography to Children* (New York, 1843).
2. Donald G. Mitchell [Ik Marvel], *Reveries of a Bachelor* (Chicago, n.d.), pp. 150–51. The line he remembers with such exultation ("Battle! battle!—and then death to the arm'd, and chains for the defenseless") is spoken by Almagro in

act I of Richard Brinsley Sheridan's *Pizarro* (*Sheridan's Plays* [New York: Every-man's Library, 1963], p. 361).

3. Among the William H. Prescott books owned by the Dickinsons and preserved in the Houghton Library are a five-volume *History of the Conquest of Mexico* (New York, 1854), another edition in three volumes (Philadelphia, 1860), and a two-volume edition of his *History of the Conquest of Peru* (Boston, 1859). Both titles had gone through many editions since their original publication in 1843 and 1847, respectively, and may have been long known to the Dickinson children through borrowed copies. The Houghton collection, for example, contains no copy of Carlyle's *French Revolution,* but Lavinia and probably Emily were reading it in 1851 (see Leyda, *Years and Hours,* 1: 195). Again, in 1851, Austin Dickinson recommended Irving's *Life of Columbus* to Sue, who would certainly share it with Emily; but no edition survives in the Houghton collection, which must represent very poorly the quantity and variety of the Dickinsons' reading.

4. See Herbert E. Childs, "Emily Dickinson and Sir Thomas Browne," *American Literature* 22 (1951): 459.

5. William H. Prescott, *History of the Conquest of Peru* (New York: Modern Library, n.d.), pp. 742–43.

6. Ibid., pp. 752, 1035.

7. See Jack Capps, *Emily Dickinson's Reading* (Cambridge: Harvard University Press, 1966), pp. 7–8. And see S. S. Cornell, *Cornell's Primary Geography,* pt. 1 of *Systematic Series of School Geographies* (New York, 1854), p. 35, where, in a map of "States of Central America," what today is called The Republic of Honduras is given as "Balize."

8. William Lewis Herndon and Lardner Gibbon, *Exploration of the Valley of the Amazon,* 2 vols. (Washington, D.C., 1854), 2:169.

9. See Leyda, *Years and Hours,* 2:134, for Dickinson's letter to Bowles.

10. The passage dealing with the butterfly is worth quoting *in extenso:*

   As rising on its purple wing
   The insect-queen of eastern spring
   O'er emerald meadows of Kashmeer
   Invites the young pursuer near,
   And leads him on from flower to flower
   A weary chase and wasted hour,
   Then leaves him, as it soars on high,
   With panting heart and tearful eye:
   So Beauty lures the full-grown child,
   With hue as bright, and wing as wild,
   A chase of idle hopes and fears,
   Begun in folly, closed in tears. [*The Giaour,* lines 388–99]

11. Capps, *Emily Dickinson's Reading,* pp. 122–23.

12. For the *noche trista,* see Prescott, *History of the Conquest of Mexico and History of the Conquest of Peru* (New York: The Modern Library), pp. 445–53; but of course the entire *Mexico* is an account of fierce struggles to gain or hold the causeways, of desperate attacks on walls, parapets, ramparts, barriers, bulwarks, and the like. The Aztecs "take refuge behind a barricade," and Cortes orders up his heavy ordnance to sweep away these "barricades" (p. 417). "Barricades thrown across the causeway" embarrass the Spanish cavalry (p. 554); the Spaniards carry "one barricade after another" (p. 574); Alderete carries "the barricades" defending the causeway (p. 575); and so on.

13. John L. Stephens, *Incidents of Travel in Central America, Chiapas, & Yucatan,*

rpt. ed. (New Brunswick, N.J.: Rutgers University Press, 1949), pp. 221, 236–37. Elsewhere there are incidental references to cochineal plantations or to the growing of cochineal (1: 43, 55, 211, 212).

14. Prescott, *Mexico,* pp. 28 and n., 83, 212, 329 and n.
15. Ibid., pp. 81, 235–36, 298, 421, 625 and n., 666 and n.
16. Ibid., pp. 84, 319 and n., 693.
17. Ibid., p. 38 and n.
18. *Don Juan,* canto 4, line 455.
19. See Frank Davidson, "A Note on Emily Dickinson's Use of Shakespeare," *New England Quarterly* 18 (1945): 407–408, for the initial suggestion that Dickinson's phrase "the mail from Tunis" owes something to Shakespeare's *Tempest.* I have discussed the indebtedness at greater length in "Emily Dickinson's Hummingbird," *Educational Leader* 22 (July 1958): 12–19, an article reprinted in *14 by Emily Dickinson,* ed. Thomas M. Davis (Chicago, 1964), pp. 140–48. I now incline to believe the poem was in rough draft as early as 1862.
20. *Aurora Leigh* 2. 519; *Paradise Lost* 12. 634; *Troilus and Cressida* 1. 3. 328.
21. Goodrich, *Peter Parley's Method,* p. 97.
22. Moore, *Lalla Rookh,* pp. 332–33.
23. James Russell Lowell, *Poetical Works* (Boston, 1887), p. 84.
24. Ibid., p. 90.
25. Jer. 13:23.
26. Song of Sol. 4:7.
27. Ibid. 1:6.
28. Ibid. 1:6, 8:11–12, 7:12 (or the vineyard could be in Italy, as in letter 222, for all these properties were peripatetic). Puritans in general were great relishers of the Song of Solomon, which they proceeded to interpret piously, much as students of Emily Dickinson relish her highly erotic poetry but piously interpret it as expressing a devotion to God and a longing to enter heaven. Verily, they have their reward!
29. *A Midsummer Night's Dream* 3. 2. 257, 263; and 2. 2. 330.
30. *Paradise Lost* 4. 281–83.
31. Song of Sol. 8:7.
32. Ibid. 8:5.
33. Ibid. 7:7–8.
34. Of the four books I discovered in the Dickinson collection at the Houghton Library, Mrs. Dickinson's Bible, published at Edinburgh by Mark and Charles Kerr, 1791, gives "Susanna" as "lily, rose, joy," as does the Reverend William Jenks's *Companion to the Bible* (Brattleboro, Vt., 1836). J. Lempriere's *Classical Dictionary* (London, 1818) states that "Susan is the name of a lily in Hebrew," but Charles Anthon's *Classical Dictionary* (New York, 1846) has a different origin for the name: "We are informed by Strabo that Susa or Susan meant in Persian 'a Lily,' and that the city was so called from the abundance of these flowers that grew in the vicinity." All this information was at the poet's hand and would have interested her; but she would not have known, because Charles Anthon apparently did not know, that the Lily-goddess Susannah was identical with Astarte, the great mother-goddess known by so many names throughout the Middle East.
35. Emily Fowler Ford's "remembrances of my schoolfellow and friend Emily Dickinson" are given in full in the revised *Letters of Emily Dickinson,* ed. Mabel Loomis Todd (New York, 1931). The anecdote of the flower names appears on p. 131.
36. *Atlantic Monthly* 2 (September, 1858): 470. Higginson's *Outdoor Papers* (1863),

in which this essay reappeared, was also originally among Emily Dickinson's books but has vanished like most of her personal library. It seems hardly necessary to add that she knew the botanical distinctions among her lilies, though she chose to make no poetic differences: a lily was a lily.

37. *Antony and Cleopatra* 2. 6. 63–65, 123; 2. 2. 226–27.

38. Ibid. 3. 11. 56–61.

39. Thomas Bulfinch, *The Age of Fable* (London: Spring Books, 1964), p. 149.

40. Still more important in shaping Emily Dickinson's poem may have been certain lines of Elizabeth Browning quoted in a September 1862 *Atlantic Monthly* article (9: 375) eulogizing the newly dead poet. In Mrs. Browning's lines the broken idols of our devotion are called Memnons:
God keeps a niche
In heaven to hold our idols; and albeit
He brake them to our faces, and denied
That our close kisses should impair their white,
I know we shall behold them raised, complete,
The dust swept from their beauty, glorified,
New Memnons singing in the great God-light.

41. William Butler Yeats, *Collected Poems* (New York: Macmillan, 1955), p. 336.

42. But see Moore's *Lalla Rookh,* p. 226:
The Persian lily shines and towers
Before the combat's reddening stain
  Hath fallen upon her golden flowers.
And in a footnote Moore quotes a traveler as saying that, after the autumnal rains, "the ploughed fields are covered with the Persian lily, of a resplendent yellow color." Perhaps the bloodstains have played tricks with the poet's memory, or Mrs. Todd's informant that the poem was sent with a gift of red lilies was mistaken.

43. See Leyda, *Years and Hours,* 1: 161.

44. Moore, *Lalla Rookh,* pp. 288–89.

45. Ibid., pp. 240–41.

46. Ibid., pp. 50, 88, 112, 213, 220, 289–91.

47. Tennyson, *Locksley Hall,* line 184.

48. See Richard Sewall, *The Lyman Letters* (Amherst: University of Massachusetts Press, 1965), p. 70.

49. Moore, *Lalla Rookh,* pp. 288–89.

50. *Aurora Leigh* 6. 81–82, 89–90.

51. See André Maurois, *Byron,* trans. Hamish Miles (New York: F. Ungar Pub. Co., 1964), p. 187.

52. Oliver Wendell Holmes, *The Autocrat of the Breakfast Table* (Boston, 1892), p. 190. Emily saw this passage on its initial appearance in the *Atlantic Monthly* 2 (June 1858): 107.

53. Mitchell, *Reveries,* pp. 82–124.

54. See Bingham, *Ancestors' Brocades,* p. 86.

55. Victor Wolfgang von Hagen, *South America Called Them: Explorations of the Great Nationalists* (New York: Alfred A. Knopf, 1945), p. 144.

56. Although Humboldt gives no connected narrative of his climb, he mentions Chimborazo repeatedly in his writings. Among the lengthier references are the following: *Personal Narrative of Travels to the Equinoctial Regions of America during the Years 1799–1804,* 3 vols., trans. Thomasina Ross (London, 1907), 1: 43–44, 93, 439; *Researches Concerning the Inscriptions and Monuments of the Ancient Inhabitants of America,* 2 vols., trans. Helen Maria Williams (London,

n.d.), 1: 230–39, 2: 13; *Aspects of Nature in Different Lands and Different Climates*, trans. Mrs. Sabine (Philadelphia, 1850), pp. 89–92. English translations of all three works were in print before 1850. In 1842 Harper and Brothers brought out *The Travels and Researches*, a condensed narrative of Humboldt's journeys in South America, Mexico, and Asiatic Russia, doubtless intended for a wider, more popular audience. Unfortunately, I was not able to examine it. Plainly, Humboldt was chagrined to learn that the Himalayas outsoar Chimborazo (*Researches*, 2: 13; *Aspects of Nature*, pp. 92, 252); but he remained convinced that his heroic climb was the greatest achievement of his illustrious career. Sitting for his portrait in 1859, he suggested that he be painted without his medals but with the great peak in the background (Hagen, *South America Called Them*, p. 147). Of Humboldt's extraordinary and lasting popularity in the United States, Victor von Hagen gives an interesting account in *South America Called Them*, pp. 160–62.

57. *Aurora Leigh* 1. 409–10.

58. Emerson, *Complete Essays*, pp. 322–23.

59. Henry Wadsworth Longfellow, *The Complete Poetical Works* (Boston, 1922), p. 60. "To a Child" originally appeared in *The Belfry of Bruges and Other Poems* (1845) and was reprinted in the two-volume *Poems* (1856).

60. "While sailing among these islands [the Canaries], the crew were terrified at beholding the lofty peak of Teneriffe sending forth volumes of flame and smoke. ... Columbus took great pains to dispel their apprehensions, explaining the natural causes of those volcanic fires, and verifying his explanations by citing Mount Etna, and other well-known volcanoes" (Washington Irving, *Life and Voyages of Columbus*, 2 vols. [New York, 1881], 1: 136).

61. *Childe Harold's Pilgrimage*, canto 3, stanza 62. Still more suggestive of poem 666 is John Ruskin's Alpine description. Of Mont Cervin (the Matterhorn), he writes that it is "a wall truly of some majesty, at once the most precipitous and the strongest mass in the whole chain of the Alps." After some further account of its great height, flanking glaciers, spurs, and sharp-angled bastions, he calls attention to a "course of living rock, of quartz as white as the snow that encircles it, and harder than a bed of steel," and adds that this steellike bed "is one only of a thousand bands, that knit the strength of the mighty mountain ... the courses of its varied masonry ... with silver cornices glittering along the edge of each, laid by the snowy winds and carved by the sunshine—stainless ornaments of the eternal temple" (*The Stones of Venice* [London, 1925], 1: 5, nos. 2–5). On a later page he speaks of the "purple walls" of some unnamed Alp (1: 21, no. 17). From this mass of words a poet might extract the starkly essential "Purples of Ages," "Mail of ices," "Thigh of Granite," and "thew—of Steel."

62. *Paradise Lost* 4. 987. This striking figure appears in the work of Carlyle and other writers Emily Dickinson read.

63. *Beppo*, stanza 44.

64. Lowell, *Poetical Works*, p. 83.

65. Robert Browning, *The Poems and Plays* (New York: Modern Library, 1934), p. 56.

66. *Aurora Leigh* 8. 358.

67. Nathaniel Hawthorne, *The Marble Faun* (New American Library, Signet, 1961), pp. 13, 35, 79, 302, 314, 327, et passim.

68. *Aurora Leigh* 5. 1266–71; 1. 232.

69. Mitchell, *Reveries*, pp. 248, 183, 184.

70. Alexander Pope, *Complete Poetical Works* (Boston, 1903), pp. 60, 26.

71. "The Prophecy of Dante," canto 3, lines 186–93.
72. Moore, *Life*, p. 267, n. It might be remarked that Edward Dickinson, a more romantic soul than his daughter's biographers have discovered, not only bought the four-volume 1821 set of Byron's poems but also acquired the two-volume first American edition (1830) of Moore's *Life*.
73. *Don Juan*, canto 13, stanza 36; "On This Day I Complete My Thirty-Sixth Year."
74. Moore, *Lalla Rookh*, p. 261.
75. Longfellow's "Enceladus" first appeared in the August 1859 *Atlantic Monthly*.
76. Emerson, *Complete Essays*, pp. 59, 762.
77. *Aurora Leigh* 5. 215–19.
78. *The Giaour*, lines 1099–1102. Dickinson's poems 601 and 646 must also have been indebted to the following:
A stranger loves the lady of the land,
Born far beyond the mountains, but his blood
Is all meridian, as if never fann'd
By the black wind that chills the polar flood.
My blood is all meridian, etc. ["Stanzas to the Po"]
and to these lines:
Happy the nations of the moral North!
    Where all is virtue, and the winter season
Sends sin, without a rag on, shivering forth [*Don Juan*, canto 1, stanza 44]
79. Surviving in transcripts piously made and preserved by Sue Dickinson, the un-dated volcano poems are concerned with precisely the same suffering as the dated poems and were probably written in the same crucial period. Of a volcanic poem transcribed by Mrs. Todd there is less certainty, although it too may well belong to the 1861–65 period of her mysterious suffering. The babbler tempted to reveal a secret is reminded that the "reticent volcano" does not confide its "projects pink" (1748). According to a volcano poem already discussed, "Etna" in a quiet mood is more alarming to "Naples" than when she displays her "Garnet Tooth" (1146).
80. William Cullen Bryant, *The Poetical Works* (New York: Roslyn edition, 1903), pp. 231–32.
81. *In Memoriam* 91. 4. In a late edition of the poem, Tennyson himself identifies his bird with the kingfisher, but this fact would not have disturbed the American poet if she had known it. After all, both birds were blue.
82. Sue Dickinson's copy of *Aurora Leigh* is in the Houghton Library collection. Emily's copy, in the Bingham collection of Amherst College Library, Amherst, Mass., is a later edition, very scantily marked, but of course she first became acquainted with the work through Sue's copy. The marked line reads in its entirety, "My Italy of women, just to breathe," which may have lent special emphasis to the several poems affirming that she breathes or does not breathe according to whether the beloved woman is present or absent.

Chapter Seven

1. Yeats, *Collected Poems*, pp. 59–60, 450.
2. See Edward H. Schafer, *Ancient China* (New York: Time-Life Books, 1967), p. 105. Cardinal-point systems are so ubiquitous that the poet could have derived her entire pattern from her reading. For example, the November 1851 *Harper's Magazine* (3: 846) makes pointed reference to the West as a "symbol of man-kind," adding, "As the North is called by a word meaning the *dark or hidden*

place, so the sea ever denotes the West," and this kind of influence could be illustrated tediously. A modern example from John G. Neihardt's *Black Elk Speaks* (as reported by Robert F. Sayre, "Vision and Experience in *Black Elk Speaks,*" *College English* 30, no. 5: 517–18) has interesting resemblances. There are "contrasting symbols of four directions, four seasons, four colors, and four ways of perceiving." The North, for example, is associated with "white horses, 'where the great white giant lives,' winter and white, a blizzard wind, white geese." Yeats too brings in the horses. Dickinson does not associate horses with cardinal points, but the several horses in her poetry are used symbolically. They portend death, as do the horses of Yeats, and are connected in some manner with Father.

3. See, for example, Anderson, *Emily Dickinson's Poetry* pp. 155, 236, 279–80; William H. Matchett, "Dickinson's Revision of 'Two Butterflies Went Out at Noon,'" *PMLA* 77 (September 1962): 440–41; Gelpi, *Emily Dickinson,* p. 83. Other students of Dickinson's work have alluded to elements of her cardinal-points symbolism, briefly and incidentally, but no one has shown any awareness of this symbolism as an interlocking system.

4. Emerson, *Complete Essays,* pp. 6, 14–16.

5. Ibid., pp. 326–27.

6. Ibid., p. 338.

7. Ibid., pp. 439, 444.

8. Ibid., pp. 54, 240, 369–70.

9. Ruskin, *Stones of Venice,* 2: 153–56, 158, 168–69 (or, following Ruskin's own division, uniform in all editions, 2: 6, nos. 7, 8, 11, 24, 25). The Dickinsons owned the 1860 American edition, but the poet was probably best acquainted with her sister-in-law's 1859 edition of Ruskin selections entitled *The True and the Beautiful,* which repeats most of the paragraphs cited above.

10. Other images, such as "Summer," "Hesperides," and "West-Indian," relate poem 1067 to the South and West as well as to the North. The original of her Hesperidean fruit, "Hugest of Core" and of "awkward Rind" and solitary growth, may well have been a pineapple from the West Indies. In late October 1862 she would have read in the *Atlantic Monthly* H. D. Thoreau's "Wild Apples," which makes a comparison of "the golden apples of the Hesperides" with "pine-apples which are imported from the West Indies." A belated recognition of the absurdity of her frost-ripened pineapple may have led to the dropping of the two final stanzas.

11. Dickinson's "teeth of Frosts" in poem 332 and her bleak island home surrounded by "Oceans—and the North" in poem 631 may owe something to a passage in *Stones of Venice,* 2: 6, no. 8 (repeated in *The True and the Beautiful,* pp. 171–73), in which Ruskin takes his reader on a flight to the far northland over irregular and grisly islands amidst the northern seas, beaten by storm and chilled by ice-drift, and tormented by furious pulses of contending tide," where the "hunger of the north wind bites their peaks into barrenness; and, at last, the wall of ice, durable like iron, sets, deathlike, its white teeth against us out of the polar twilight."

12. Ruskin, *Stones of Venice,* 2: 6, no. 8 .

13. John Ruskin, *Modern Painters* (New York: International Book Company, n.d.), 5: 100 (or, 6: 9, no. 11).

14. *Aurora Leigh* 2. 102.

15. *Paradise Lost* 5. 689, 726, 755; 6. 79; 4. 569; 2. 710.

16. The "South," "Breeze," "Cinnamon," and "Spices" of her last two stanzas allude to the Song of Solomon 4:16, 16.

17. *Samson Agonistes,* lines 80–83, 99–104.
18. *Paradise Regained* 2. 155–57.
19. *Paradise Lost* 4. 564, 569, 29–30; 9. 401–404, 406–407, 739–40, 780.
20. *A Midsummer Night's Dream* 2. 1. 166–67.
21. Bianchi, *Face to Face,* p. 157.

INDEX

This index is divided into three sections: First Lines, Letters (by recipients), and Prose Fragments.

FIRST LINES

Numbers in parentheses are those assigned to the poems in the Johnson three-volume edition.

LETTERS (BY RECIPIENT)

The numbers in parentheses are those assigned to the letters and the prose fragments in the Johnson three-volume edition of the letters.

PROSE FRAGMENTS